BRIDGE, PROBABILITY & INFORMATION

MASTER POINT PRESS / TORONTO, CANADA

Master Point Press
331 Douglas Ave.
Toronto, Ontario, Canada
M5M 1H2   (416)781-0351

Email: info@masterpointpress.com

Websites: www.masterpointpress.com
                 www.masteringbridge.com
                 www.bridgeblogging.com
                 www.ebooksbridge.com

Library and Archives Canada Cataloguing in Publication

MacKinnon, Robert F.
        Bridge, probability and information / Robert F. MacKinnon.

ISBN 978-1-897106-53-2

        1. Contract bridge. I. Title.

GV1282.3.M324 2010   795.41'53   C2009-906752-8

We acknowledge the financial support of the Government of Canada through the Book Publishing Industry Development Program (BPIDP) for our publishing activities.

Editor	Ray Lee
Copy editor/interior format	Suzanne Hocking
Cover and interior design	Olena S. Sullivan/New Mediatrix

1 2 3 4 5 6 7   14 13 12 11 10
PRINTED IN CANADA

TABLE OF CONTENTS

INTRODUCTION

'Begin at the beginning,' the King said, gravely,
'and go on until you come to the end, then stop.'
- from *Alice in Wonderland* by Lewis Carroll (1832-1898)

Perhaps nothing in bridge is as misunderstood as the correct application of Probability to the game. This book represents an attempt to correct some of the worst misconceptions, and at the same time introduce some ideas from the realm of Information Theory, a related branch of mathematics that deals with (among other things) how to make the best guess in the face of partial information. The application of the latter to bridge is self-evident to any moderately experienced player.

What is not self-evident, however, is how to present these mathematical ideas in a way that won't immediately provoke the average reader into closing the book for ever. On the face of it, no advice to a budding author is easier to follow than that given by the King to Alice, for everything must have a beginning, a middle and an end, with the possible exception of time itself. If this were a historical novel, we would be starting in 17th century France where a rich young man, Blaise Pascal, is worried about his gambling debts. The opening scene is set in a Paris tavern.

> As he sipped his wine, the young man's handsome face became distorted with concern. 'Believe me, Chevalier,' moaned Pascal, 'if I don't find the winning formula soon, my father's vast fortune will disappear into the pockets of unscrupulous gamblers.'

The subsequent invention of the Theory of Probability could be described in a chapter or two, ending with Pascal's early death in 1662. However, Bridge as we know it wasn't played until 1925, so you see the problem — there would inevitably be dull stretches over the intervening 263 years with only the invention of whist, the precursor of bridge, to lighten the pages.

Whist, bridge without bidding, allowed scientific card play to develop. Some great whist players arose over the centuries: Deschapelles, Yarborough, and Talleyrand are three whose names survive in posterity. The French diplomat made the following famous comment to a colleague: 'You do not play at whist, *monsieur*? Alas, what a sad old age you are preparing for yourself.'

One of the more familiar stories related to whist comes from a London club frequented by aristocrats. The second Earl of Yarborough had a good understanding of *a priori* probabilities. As he sat down for a game of whist, he would offer to give any player £1000 if during the evening they picked up a hand that contained no card higher than a nine. All he asked was that the player pledge him £1 before each deal. This was a very good proposition for his Lordship as the *a priori* probability of the occurrence of such an event on any given deal is 1826:1.

Back at your author's dilemma, there are, unfortunately, no good novels revolving around whist playing. It is a pity that Jane Austen didn't apply herself better to the cause. However, for the purposes of this book, we are free to drift in time. If we assume that the reader knows a lot about Bridge and thinks he knows something about Probability, we can start our work in the middle with the discussion of some bridge deals. In Chapter 1, we shall therefore go over some concepts (such as Restricted Choice) that are familiar, although not necessarily completely understood, with the aim of later describing how these concepts arise from consideration of probabilities. However, if we are to correct wrong impressions, we must sooner or later tackle the basics; that means going back to the beginnings with Pascal, which we do in Chapter 2. Throughout the book, we are going to emphasize that the modern concept of Information is closely linked to Probability. After exploring the application of Information Theory to card play, we shall discuss bidding, a topic that often comes first in bridge books, but here comes at the end.

There are many examples discussed throughout the book, deals played by club players and experts alike. The errors they make are surprisingly similar in nature, which is one lesson the improving player (in which category I place myself, somewhat hopefully) should absorb. Of course, experts make fewer mistakes, but there is a commonality of fallibility that begs to be investigated. When uncertainty is involved, one can't always make the winning decision. The purpose throughout is to guide players into a way of thinking that allows for continuing improvement. Along the way, the reader will, we hope, discard some misconceptions and learn something of Probability and Information Theory, subjects that have wide application outside the bridge world.

CHAPTER 1

WHEN THE DUMMY COMES DOWN

Whenever you can, count
- Sir Francis Galton (1822-1911), Victorian Scientist

At the core of all sciences are numbers. The central process of bridge playing is counting cards. At the heart of Bridge Probability are ratios of card combinations. That's enough to set us on the right track. Off we go!

When the dummy comes down, a declarer's first duty is to assess his contract, count winners and losers, and begin the process of forming a plan for the play. Next he may scan the cards suit by suit to see which positions need to be tackled early and which guesses should be delayed. Tempting as this approach is to the impatient mind, it is the wrong approach — an essential first step in the counting process has been missed.

Not many bridge books will tell you this, but even before considering the implications of the opening lead, declarer should count the number of cards held *jointly* with dummy in each suit. If between his hand and the dummy he finds eight spades, then the defenders must hold the remaining five; if seven hearts, the defenders hold six, and so on. This is known as **counting the sides**. As play progresses, changes occur, but the division of 'sides' is the firm framework within which such changes occur, as cards can't jump from one suit to another.

Bridge players are very familiar with individual hand patterns. They recognize as 'normal' a 4432 shape which occurs for 21.5% of the hands, and as 'flat' a 4333 shape, which occurs 10.5% of the time. The divisions of sides have corresponding patterns. An 8765 pattern is the most common, occurring in 23.6% of deals, and next is the 7766 pattern, which occurs in 10.5% of deals. The former is considered 'normal', the latter 'flat', requiring special treatment.

Let's consider a 7-7-6-6 pattern first as it occurs in the defenders' side. (The hyphen signs indicate that the numbers relate to the suits in strict order, thus seven spades, seven hearts, six diamonds and six clubs.)

I	II	III
♠ 4 - 3	♠ 3 - 4	♠ 5 - 2
♡ 3 - 4	♡ 4 - 3	♡ 1 - 6
♢ 3 - 3	♢ 3 - 3	♢ 4 - 2
♣ 3 - 3	♣ 3 - 3	♣ 3 - 3

In the absence of bidding, Conditions I and II are the two most likely distributions of the suits among the defenders. The strings of numbers represent the double helix of the deal's composition. They determine whether you have encountered something ordinary or something more unusual, like the one shown in Condition III. If the bidding has gone 1NT-3NT and the lead is a low spade, declarer should assume Condition I as a working hypothesis, and if the lead is a low heart, Condition II. Begin with what is most likely and work from there, keeping in mind the Scottish proverb 'What may be may not be'.

I	II	III
♠ 4 - 4	♠ 4 - 4	♠ 4 - 4
♡ 3 - 4	♡ 4 - 3	♡ 3 - 4
◇ 3 - 3	◇ 3 - 3	◇ 4 - 2
♣ 3 - 2	♣ 2 - 3	♣ 2 - 3

With 8-7-6-5 as the defensive sides, both 4333 and 4432 are common hand patterns. On a low spade lead, Condition I is more likely than Condition II, because in the latter case, a heart might have been led. Under Condition III, a diamond might have been led, but it is normal to lead a major against a 3NT contract.

Eventually, these observations could determine in what manner declarer plays the club suit. This is not much to go on, we agree, but it is what's available. The next step is to gather more information at minimum cost, since the information gathered may alter one's estimate of the splits within a suit.

This concept of counting sides will be treated in greater detail later in the book, especially in Chapter 5, but for now the time has come to provide some sustenance in the form of examples of how the process works. If you should find these no more than demonstrations of common sense, then you have captured the essence of Probability.

Counting Cards - Alice in Bridgeland

'Can you do Addition?' the White Queen said. 'What are one and one and one and one and one and one and one and one and one and one?'
'I don't know', said Alice, 'I lost count.'
'She can't do Addition', the Red Queen interrupted.
-from Through the Looking Glass by Lewis Carroll (1832-1898)

Behind this abstract, one can imagine a kindly, middle-aged Professor Charles Dodgson attempting to teach little Alice how to count out the trumps during the play of a hand of whist. Not easy for a young person just introduced to a complex game, and not, incidentally, the best approach at bridge where one gets to see the cards in the dummy. No, the best way is to introduce a pattern made up of your cards plus the dummy's cards, the division of sides, and to count all four suits at once by modifying the pattern as new cards appear during the play. This is a much easier way to keep track than by counting cards one by one, suit by suit, which overtaxes the memory.

There is a further advantage to this approach, besides ease of calculation, which is that it gets a declarer to look at the deal as a whole. The play in one suit may be affected by the distribution of cards in another suit, as we shall demonstrate with two deals played in 6NT, one where a complete count can be obtained and a second where an inferential count is used. (Yes, we know you could count the hand in the time-honored way too: we are just trying to show you the 'sides' process.) Both deals involve playing the combination of ◇KQ9 opposite ◇A1074. The correct play in the suit depends on the conditions in the outside suits at the time of decision. It is not true that finesses are destined to fail half the time.

Here is a deal played by Alice later in life, her golden ringlets now a tarnished silver.

Dealer South
NS Vulnerable

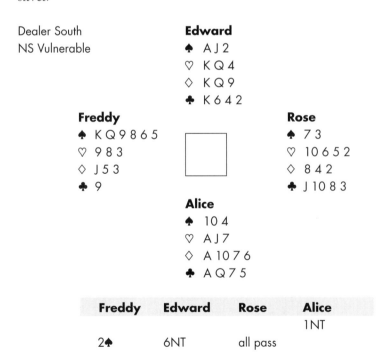

Edward
♠ A J 2
♡ K Q 4
◇ K Q 9
♣ K 6 4 2

Freddy
♠ K Q 9 8 6 5
♡ 9 8 3
◇ J 5 3
♣ 9

Rose
♠ 7 3
♡ 10 6 5 2
◇ 8 4 2
♣ J 10 8 3

Alice
♠ 10 4
♡ A J 7
◇ A 10 7 6
♣ A Q 7 5

Freddy	Edward	Rose	Alice
			1NT
2♠	6NT	all pass	

Aunt Alice is hosting her weekly game at home with her feckless nephew, Freddy, and his spouse. Now a grandmother, she is still quite capable of opening a strong 1NT with less than the required strength (in those days, 16 HCP was considered the absolute minimum). Freddy, who is showing signs of restlessness, tries to upset her with a silly overcall, but her ever-trusting husband gives her a sporting raise. Freddy leads a straightforward ♠K and awaits developments with a stifled yawn.

'I thought the clubs might split badly,' says Edward apologetically as he puts down the dummy. It is always wise to cover yourself with Alice.

'Thank you, Edward. Your values are quite suitable,' replies his mate reassuringly.

This looks like an easy twelve tricks: two spades, three hearts, three diamonds and four clubs on the expected 3-2 split. The defenders' cards are most likely divided as shown under Condition I below.

I	II	III	IV
♠ 6 - 2	♠ 6 - 2	♠ 6 - 2	♠ 6 - 2
♡ 3 - 4	♡ 2 - 5	♡ 2 - 5	♡ 3 - 4
◇ 2 - 4	◇ 3 - 3	◇ 4 - 2	◇ 3 - 3
♣ 2 - 3	♣ 2 - 3	♣ 1 - 4	♣ 1 - 4

Still, Edward may be right, and if the clubs don't split 3-2, Alice will need to make four tricks in the diamond suit. This can be done in three ways: finessing in either direction or playing for the jack to come down in three rounds. It is all a matter of counting and planning ahead for each eventuality.

Alice takes the ♠A and returns the suit, Freddy taking his ♠Q and exiting safely with the ♠6, a card signifying nothing. His long-suffering partner discards the ♡2. This looks like it might be a count card from a five-card suit. In that case, the distribution of sides might be that listed under Condition II. There is still no problem as long as clubs behave, but when Alice cashes the ♣KQ, leaving the ♣A in dummy for the purposes of transportation, Freddy discards the ♠8. Now one must consider the possibility of the distribution under Condition III where the percentage play is to finesse Freddy for the ◇J.

Thanks to her foresight in not releasing the ♣A in her hand, Alice is able to play off the top hearts to confirm the expected presence of a doubleton heart in the West hand, but to her mild surprise, the hearts split evenly, so she obtains the full count represented by Condition IV. The hand has become an open book and Alice plays off the top diamonds for twelve tricks.

'Jolly well done, Aunt Alice,' says Freddy. 'I don't really see how you figured out to drop my ◇J. Against the odds, but your only chance, I imagine.'

'It was largely a matter of Luck,' says Alice, graciously ringing for brandy and chocolate biscuits. With his wife present, it was not the time to advise her nephew on the need to count out a hand and draw the obvious conclusion.

The Inferential Count

We may not be able to get certainty, but we can get probability,
and half a loaf is better than no bread.
- C.S.Lewis (1898-1963)

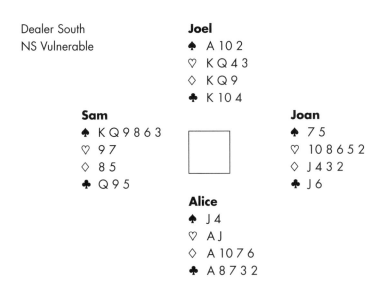

Dealer South
NS Vulnerable

Joel
- ♠ A 10 2
- ♡ K Q 4 3
- ◇ K Q 9
- ♣ K 10 4

Sam
- ♠ K Q 9 8 6 3
- ♡ 9 7
- ◇ 8 5
- ♣ Q 9 5

Joan
- ♠ 7 5
- ♡ 10 8 6 5 2
- ◇ J 4 3 2
- ♣ J 6

Alice
- ♠ J 4
- ♡ A J
- ◇ A 10 7 6
- ♣ A 8 7 3 2

Sam	Joel	Joan	Alice
			1♣
2♠	3♠	pass	4◇
pass	4♠[1]	pass	4NT[2]
pass	6NT	all pass	

1. RKCB for diamonds.
2. Three keycards.

Let's jump ahead to London in the swinging sixties. In 1964, Great Britain has won the Women's Team Bridge Olympiad and hopes are high that the men can rise from their third-place finish and regain their former supremacy in next year's world championships. The great-grandchildren of Alice and the rest are playing for high stakes in a Mayfair club. The new Alice, a smashing boy-cut blonde, is affectionately known as 'Mousetrap' because of her penchant for sharp penalty doubles when lesser beings stray. Sitting West is a rich real estate developer from New York. The bidding systems are ever-changing, and sometimes misunderstandings arise, but good contracts are often reached nonetheless. Due to an accident of good fortune arising from a hazy recollection of the latest craze from Italy, Alice gets to play in a 6NT contract with a decision to be made on the same diamond holding. Although West's overcall is now part of a system and not a mere flight of fancy, it nonetheless still proves ineffective and the lead is the same ♠K.

'Sorry if I got this wrong,' says gentlemanly Joel as he lays down his excellent dummy.

Alice wins the ♠A in dummy and plays off the ♡AJ before establishing a second spade trick. Sam exits with the ♠6 as East discards the ♡2. A group of admirers who include Maurice Harrison-Gray lean forward in their chairs to see if this petite blonde can make twelve tricks where the Losing Trick Count predicts just the obvious eleven. The top hearts are cashed; when West shows up with six spades and two hearts and East with two spades and five hearts, the remaining manageable possibilities include:

I	II
♠ 6 - 2	♠ 6 - 2
♡ 2 - 5	♡ 2 - 5
◇ 3 - 3	◇ 2 - 4
♣ 2 - 3	♣ 3 - 2

Alice needs to get the diamonds right, but she can't get a full count because her clubs are not sufficiently robust. However, an inferential count is available using the Principle of Restricted Choice, which has become all the rage after Terence Reese showed everyone how it works. Playing off the ♣A and ♣K, she arrives at this four-card ending:

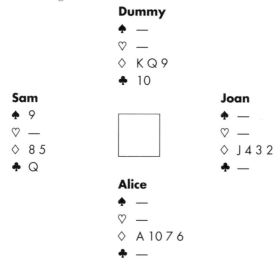

With no one having thrown a diamond yet, it's clear neither defender started with four diamonds and the ♣Q, but there is another inference to be drawn. On the second round of clubs, Joan played the ♣J. The Principle of Restricted Choice tells us that Sam is twice as likely to hold the missing queen as is Joan. Thus Joan most probably began with two spades, five hearts, four diamonds and just two clubs (Condition II). The diamond finesse through East is a 4:2 favorite, and so it transpires.

'Well done, my dear,' whispers Harrison-Gray as Sam makes some notes in a little black book. 'Let me put your name before the selection committee for Buenos Aires. We pre-war ancients need rejuvenation if we are to uphold Britannia's honor.'

'Young lady, you should take up Maury on his offer,' advises the New Yorker. 'The US of A will have Mrs Hayden on the Open Team, who you very much remind me of. She plays as well as any man.'

'And better than most,' sniffs Joan.

'You're so sweet, Maurice and Sam, and I do so love the tango...' smiles Alice. 'Help me here, Joel. You be the judge: can women today consider themselves the equal of men?'

'I myself rate them above men, always have,' replies Joel drily, 'although I consider it largely a matter of personal preference.'

Percentage Play

Principle and fact are like eyes and feet.
- Zen Master Fayan Wenyi (885-958)

JAYNES' PRINCIPLE: In making inferences on the basis of partial information we must use the probability distribution which has maximum uncertainty subject to whatever is known.

The above statement is one of the outstanding achievements of the 20th century with regard to the application of probability theory to scientific endeavor. The consequences to playing a bridge deal are easily stated. Whether we think of maximum uncertainty or ratios of card combinations, it comes to the same thing: play for splits that are as even as possible under the circumstances — there are more cases, and therefore they are more likely. Of course, circumstances may change dramatically when the defenders are forced to make a revealing play, either by showing out of a suit, or playing a card that damages their chances (Restricted Choice).

Of course, the more information at one's disposal, the better will be the basis for a decision and the more likely the even split, so the process feeds on itself.

An imbalance of vacant places or the unexpected fall of an honor must be taken into account as these are indications of uneven splits. This leads to the following general advice for declarers:

BOB'S BLIND RULE: Gather as much information as you safely can, then play for as even splits as are still possible under the circumstances.

This rule is 'blind' because no attention is given to the relevance of the spot cards. The unknown cards may remain as anonymous as they were during the deal. Another way of looking at this is that Jaynes' Principle applies to the combinations of the deal without regard to restrictions in the play, each card being an insignificant card played at random. Thus, the rule is equivalent to playing according to the nature of a blind deal.

Significant cards in side suits may be revealed through the phase dubbed 'the gathering of information'. If the defenders follow with low cards, not much information is revealed, as this is the normal occurrence; however, when a defender shows out of a suit, the information content is high and accurate. The point is that a declarer should make a conscious effort to obtain information in other suits that affects the probabilities of a critical choice, the split in one suit being dependent on the split in another.

Bob's Blind Rule is contrary to the normal advice given to readers of bridge literature, which is first and foremost that a declarer should guard against possible disasters. In many books, one finds problems in which the author suggests a play that is contrary to the most probable lie of the cards, the purpose being to assure a contract that would fail in some circumstances. That is especially relevant to IMPs scoring where assuring the contract takes precedence. Matchpoints, on the other hand, is a game of frequency, thus more closely tied to probabilities. Guarding against bad splits is not often the main concern, so if one plays against the odds and holds oneself to fewer than the normal number of tricks, the results will seldom please one's partner.

When Virtue Goes Unrewarded

No Victor believes in Chance.
- Friedrich Nietzsche (1844-1900)

Bridge is a game of percentages, and as with any such endeavor, success or failure on a given occasion shouldn't be taken personally. Favorable odds are not certainties. It is said that Napoleon considered himself a Man of Destiny, but did he consider losing the Battle of Waterloo a result of bad planning, bad digestion, or fate? Wellington famously said it was won on the playing fields of Eton, but earlier had noted, 'I don't think it would have done if I had not been there.' No public credit was given to the timely arrival of Blücher's German infantry. Actually, Information was the key: the battle was lost due to a lack of information on the French side regarding the imminent arrival of these reinforcements.

For those readers with a taste for irony, here is a deal played on November 18, 2007 by Ulf Tundal, a player who a month earlier in Shanghai had been crowned a world champion. Optimistically, he opened a light 1♡ and subsequently showed long hearts and a singleton club. The opening lead against 6♡ was the ♠2, third-and-fifth best. How might you go about gathering twelve tricks?

Groetheim
♠ A J
♡ Q 7
◇ A Q 7 3
♣ K Q 9 8 6

	Opposition Sides	Splits	
	9	5 - 4	3 - 6
	4	2 - 2	2 - 2
	6	3 - 3	4 - 2
	7	3 - 4	4 - 3

Tundal
♠ 10 6
♡ A K 10 9 8 4 3
◇ K 10 4
♣ 7

Both sides are 9764. Given the lead is from an odd number, the two most likely distributions of the defenders' suits are given on the right. The leftmost encompasses twice the number of combinations as that on the right, hence is represented by twice the probability. (We shall show later how this can be easily calculated at the table.) Notice the effect of thinking about sides, as opposed to isolated suits. Yes, *a priori*, the diamonds are more likely to break 4-2 than 3-3. But *in context*, given what we know about the remaining suits, the leftmost division of sides (which includes a 3-3 diamond break) is the more probable.

Bob's Blind Rule gives reassurance that the chances are good that a losing spade or club in hand can be discarded on the fourth diamond in dummy. Declarer obviously does not wish to rely completely on 3-3 diamonds, but it is difficult to modify the initial assumptions about the splits due to a lack of communications. The Man of Destiny might draw two rounds of trumps ending in dummy and not be surprised when they split 2-2. Thinking the ◇10 was put there for a purpose, he would take an immediate finesse for the ◇J and claim his contract. Joan of Arc might have played it that way, or Alexander the Great, but they both died young. Those of us with fainter hearts prefer not to go down at Trick 4.

The safest way to gather information is by reading discards when one runs a long trump suit; it is also the most unreliable, because the defenders soon become aware of what you are trying to do and will discard in the most uninformative way possible. However, it doesn't hurt to play off a string of hearts and see what happens. Preparation and Information. If one defender parts with two diamonds, then playing to drop the ◇J may become the better play. This is how the declarer in the other room played the hand and he was rewarded with twelve tricks. However, he had opened 4♡ and played there, so the extra tricks were merely thick icing laid on a rather unappetizing cake.

Ulf Tundal was not willing to risk everything on an early finesse or an even split. He, too, ran off the hearts before broaching diamonds. Defending a slam, armed with the knowledge that declarer was very likely the possessor of the ◇K, the opponents were less willing to part with a diamond. This was the full deal.

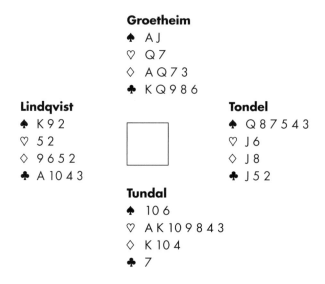

Groetheim
♠ A J
♡ Q 7
◇ A Q 7 3
♣ K Q 9 8 6

Lindqvist
♠ K 9 2
♡ 5 2
◇ 9 6 5 2
♣ A 10 4 3

Tondel
♠ Q 8 7 5 4 3
♡ J 6
◇ J 8
♣ J 5 2

Tundal
♠ 10 6
♡ A K 10 9 8 4 3
◇ K 10 4
♣ 7

Declarer won the opening lead with the ♠A and ran off hearts to reach this six-card ending:

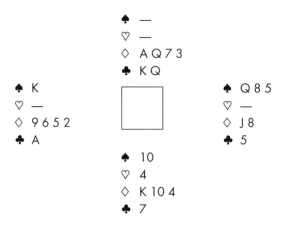

♠ —
♡ —
◇ A Q 7 3
♣ K Q

♠ K
♡ —
◇ 9 6 5 2
♣ A

♠ Q 8 5
♡ —
◇ J 8
♣ 5

♠ 10
♡ 4
◇ K 10 4
♣ 7

Now on the play of the last heart, West parted with the ♠K, dummy threw the ♣Q and East the ♠5. The stage had been set for an elegant winning play, which is to exit with the ♣7, endplaying West into breaking the diamond suit. The stuff that dreams are made of.

However, Tundal could not be sure that East didn't have the ♣A along with a spade winner. He also had a shrewd idea that the diamonds were split 4-2, so elected to play for West to hold the ◊J along with the ◊9 or ◊8. The combinations involved are:

◊ J9xx   ◊ 8x   ◊ 8xxx   ◊ J9   ◊ 9xxx   ◊ J8
◊ J8xx   ◊ 9x

Running the ◊10 works in six combinations, while the ◊J drops in only two, so Tundal made the correct but losing play of running the ◊10, losing to the ◊J and going down three. Unfortunately, the lack of entries prevented him from cashing the ◊K first and seeing East's ◊8, which might have caused him to rethink his line of play.

We may imagine the postmortem with his teammates.

'Board 20, minus 680.'

'Lose 14.'

'You went down three in 6♡?'

'Yes, not doubled.'

'I see. Well played, Ulf.'

That conversation is hard to believe, isn't it? Usually, a play is not considered brilliant unless it coincides with reality. This is unfair; surely a play can be judged to be optimal without reference to the outcome. A 75% finesse will fail 25% of the time; it's no one's fault. If a 25% finesse works, the victims shouldn't feel they have been robbed. An inferior line has given them a chance they didn't in theory deserve. A stoic reaction is best, softened by the hope that next time justice will be served and the better side (yours) will be given redress. Short-term pain, yes, but long-term gain, if time doesn't run out first.

How Probabilities Accumulate

When the mind is in a state of uncertainty,
the smallest impulse drives it to either side.
- Terence (185-159 BC)

It is often said of a close decision that it is a 'coin-toss'. We don't actually get out a coin at the bridge table, preferring instead to make an impulsive guess, perhaps based on a slight hesitation or gesture on the part of an opponent, but often based on our own psychological responses to a crisis situation. There is no harm in this, and in fact such guesses are a large part of the fun that the game provides. No harm is done as long as the decision is truly close to 50-50.

Quite often one encounters in the bridge literature an analysis that shows that one line of play, call it Option A, is better than another line of play, Option B, by a small percentage. The author may then comment that 'the difference, although small, adds up quickly'. Gambling casinos do indeed make fortunes on small percentage advantages, but they are operating 24 hours a day, 365 days a year. The argument is less convincing as far as bridge is concerned, where advantages gained are wiped out once a match is completed. Suppose Option A is correct 52% of the time and Option B only 48% of the time. Over 100 plays on average the difference between choosing A over B adds up to just four cases. That hardly seems significant, especially when in practice the difference can run in the other direction in such a small sample.

To see how probabilities accumulate over several 'trials', let's first look at the well-known case of a split in the defenders' cards when declarer and dummy hold eleven cards in a suit. The defenders' cards will split 1-1 with an *a priori* probability of 52% and will fail to do so with an *a priori* probability of 48%. Suppose that someone uses a computer to generate random deals and isolate a sequence of deals in which the defenders hold two cards in a suit in each deal. Now you are asked to bet on whether the first deal generated is a 1-1 deal or a 2-0 deal. Naturally you will go with the odds and bet on Option A, a 1-1 split. Proceeding to the second deal, you are again asked to bet, and, naturally, once more, you will choose Option A. And so on down the line: one always chooses the option with the better odds. However, choosing the correct option does not mean you have chosen the 'right' option, for Option B will occur a certain percentage of the time. It is easy enough to calculate the percentage for any number of deals, starting with two:

Two 1-1 splits	27%
One 1-1 split, one 2-0	50%
Two 2-0 splits	23%

For two deals, half the time, one of the deals has a 1-1 split and the other has a 2-0 split. The advantage to betting on the 1-1 split is evident only in the cases of two-of-a-kind, where two 1-1 splits outweigh two 2-0 splits by 4%. If one bets on Option A on each deal, one has to expect to suffer losses on both deals 23% of the time.

Of course, one has to wait a long time to play hands with eleven-card fits, so this result does not appear to be of much practical use. However, the same argument applies to choosing options in the play of the cards. Suppose that during a session you have to choose between two lines of play, one with a 52%

chance of success and a second with a 48% chance of success. Naturally you will choose the one with the higher percentage, Option A. Later in the session you are called upon to make another close decision. It may not be exactly 52-48 again, but suppose that is a close approximation. The chance of getting both decisions right is 27%, because you have chosen the optimum line twice in a row, but the chance of both decisions being wrong is 23%. Half the time you will succeed once and fail once.

Let's extend the sequence to six deals in a session. Here are the percentages for winning decisions when one always chooses the correct option. For comparison, we give the percentages when each choice represents a 50-50 toss-up.

Results	50-50	52-48	Difference	57-43	Difference
6 right - 0 wrong	2%	2%	–	3%	+1%
5 right - 1 wrong	9%	11%	+2%	16%	+7%
4 right - 2 wrong	23%	25%	+2%	29%	+6%
3 right - 3 wrong	31%	31%	–	29%	-2%
2 right - 4 wrong	23%	22%	-1%	17%	-6%
1 right - 5 wrong	9%	8%	-1%	5%	-4%
0 right - 6 wrong	2%	1%	-1%	1%	-1%

If you always choose the higher probability option from a 52-48 differential, you will be right more than you are wrong in the ratio of 38% to 31%, and be neutral 31% of the time. If you chose the incorrect option half the time, the effect would be the same as if you faced a 50-50 choice. In that situation, the rights and wrongs are balanced out. The same applies if Option A is 52% on half the deals and 48% on the other half, the overall effect being that the choice between Option A and Option B becomes a 50-50 toss-up taking all six deals into account.

The upshot of this analysis is that there is no great reward to be earned from playing 'correctly' when the odds are close to 50%. The uncertainty is high and the cards will be unfriendly almost as often as they are friendly. The decisions you must strive to get correct are those for which the odds strongly favor one option over the other. Such a case is shown by the 57-43 column on the far right, for which the majority 'rights' outnumber the majority 'wrongs' 48% to 23%. This represents a big increase over the original difference. In bridge terms, this is a difference one encounters in the following situation:

A 10 x ⬜⬜⬜ K J x

Declarer has a choice of finessing for the queen by cashing the ace and leading towards the jack or cashing the king and leading towards the ten. If it is known that one defender holds four cards in the suit and the other only three, the correct play is to play the defender with the four cards for the queen, the favorable odds being 57% versus 43%. If it is not known how the cards are split between the defenders, then declarer may guess either way with a 50-50 chance of getting it right, given the lack of knowledge available at the time of decision.

Good technique requires that declarer gather information to aid in his decision about which way to finesse. This is not always possible to accomplish with safety, in which case one can expect to get it right only half of the time. If one neglects the gathering of information, there is a stiff price to be paid, a price that increases over several such deals. *It is important to attempt to count out the hands.* Playing a 57-43 decision as if it were a 50-50 decision results in significant losses even in the short term. So the conclusion one draws is that one should work on getting the clear-cut ones right and not worry about the truly close decisions that didn't work out in your favor. Indeed, in close decisions, one should prefer the option that, if right, produces the greatest reward.

The Enlightenment of Scrooge

Bah! Humbug!
- Ebenezer Scrooge, A *Christmas Carol* (1843)

The writings of Charles Dickens can teach us something about the proper spirit in which to approach the game of bridge. Recall, for example, what Ebenezer Scrooge experienced one Christmas Eve long ago. Before that night, Scrooge would have been in line for the Nobel Prize for Economics, if it had existed in his time. In our more enlightened times, we recognize that the post-Christmas Scrooge was the better man, and the better economist to boot — a pre-Keynesian, no less. As with Scrooge and Christmas, so with those who say 'Humbug!' to Bridge Probability. Yes, one may struggle on miserably without it, but how much richer our lives become when we can enjoy its benefits to the full!

A bridge Scrooge deserves a night visitation from the three spirits of Probability: Past, Present, and Future. The Ghost of Probability Past will speak of what cannot be changed and is forever fixed, the *a priori* odds with which every deal begins. One has great expectations, but alas, sometimes one is dealt a yarborough. Furthermore, the Ghost will recall the numerous deals when Scrooge played against the odds and went down in contracts that should have succeeded.

Probability Present will show Scrooge the partners he threw away by a stubborn refusal to change his ways. At this year's Christmas party, he will see his ex-partners having a good time without him. Some are obviously happy with their new partners, others, like Alice, are not, although her bridge seems to have improved remarkably since their breakup. The Spirit will tell him, 'The past is ever lost, the future is beyond reach, so all you have left is the present. Learn to live in it.'

Lastly, Probability Future will speak of the uncertain times to come when one can only speculate on what is likely to happen — good and bad, but mostly bad if Scrooge keeps going along the same track. The Spirit will pose questions like, 'If I play ace-king and a low club, what are the chances I can endplay an unwary Fred?' Scrooge will be let in on a future post-mortem in which the discussion of his abilities becomes pretty frank since he's not there to defend himself. He may say to the Spirit, 'Despite what Mrs. Dilber says, I'm sure I would always do what was proper at the time,' but that just doesn't cut it in the face of the harsh comments of accusatory team-mates.

Let us hope that the Scrooges of the bridge world will have a change of heart, learn the basics of probability, endeavor to be sympathetic to their partners, and live happily ever after in their new-found state of self-awareness. As Tiny Tim might say, 'God bless us every one, even those unfortunates who do not play bridge.'

In Conclusion

Chance is the name fools give to Fate.
- Fred Astaire to Ginger Rogers in *The Gay Divorcee* (1934)

Hollywood fantasy is a pleasant entertainment, or used to be, but it is unrealistic. Here the writers got it the wrong way around. It's not the sort of admission one makes when holding hands over a candlelight dinner in celebration of twenty years of happy marriage, but fate has more to do with preparedness than opportunity. It is safe to speak of fate when referring to the past, but it is dangerous to count on it in the future.

The whole idea behind the scientific approach is to execute bridge play and bidding in a systematic way, putting emphasis on what is most probable. In this introductory chapter, we've looked at some fundamentals of declarer play as they pertain to card combinations. The most important concept introduced was the idea of counting out a **side**. We also discovered that the most probable split of the sides may involve a specific suit breaking in a way that does not conform to the odds in isolation. Bob's Blind Rule (*Play for suits to split as evenly as possible, consistent with the information you have*) is the simplest form of percentage play. Later we shall discover exceptions to this simplification.

If a theory is misunderstood, it will be misapplied, and from this will arise misunderstanding, confusion and disillusionment. If the theory is understood, as this one can be by most players, it is no longer necessary to play according to slogans without knowing why. That is the rationale behind developing basic probability theory step by step, with many examples, to guide the reader along a path of learning. We can explore such concepts as 'restricted choice', 'losing trick count', 'vacant places' and 'the law of total tricks' to the benefit of the committed reader. Indeed, one derives great pleasure from exclaiming, 'Ah, yes, now I understand.'

We also want to cure the experienced player who has been led astray into an over-reliance on (1) the *a priori* odds, and (2) rules for single-suit card combinations, so as to move him onward to application of (3) the *a posteriori* odds, and (4) whole-hand analysis. At the very least, we can stress that quoting probabilities to two decimal places gives the wrong impression of how much accuracy can be attributed to them. In a practical sense, their accuracy depends on the assumptions incorporated in the mathematical models to which they apply. As more is learned about a given deal from the bidding and play, the farther one should move from (1) and (2) towards (3) and (4). The following chapters tell the reader how to accomplish this effectively at the bridge table.

CHAPTER 2

EMOTION, LOGIC, AND HOW WE DECIDE

Each of our major 'emotional states' results from turning certain resources on while turning certain others off — and thus changing some ways our brains behave.
- Marvin Minsky (1927-) in *The Emotion Machine* (2006)

Before we consider probability in the play of the cards in detail, we should talk about the broader problem of how one arrives at decisions. Most bridge players operate in this context without feeling a great desire to solve equations, so we have to consider what they are doing instead. To do this, we go to the most advanced theories on human thought processes as formulated by experts working in the field.

Several days a week, a roomful of senior citizens of legally sound mind get together at my local bridge club to play 26 boards. Only very rarely do they all arrive at the same contract on a given deal and even then the sequences of play are never matched throughout the room. What does that tell us? From the outset, there is no consensus on how to bid and play a deal. Why is that so? Partly because the actions at each table depend to a great extent on the emotional reactions of the individual players. We can analyze the results looking at all four hands, but the analysis won't make complete sense unless we take into account how emotions around the table played a part.

The quote at the start of this chapter is from Dr Marvin Minsky, a pioneer in the development of Artificial Intelligence. He and others, in their attempts to make computers think like us, have developed a modern theory of how our brains work. Their view is that one cannot separate emotions from the way we reason; the human capacity for emotional response is ever present in full potential. After all, we need to react instinctively in order to be able to jump out of the way when someone spills hot coffee in our direction. In a less obvious way, our emotions play a part in our thought processes when we tackle bridge problems. The way we think evolves from a suppression of certain emotions, leaving other emotions freer to engage in the decision-making process.

How is this achieved? Here I shall interpret freely what the MIT professors tell us. There is a facility in the brain that acts as a controller of emotions, a 'Critic' in Minsky's terminology, with three recognizable components. It has been developing from early days (300 million BC) to the present, so we owe our brains, as well as other bodily parts, to our ancestors. When you sit down at the bridge table, you do not sit alone — your ancestors, who have contributed throughout the eons to the structure of your brain, sit with you. I shall denote these ancestors as the YAKs: 'Your Ancestral Kibitzers'. The YAKs give advice of a general nature as they are not adept at playing the game — which doesn't mean they don't have an opinion. This is what they may be telling you as you select your opening lead against 3NT:

Function	General Guidance	Bridge Translation	Traffic Light
Censure	Stay in the cave	Stop! Top of Nothing.	Red
Correct	Run for the hills	Go! Get active.	Green
Suppress	Do what the others do	Wait! Fourth Highest.	Amber

I suspect that the vast majority of our forebears are assembled under the Amber category. Duplicate bridge was made for them. After failing to take full advantage of the lie of the cards, these types may comment as they open the scoresheets, 'Not so good, but I suspect we'll have lots of company — yes, actually, some went down two.'

Where does probability theory come into all this? It is a question of *abstraction* versus *distraction*. By thinking abstractly about the position of the cards around the table, one distances a decision from personal concerns, such as anxiety or optimism, thus reducing their effects. One's ancestors can't complain as much if a failed finesse had a 60% chance of success. Probability acts to overcome fear and moderate intuition. One suspects that the experts, who are the most analytical, are the ones who have the best control over their emotions. So let's consider why even experienced players go wrong.

Where Do Blunders Come From?

Where emotions arise, knowledge of reality gets blocked off.
- Zen Master Huanglong (1002-1069)

Often at the table it seems that a blunder has occurred out of nowhere. Why is that? The great Howard Schenken knew that when it comes to decision-making, emotion is the ever-present threat, and advised players to suppress their emotions. That was the old view.

The modern view of the role emotions play is closer to the view of ancient Chinese Zen Masters than it is to the traditional Western view of a conflict with Reason. Today, the consensus is that one shouldn't struggle against emotions from which benefits may derive. Emotions are like the force of a river we are trying to navigate in a canoe. It is better to paddle downstream using the force of the water as an aid rather than to struggle upstream against it, but one should never let the river take control — that leads to upsets. This is neatly expressed in the advice 'It's okay to have butterflies, as long as they are flying in formation.'

Experts speak of a certain happy state of mind as being 'in the zone'. This is a time when correct decisions come easily without apparent effort. There are no distractions and solutions spring quickly to mind. However, a player in the zone is not feeling robotic. It is not an emotionless condition, but one of happiness with feelings of general well-being. Pre-game nerves are under control, and the player has channeled the extra adrenaline into being alert and on top of his game — the butterflies are flying in formation. There are other times when nothing comes easily and the choices made are often inferior. This is a time of frustration and conflict, a time to fall back on general principles and attempt to give nothing away. Don't struggle against the stream of emotion: there may be some unresolved issues that are causing a debate within your brain that has nothing to do with the action at the table. Clear the mind and convince yourself that here is where you want to be and this is what you want to be doing at this particular time.

It may be necessary to form habits of disengagement from one's natural inclinations. To illustrate this point, let's take an example from recent play at my local duplicate club with the usual cast of characters. The occasion is the 2007 WBF Charity Pairs.

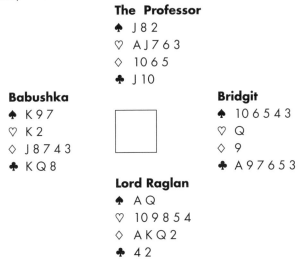

The Professor
♠ J 8 2
♡ A J 7 6 3
♢ 10 6 5
♣ J 10

Babushka
♠ K 9 7
♡ K 2
♢ J 8 7 4 3
♣ K Q 8

Bridgit
♠ 10 6 5 4 3
♡ Q
♢ 9
♣ A 9 7 6 5 3

Lord Raglan
♠ A Q
♡ 10 9 8 5 4
♢ A K Q 2
♣ 4 2

South opened a Precision 1♡ and I raised to 4♡, shutting out East-West from a makeable contract of 3♠. West chose to attack with the ♣K, overtaken by East, who returned the ♢9. This would have worked well if West could have won to lead a diamond back for a ruff, not a highly likely possibility. In fact, East had given declarer a chance to make his contract — a chance his emotional state was not going to let him seize.

When the dummy came down, my partner gave me the same resigned look of disapproval the real Lord Raglan, commander-in-chief during the Crimean War, might have given Lord Cardigan as he returned from leading the Charge of the Light Brigade. I could read his thoughts as if he had spoken them aloud: 'Sir, you have over-committed your meager resources to a lost cause. A bid of 2♡ was quite enough for the purposes of reconnaissance, followed by an advance to the three-level if that were deemed prudent.'

With this background to his thinking, declarer was doomed. A heart to the ace at Trick 3 and a finesse for the ♠K quickly led to down one.

'You know, I could have made that,' remarked Raglan with belated insight as his bottom score was being recorded. 'First I eliminate the diamonds, then I throw West in with the ♣Q.'

He was right of course — too late for it to help. When East followed to the ♡A with the ♡Q, bells should have rung in the Bell Tower of the Prepared Mind, especially one built from the rubble of hundreds of destroyed stone-cold contracts like this one. No doubt the peal of bells went unheeded, lost in the din of Ancestral Voices.

When East dropped the ♡Q under the ♡A, declarer's thoughts should have turned to the Principle of Restricted Choice. This tells us that West now is much more likely to hold the ♡K, as with both the ♡K and the ♡Q, East could have played either. Placing West with the ♡K suggests immediately the elimination and endplay that stares declarer in the face. A low diamond from the dummy confirms the position without cost, and all goes smoothly from there as a potential bottom is turned into a top.

Of course, it is always easy to manufacture a valid reason to back one's natural inclination to err. East has shown up with a singleton diamond and a singleton heart, so the odds greatly favor her holding the ♠K, justifying the finesse. That is true, but a mere 5:3 probability is never as good as a sure thing.

Of course, the defense had slipped up also. True to her ancestral pool and consistent with her desire to take action, Bridgit jumped at a slim chance for a top board. If West is allowed to hold the first trick, then the ♣Q can be used at Trick 2 (rather than the ♣2) to signal subtly that a spade return would be welcome. East overtakes and leads a spade. The increase in *information* inherent in the second club lead is what is needed to achieve, without a guess, the best result possible under the circumstances. Overtaking and playing a diamond at Trick 3 would have been equally fatal to the defense, so it was not the overtaking *per se* that was the problem; it was the choice of switch.

Luck, Chance and Design

In the field of observation,
Chance favors only the prepared mind.
- Louis Pasteur (1822-1895)

'You see, Watson, but you do not observe.'
- Sherlock Holmes in A *Scandal in Bohemia,*
Sir Arthur Conan Doyle (1859-1930)

Bridge hands are dealt at random. This element of uncertainty influences some players into thinking that the results of each deal are somehow determined largely by luck. For example, in a team game where 3NT is the contract at both tables, the result may be determined by the opening lead, so it may be important which player is declarer. The belief is that good or bad results often have more to do with the opponents' actions than with our own.

I do not subscribe to this chaotic view of Bridge. Yes, there is an element of Chance in the game, and emotions often intervene, but we cannot let this poison our approach. The remarks made by Pasteur and Holmes are appropriate to any reasoning process. It does not matter whether you are thinking about scientific experiments, detection or card play: the mind must be ready to place the observations into a wider context. You may see and note the cards as they appear around the table, but unless you can make use of those observations within some more general organized way of thinking, you miss their significance. The mind must be prepared to see the advantages that might result from a probable lie of the remaining cards. It is a question of having an open mind and a flexible approach.

Luck is personal whereas Chance is not. I like to believe that whatever luck there is lies in the distribution of the cards and it is the task of the players to take advantage of it. We must develop the techniques and recognize the opportunities. This is best done through an understanding of how Chance plays its regulated part — that is, we have to grasp the fundamentals of Probability Theory and its extension, Information Theory.

As beginners, we all sometimes make plays that turn out to be unexpectedly beneficial. Not seeing much hope for success, we play off a long suit more in an atmosphere of embarrassment than of optimism, and discover that our opponents have unaccountably discarded their winners. By accident, we have executed our first squeeze. First time lucky, but can we repeat the process on some future deal? If we do so by design, can we still attribute our good result to Luck? No, we conclude that the subsequent result was obtained by extracting the luck inherent in the lie of the cards.

Let's see a simple example where declarer had all the clues necessary to take the winning action. As it happened, he failed to extract the good luck that was available to him because his mind was not prepared. This can happen on any given day in any given bridge club, but on this occasion it was reported on a Bridge Base Online (BBO) broadcast of the 2006 DongMing Knockout Teams in Shanghai.

The Gods Love the Odds

I am a great believer in luck, and I find the harder I work
the more I have of it.
- Stephen Leacock (1869-1940)

The bridge gods love the odds and those who play by them, but the goddesses love the daring ones who can get themselves in and out of a tight spot. Too often we are too lazy or too distracted to take full advantage of the slim chance these divine lovelies afford us.

NS Vul

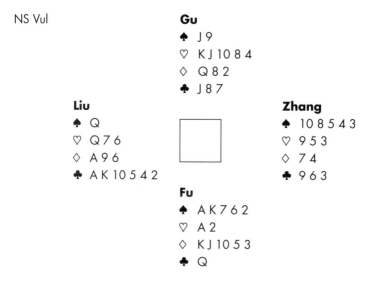

Gu
♠ J 9
♡ K J 10 8 4
♢ Q 8 2
♣ J 8 7

Liu
♠ Q
♡ Q 7 6
♢ A 9 6
♣ A K 10 5 4 2

Zhang
♠ 10 8 5 4 3
♡ 9 5 3
♢ 7 4
♣ 9 6 3

Fu
♠ A K 7 6 2
♡ A 2
♢ K J 10 5 3
♣ Q

Liu	Gu	Zhang	Fu
1NT	pass	2♡*	pass
2♠	pass	pass	dbl
pass	3♡	pass	3NT
dbl	all pass		

Once West starts with a flawed 1NT, the auction proceeds with the inevitability of a Greek tragedy, the BBO commentators acting as the Chorus forecasting disaster. North-South can make 5◊ easily, but they are blown off course, landing on the rocky shores of 3NT.

West begins by playing clubs from the top, yielding a trick in the suit to declarer. The bidding has indicated that West holds all the defenders' high cards, including the ◊A as an entry to the remaining club winners. Meanwhile, even if hearts behave, declarer seems to have only eight tricks without playing on diamonds. Yes, the contract has little hope, but must Fu give up? Too often we despair and spurn the goddesses' gifts.

What are the clues that should give rise to a suspicion that all is not as it seems? A major clue is that East transferred to spades, promising five, when there are only six spades held by the defenders. This fact would have come to mind readily if declarer had routinely counted the sides: 7-7-8-4 and 6-6-5-9. The situation may appear as near hopeless as makes no difference, but it costs nothing to lay down the ♠A before playing on diamonds — and lo, the ♠Q falls singleton from the hand of the player who opened 1NT!

As West is marked with the ♡Q, declarer can now succeed by cashing the ♠J, then returning to hand with the ♡A, laying down the ♠K and finessing in hearts to gather nine tricks without touching diamonds. Making 3NT would have been a triumph, but, alas, declarer blindly accepted his failure by leading a diamond from the dummy at Trick 4, losing 14 IMPs in the process. A tragedy, then, but one that could have been avoided.

Some observers may wonder if any lessons can be derived from outcomes in which dubious actions played such a large part. These situations arise at all levels of play from the world championships down to the local level. They must be dealt with. Departures from normalcy can work in both directions, as the above deal illustrates. Those who keep a cool head and act according to sound principles are better equipped to cope.

Is Bridge a Science?

> When you can measure what you are speaking about, and express it in
> numbers, you know something about it; but when you cannot measure
> it, when you cannot express it in numbers, your knowledge is of a
> meager and unsatisfactory kind; it may be the beginning of knowledge,
> but you have scarcely, in your thoughts, advanced to the stage of science.
> - Lord Kelvin (1824-1907)

Many bridge experts have expressed the opinion that bridge is not a science. Certainly, bridge is all about numbers and although it is true that bridge bidding and play are not exact processes, that does not rule them out as being subject to the rules that govern uncertainty — in particular, the laws of probability.

Scientific theory provides us with models of our universe, the usefulness of the models being related to the degree to which they can predict future events. The accuracy of a model of a bridge game depends on the extent to which it incorporates details concerning the uncertainty of the processes. There is a limit to what can be achieved at the bridge table without the use of a computer, and past theoretical models have been too simple to provide consistently accurate results. It is possible to imagine complex models running on modern computers that can very closely approximate what we observe at the bridge table. As with all human mental activity, allowances must be made for errors, but that does not rule out the game as a science. As players, our task is to observe what is happening and then to apply as accurate a model as we can to the situation at hand, hoping for success in an uncertain environment in which many factors play a role.

CHAPTER 3

THE CONCEPT OF PROBABILITY

The theory of probabilities is basically only common sense reduced to
a calculation. It makes one estimate accurately what right-minded people
feel by a sort of instinct, often without being able to give a reason for it.
- Pierre-Simon Marquis de Laplace (1749-1827)

Stock market — up or down? Weekend — wet or dry? Queen of spades —
finesse or drop? These are just a few of the uncertainties that give us daily pause.
Although there are no guarantees, most would agree that the more information
we use, the more accurate the prediction is likely to be.

Let's look at forecasting the weather, always a topic of interest. A simple
predictor is to assume that the weather tomorrow will be the same as it is today:
look out of the window and there's your prediction. The farmer in the field can
do better than that. He has observed what has occurred over the past few days
and can follow the trend. Years of experience and a throbbing in his joints in
response to rapid changes in the atmospheric pressure back his prediction. The
most sophisticated analysis comes from the weather service, which guardedly
announces a 50% probability of precipitation. Really? 50%? Taxpayers have
put millions of dollars into a computer system that analyzes data from thousands
of sensors using the best atmospheric model available in order to arrive at a
prediction, and all we get is a 50-50 toss-up? Isn't it better to flip a coin, and
put the money back into the taxpayers' pockets? No, actually it isn't, because
the theoretical atmospheric model systematically takes into account all the
knowledge that is currently available. If the results are inconclusive, blame the
weather, not the predictor. Bridge is like that: put all the time, money and effort
into prediction that you like, but at times it will still come down to a coin-flip.
Nonetheless, the more information one can make use of, the more likely it is that
the prediction will prove accurate within an appropriate degree of uncertainty.

At the bridge table, the equivalent to 'looking out of the window' is taking
all the finesses without much thought as to how one suit relates to another. At

matchpoints, a winning finesse not taken often converts to a bad score, so this approach is not as frivolous as it appears. The bridge-playing 'farmer in the field' has a long-term plan based on the *a priori* odds, but he tends to carry out the plan without much flexibility. The 'weatherman' has a probability model he follows as he collects information from around the table, and the 'expert forecaster' carries this one step further and adjusts according to 'local conditions'.

Probability is a quantity that exists in the wonderful world of mathematics. The extent to which probability is useful depends on how closely the theoretical assumptions of the model match conditions in the real world. At the bridge table, the match is rather good, as one is dealing with the finite world of fifty-two cards. In fact, probability theory was developed in the 17th century to establish gaming odds. Keep in mind as you read on that it is easier to teach probability to a bridge player than it is to teach bridge to a mathematician.

A great benefit of thinking about card play in terms of probability is that one can apply structure to one's thinking, and mathematics is nothing if not structured in its approach. Math is the closet organizer for the brain. As each new fact is acquired, it is placed next to the other relevant facts to be recovered as needed. Neat! There is a space between the ears in which to store away what has been observed at the bridge table, so useful items can be accessed with ease as required. Every deal has its history.

Probability applied to declarer play involves little more than organizing one's thoughts around a count of card combinations. There is a technique involved, which we shall explore, but mainly it is a matter of a commitment to counting. The aim of this effort is to make choices that conform to the most likely situation at the time of the decision. We start with a prediction based on what can be expected ahead of time in a state of a total lack of information. This takes the form of the so-called *a priori odds*. As play progresses, we must balance what we have discovered against what was expected. A new probability is created based on the subsequent knowledge acquired that takes the designation of *a posteriori* odds. Ultimately, observation prevails over expectation as the *a priori* odds go up in smoke. All ends in certainty.

Mathematics and Bridge

Crafty men condemn studies, simple men admire them,
and wise men use them.
- Sir Francis Bacon (1561-1626)

Bridge is a game based on numbers, so by and large it lies within the domain of mathematics. Numbers in the form of HCP are used to evaluate the potential for taking tricks. The predictions based on HCP alone are sometimes good, sometimes bad, depending on other conditions; nonetheless, players use HCP as a convenient descriptor as well as a starting point. Other numbers are often bandied about, like 'losing trick count' and 'total tricks'. Their predictive value is variable and often open to question, yet when one player talks to another, a certain quality of the hands involved is expressed numerically.

Counting cards during the play yields concrete numbers without ambiguity. The aim is to use the card count for choosing the best option on the basis of probabilities. In his book *Probabilities in Everyday Life*, published in 1986, John D. McGervey wrote as follows about bridge and probability.

> Bridge is an easy game. There is no house percentage to beat, and you can choose the bid or play that give you the best odds. The opponents can do that too, but these are the same people who give a big edge away to lotteries, racetracks, casinos, and bookies. Why shouldn't they be generous to you, too?

> Bridge probabilities are simpler than those of blackjack... You can see two of the four hands and your most common problem is to determine whether a specific unseen card, say the queen of spades, is on your left or on your right.

That is reassuringly simple, but not everyone agrees. John Boeder, in *Thinking About IMPs*, echoes the philosopher Nietzsche in his statement 'Mathematics is the excuse that losers resort to in the post mortem'. Presumably he refers to probabilities, not to card counts. Nonetheless, the analysis in his book is full of percentages. For example, he refers to a poor slam as one having a chance of success between 41% to 49% and a reasonable slam as one between 50% to 59%. That 1% difference between 'poor' (49%) and 'reasonable' (50%) implies a great deal of faith in being able to calculate probabilities to this degree of accuracy. I don't believe it can be done, because such accuracy requires a great deal of certain knowledge. If one misuses mathematics, it is not surprising that one begins to lose faith in its utility. Given his expressed attitude, it would be more appropriate for Boeder to adopt Bob Hamman's dictum 'A good slam is one that makes', and leave it at that without resorting to pseudo-numerical treatments that are impractical. How does one judge at the table that a potential slam is only 45% probable and so not worth bidding?

It is understandable that even good players may rely on table feel rather than an objective approach based on probability, as the subject has not been well treated in the past. Oswald Jacoby, one of the all-time bridge greats, was an expert on combinatorics, having been a code breaker during WWII, yet he claimed that the hardest thing to teach bridge players was probability. He tried it in a 1947 book entitled *How to Figure the Odds*. Jacoby knew his subject as well as any bridge player, but he still encountered difficulties getting the ideas across. Why? One reason was that the thinking at the time was bound up with the *a priori* odds, that is to say the odds calculated for the dealing of the cards before anything is known of the particular hand that has been dealt.

Another attempt to correct faulty thinking appeared in the October 1961 issue of *The Bridge World*. The article, entitled 'Bridge Probabilities', was actually written by a professor of mathematics, Dr. D. Divinsky. Unfortunately, it still contains many statements that are misleading in their general sweep and merely add to the confusion. For example, 'Probabilities do not change with the play of the cards... only the *a priori* odds matter.' This is simply wrong — probabilities change with each card played. Later, 'Each round rules out certain cases and thus gives us information which we did not have before. The probabilities do not change...' Is this possible? Surely probabilities reflect uncertainty, which is reduced by the addition of information.

It is better to establish the correct basis for calculating probabilities rather than to argue against the many false concepts that one encounters in the bridge literature, but it may be worthwhile to consider one example to illustrate how careful one must be when it comes to vague arguments that appear at first glance to be reasonable. Some years ago, a world champion justified her declarer play with an argument that went something like this: 'After my LHO showed up with the ♠A, naturally I played for the ♡A to be in the other hand'. The probability of the deal is that any two given cards are more likely to be placed in different hands than in the same hand; however, once the ♠A was found to be held by LHO, the probability of the location of the ♡A depended on how many hearts were held in each hand. If LHO were found to hold two spades and RHO four spades, it would be more probable that LHO held more hearts, and hence more probable that the ♡A would be found among them. It has nothing to do with the rank of the cards involved.

It wasn't until 1960 that Terence Reese in *The Expert Game* (published as *Master Play* in the USA) famously presented the Principle of Restricted Choice, which dealt with how probabilities change with the play of the cards. The concept had been described earlier by Alan Truscott; it became the subject of much speculation and a prize was offered to anyone who could explain it clearly. Reese may have thought his exposition missed the mark as he observed 'arguments of this sort can be confusing'. He clung to the notion that one need not do more than consider the *a priori* odds and in his quintessentially snide manner sneered at players who believe 'that the odds change with every card played'.

Despite this view, Reese gives us this advice: 'A defender should be assumed not to have had a choice rather than to have exercised a choice in a particular way'. This was not a call to go back to the *a priori* odds, but rather to make a judgment based on the current state of affairs as observed after the bidding and several rounds of play. The current probabilities are the *a posteriori* odds, so it is not clear how this jibes with the view that only *a priori* odds matter. Reese himself must have become aware of a problem, for in the foreword to a later (1975) edition of his classic *Reese on Play*, he explained he had 'expanded the account of "Probabilities" to accord with modern theories'. Then in the first chapter he writes, 'the odds vary every time a card is played'. As the reader will discover shortly, the theory of probability was well established by the middle of the 18th century, so what was actually 'modern' was a revised and better understanding of its application to bridge.

Probability Is Synonymous with Information

The attitude that probability is a post-mortem excuse for losers is derived from a misunderstanding of the concept of probability. Probability is no more than a numerical way of expressing the degree of uncertainty involved in a decision. The odds reflect the amount of relevant information available at the time of decision. If the odds are 50-50, there is not enough information available to make a confident choice one way or the other. This is a state of maximum uncertainty.

Take, for example, a two-way finesse for the ◊Q. If it is known the outstanding diamonds are split 3-3, the location of the ◊Q is maximally uncertain and the choice of finesse is subject to a 50% probability of success. If it is known the diamonds are split 4-2, the chances are that the ◊Q lies with the four-card collection, so the finesse through that holding is a 2 to 1 proposition. The probabilities merely reflect what one knows at the time of decision.

Of course, uncertainty still exists. Even with 2:1 odds in its favor, there are no guarantees, and the finesse will fail a fair proportion of the time. This is neither lucky nor unlucky, just a reasonable expectation. One can expect benefits over the long term, but there will be times when a cost must be incurred because of uncertainty. This is not a cause for complaint. One should play in a manner consistent with what one knows at the time (or can discover without undue risk), which means playing for favorable odds that reflect the current state of knowledge. The trick is to develop a way of thinking that allows for the full use of whatever information is available.

A truly modern development is the application of Probability to Information Theory, a subject little known before the sixties outside a small community of scientists, who realized that probability and information are related mathematically. We are going to return to the basics of probability by going back in time to trace how the ideas developed. In later chapters, we shall discuss the application of Information Theory to bidding.

A Glimpse into the History of Probability

Nothing occurs at random.
- Leucippus (5th century BC)

It is remarkable that a science which began with the consideration of games of chance should have become the most important object of human knowledge.
- Marquis de Laplace (1749-1827)

It is possible to argue that there is no such thing as a random deal. If you ask a computer for a sequence of numbers ranging from 1 to 52, the computer will oblige, provided you ask nicely, but once the list exists, the sequence can no longer be random, can it? This is a bothersome conclusion that misses the point, which is that the order of the numbers can't be predicted ahead of time, and that one sequence is as likely as any other.

Saint Augustine, the great synthesizer who blended compatible parts of Plato's philosophy with Christian dogma, found no grounds for 'accidents'. In his philosophical mix, an event might appear random to an observer, but that appearance arose solely from the ignorance of the observer, and was not a property of the event itself. It therefore made little sense to record the results of a great number of trials with a view to predicting the result of the next trial. Ignorance was considered the attribute of an unclouded mind. 'Don't confuse me with the facts' is indeed an appropriate motto for the medieval mind, past and present.

One can see that in the past, it might even have been dangerous to advocate that events can occur randomly; however, it is interesting that today's scientists share with Saint Augustine the view that randomness is related to information. 'The less we know, the more random the event appears to be' was the view of the ancients, a view turned around in the 20th Century to read, 'The more uncertain an event, the less information we have on it'.

One of the first to write about how to predict the future probabilistically was an Italian mathematician and physician, Girolamo Cardano (1501-1571), with regard to the throwing of dice. The illegitimate son of a well-to-do lawyer and geometer who was a close acquaintance of Leonardo da Vinci, Cardano led a most interesting and unhappy life on the edge of disrepute. Excluded from many posts because of the circumstances of his birth as well as his cantankerous nature, he lived by his wits at gambling. He was not greatly successful, however, at one time being compelled to sell his household furniture to cover debts. Luckily, he managed some miraculous cures of people of influence by using alternative methods of medicine, which compared to standard methods of the time had much to commend them, since at least they did his patients no harm. Prominent families backed him to the extent that he was able to function as a lecturer in mathematics. In 1545, he published a book, *Ars Magna*, that made him famous throughout Europe, although the work contained material stolen during a drinking bout from a fellow mathematician of lesser ability, Tartaglia by name. Cardano also spent many an hour throwing dice against the wall and puzzling over the results. He completed some notes on the matter in 1563, but these were not published until 1663 under the title *De Ludo Aleae* (On Dicing), a decade after the work of Pascal had raised interest in the subject of mathematically-based predictions of probable events.

The cornerstones for the theory of probability as we know it today were in fact laid in 1654. The essential building materials were seven letters exchanged by two great French mathematicians: Blaise Pascal, the son of a wealthy man who contracted for tax collections in the name of the King of France, and Pierre de Fermat, a jurist by trade, whose famous Last Theorem took four centuries to prove. The correspondence between Pascal and Fermat concerned an interesting problem involving the throwing of dice.

Pascal was a brilliantly simplistic thinker: the barometer, the speedometer and a mechanical calculating machine based on cogs and wheels were all products of his insight and genius. Here is another. In the 17th century, gentlemen wore coats of many pockets which resulted in the frustration of fishing about for needed items, such as handkerchiefs, wallets, papers, coins and so on. One day, Pascal amused his friends when he appeared with his pocket watch strapped to his wrist. He had invented the wrist watch.

But we are getting ahead of ourselves. A nervous, introspective young man, Pascal fell into a depressed mental state after the death of his father in 1651. His doctor, somewhat of a pre-Freudian psychologist it seems, seeing no physical reason for Pascal's partially paralytic condition, suggested that squandering some of the inheritance on nights on the town might effect a cure. It was worth a try: Pascal loved staying up late and gambling till dawn, so that became the prescribed regimen. It worked wonders! His heath was restored. On his journeys through nighttime Paris, he fell in with a smart young gambler much like himself: Antoine Gombauld, the Chevalier de Méré, who was a master of betting on dice and cards. Instinctively, de Méré always seemed to choose the right side of a bet. Well, most of the time. In 1654, he failed in one of his enterprises and asked Pascal for insight. Thus history was made.

For some time, de Méré had made money on this proposition: 'I will give you even money that you will roll a six at least once in four successive tosses of one die.' This is a well-known bet, even today. For the sake of variety, and desiring to win more money from people who had lost interest in his previous proposition, he later changed to this wager: 'I will give you even odds that you will roll a double six on at least one of twenty-four tosses of two dice.' It troubled de Méré that he was losing money in this new situation.

When Pascal took on his friend's problem, he transformed himself from a bright, young wastrel into what in modern terms we call a risk management consultant, a thoroughly reputable profession whose members often give advice on television. He reasoned as follows. On one throw of a die, there is an equal chance of rolling any number one through six. The chance of not throwing six must be 5/6. As each throw is independent of any other throw, the chance of not getting a six on four throws is clearly 5/6 x 5/6 x 5/6 x 5/6, which comes to 0.4822 or 48.22%. In modern parlance, the probability of throwing a six is 51.77%, a difference of 3.55%. On the other hand, throwing a double six in twenty-four tosses has a probability of 49.14%, so the odds are slightly against the proposition, as de Méré had guessed. No wonder he was losing money.

In order to move the odds in his favor, de Méré needed to change the bet from 24 throws to 25. However, it has been estimated by R.W. Hamming (in *The Art of Probability*) that to see the difference in outcomes between 24 throws and 25 throws would have required at least 78,000 tosses of the dice. So the Chevalier's suspicions were aroused more by his short-term losses than by any long-term experience. In bridge, there are many 'correct' technical plays that are favored by fewer percentage points than this, so one can hardly imagine how many years one would have to play to master them all on the basis of experience alone. Clearly some theory is needed as an aid. Short-term experience may leave one none the wiser.

Pascal's Triangle

All the ills that affect a man come from one sole cause,
namely that he has not learned to sit quietly and contently in a room.
- Blaise Pascal (1632-1662)

Pascal's way of thinking about probability is commonplace now, but first someone had to cut a narrow path of logical procedure through the twisted undergrowth of fallacious argument. Pascal himself did not claim he had invented anything new, asserting that he was merely arranging previously held concepts into a systematic framework. That points to the reason why bridge players should have a working knowledge of probability theory — first, as a practical application of relevant results that occur frequently during normal play (knowledge they may acquire through painful trial and error), and second, as a means of acquiring a systematic, general approach to decision making that may be applied to many situations, especially those that may be encountered only rarely.

One of Pascal's 'arrangements' is the so-called **Pascal's Triangle**, which starts as follows:

```
                              1
                      1               1
                 1          2               1
            1          3          3          1
       1          4          6          4          1
   1         5         10         10          5          1
 1         6        15         20         15         6          1
                              etc.
```

The numbers can be continued down as far as one wishes. Each line can be derived from the one above as follows: each number in a lower line equals the sum of the two closest integers above it in the previous line, one to the left and one to the right. (This diagram was known in China in the 14th century by the name of *The Precious Mirror of the Four Elements*.)

The importance of this diagram to bridge is that these integers represent the numbers of ways of choosing m cards from a pool of N cards. Without going into the exact method of calculating these combinations, let us just state that they are the Lego blocks in the mathematician's Playbox of Probability. The last line of the diagram represents the combinations of cards taken from a pool of six cards: 6 is the number of ways one card can be chosen; 15 represents the number of combinations for two cards chosen out of six; 20 represents the number of combinations of three cards chosen. Symmetry about the vertical can be grasped at a glance. So it is that the number of combinations of four cards chosen from six is equal to the number of ways two cards can be chosen from six, because choosing two cards and leaving four behind is equivalent to choosing four cards and leaving two behind. The ones at the extremities are respectively the number of ways of choosing no cards and all the cards available.

Information and Probability in the 20th Century

Words are but the images of matter.
To fall in love with them is to fall in love with a picture.
- Sir Francis Bacon (1561-1626)

Words, words, words... by the time the 20th century rolled around, Probability Theory had evolved into a state of linguistic confusion. The French view was that they had shipped the theory across the English Channel in good shape back in Laplace's time and a century later the British had messed it up greatly. The mathematician Émile Borel, after attempting to read a 1921 treatise on subjective probability by the economist John Maynard Keynes, said he couldn't understand a word of it, and put forth the hypothesis that English and French brains were differently constructed. Borel suggested returning to an analysis of games in order to study the problem in its simplest form, as Pascal and Fermat had done at the very beginning. He chose bridge as a suitable subject and with André Chéron, a leading French player, produced the classic *The Mathematical Theory of Bridge*, first published in English in 1955 with the financial backing of C. C. Wei, the inventor of the Precision bidding system.

Meanwhile, isolated from cross-channel condescension and vituperation, Soviet mathematicians had come up with a way to firm up the foundations. Andrei Kolmogorov said that it didn't matter what probability was as long as one could describe its mathematical properties in a few simple axioms in a manner consistent with the mathematical formulations of the past. It was as if Euclid had drawn a line in the sand and said, 'Lads, I define a straight line as the shortest distance between two points, and now let's get on with the rest of it.'

The same service with regard to information was provided in 1954 by the American engineer, Claude Shannon. 'What is information?' Shannon pondered. 'How are information and probability related?' Inspiration provided this simple mathematical answer:

$$\text{Information} = -\log(p)$$

What is p? Probability, of course! Thus Shannon made an unambiguous inverse link between probability and information. In other words, the less likely an event, the more information it conveys when it occurs. We should note before going farther that what Shannon was referring to is the *amount* of information in a message, not the actual information contained.

To put this idea in a bridge context, let's consider the situation where one is playing a natural system and opens with a bid of 1◊. Partner responds up the line with 1♡ or 1♠, promising at least four cards in the suit named. Which bid is the more informative? As partner would bid 1♡ any time he has four hearts, whether or not he has four spades, and 1♠ with four spades and fewer than four hearts, it is more likely the response will be 1♡ rather than 1♠. The 1♡ response therefore has a higher probability than 1♠. However, the 1♡ bid is less informative and possesses more uncertainty, as it does not exclude the frequent case of 4-4 in the majors. The 1♠ bid is more informative but less probable.

Shannon chose the term **entropy** (a term used in physics to express the amount of disorder in a system) to express the amount of uncertainty in many situations involving probability. Just as, in physics, systems tend to maximize disorder, we shall find that our mathematical models prefer to maximize uncertainty. At the table, the lie of the cards that generates the most possible cases, and therefore maximum uncertainty, is the most probable. We shall refer to 'entropy' when the reference is directly related to the mathematical quantity, but the reader is allowed to say 'uncertainty' under his breath. It is worthwhile to know this mathematical definition exists even if we needn't calculate its value, because the concept of uncertainty and its relationship to knowledge is fundamental to a full understanding of the applications of probability to bridge.

Interlude of Movie Madness

Tonight's Presentation: Bridge on the Orient Express (1939)
Starring Basil Rathbone as Holmes and Nigel Bruce as Watson

Scene: Holmes and Watson are kibitzing two suspicious characters posing as Levantine businessmen who have sat down in the lounge car for a game of bridge with a Turkish government official and an Arab sheik.

Watson: Holmes, at this rate we won't find out who holds the queen of spades before reaching Constantinople.

Holmes: Patience, old fellow. Why, we've already reduced the possibilities by half.

Watson: I don't see what you mean. All that's happened in the past five minutes is that the fellow beneath the fez has led the ♡8. That's just one card out of fifty-two, the way I see it.

Holmes: I mean that by playing the ♡8, he has eliminated the possibility of his partner holding that card, thus removing from consideration half of all possible deals.

Watson: Amazing! A reverse probability, or something of that sort. Now I see his partner with the false beard has followed with the ♡5, thus removing half of the remaining deals and reducing the possibilities to one-quarter of what we started with when we left the station at Budapest.

Holmes: Very perceptive, Watson, and only slightly inaccurate. Once the dummy appeared, West could have held 10,400,600 different hands and the same applies to East, so one round of hearts has reduced the possibilities to two and a half million, not much less than the one-quarter you mentioned. The next defender's card will produce another one-half reduction in a symmetric situation.

Watson: If these fellows would play a bit faster, we could catch a good night's sleep while passing through Bulgaria.

Holmes: Exactly. As I have always told you, Watson, eliminate the impossible and whatever is left, however improbable, must include the true situation.

Watson: Two and a half million possibilities still to be eliminated, minus one, that is.

Is Bridge Beautiful?

Accuracy is essential to beauty.
- Ralph Waldo Emerson (1803-1882)

I do not know what the philosopher was thinking of when he wrote the statement above — perhaps the beautifully carved but unpredictable clock on his mantelpiece. Nothing can be potentially more annoying than a cuckoo (or a partner) who continually mis-times his leaps. I have always thought of accuracy as merely a higher form of counting, a cool kind of perfection that appeals to the part of the brain capable of reasoning, a part that has a depressingly small role to play in our everyday decision making, as we learn from the highly entertaining book by neuroscientist Jonah Lehrer, *How We Decide* (2009).

Many bridge commentators are idealists; they wish the game would provide a refuge, within which what might be termed 'the higher functions' can freely roam like unicorns in the Elysian Fields. The Platonists take the view that out there somewhere there must be the perfect play, if one could only find it. To satisfy their desire for perfection, they promote the idea that at IMP scoring a player should envision a set of circumstances, no matter how unlikely, in which a contract may fail, then form a plan that avoids the imagined dangers, even at the cost of overtricks. Under such circumstances they may observe, 'She played it beautifully', without mentioning that the final trick total was well below its full potential. To them, that's where Beauty resides.

To such idealists I say, 'Embrace probability, glorify doubt.' The closer the world of bridge resembles the real world, the more amusing it becomes. There is beauty and excitement in uncertainty. Shakespeare wrote, 'Shall I compare thee to a summer's day?', which is much more evocative than a factual, 'I shall compare thee favorably to a summer's day and go on at length from there.' What poetry resides in the word 'perchance', as in 'to sleep, perchance to drop a trick that will not return'! There is no stigma to be attached to a guess, only to a bad guess.

How does the statement 'She played it beautifully' differ from 'She guessed well'? Perhaps at IMPs one can afford to play beautifully, whereas at matchpoints one must guess well to win. Probability plays a large part in the latter process. It therefore plays an increasingly large part even at IMPs, as modern players reach more dubious contracts that simply call for adopting the most probable winning line.

CHAPTER 4

COMBINATIONS AND PERMUTATIONS

I believe the calculation of the Quantity of Probability might be improved to be a very usefull and pleasant Speculation and applied to a great many Events which are accidental, besides those of Games.

Where a mathematical reasoning can be had, it's a great folly to make use of any other, as to grope for a thing in the dark when you have a candle standing by you.
- John Arbuthnot (1667-1735) from
Of the Laws of Chance, or, a Method of the Hazards of Game (1692)

Such was the admonition to the reader in the introduction to the first book on probability written in English. Why had it taken so long for this idea, commonplace in our day, to be given full public acceptance? Let's allow philosophers to argue over the reasons, and focus our own attention on the bridge player. It is essential to an understanding of how probability applies to card play to see how it derives from the number of card combinations involved.

There are two characteristics of card placements that need to be recognized: the number of combinations into which the cards can be dealt to two defenders and the number of permutations in which the cards can be played. Notice the distinction here, important in mathematics but often blurred in everyday usage: if the order of a selection is important, it is a **permutation** — if not, it is a **combination**. As we saw earlier, Pascal's Triangle can help us with the number of ways m cards can be selected from a group of N cards. Take the case of a group of four cards. The entry in the Triangle for four cards is 1-4-6-4-1, meaning that there are in total sixteen possible combinations (1+4+6+4+1), divided into groups of 4-0, 3-1, 2-2, 1-3 and 0-4, respectively, according to the splits between two hands.

Let's denote the four cards in the defender's hands by the letters u, w, x, and y. Here are the sixteen possible combinations expressed in terms of those letters.

4 - 0	3 - 1	2 - 2	1 - 3	0 - 4
uwxy - 0	uwx - y	uw - xy	y - uwx	0 - uwxy
	uxy - w	ux - wy	w - uxy	
	uwy - x	uy - wx	x - uwy	
	wxy - u	wx - uy	u - wxy	
		xy - uw		
		wy - ux		

If the cards are dealt at random, each possibility within each split is equally probable, but the splits themselves are not equally probable: an even split is more likely than a specific uneven split. The rank of the cards is not relevant.

When it comes to the play of the cards, however, the rank of the cards may be relevant, as a defender should not play a card that gives away a trick unnecessarily. An important characteristic is the order in which the cards can be played under such a condition. If cards u, w, x and y are of equal significance, then they can be played at random (if we ignore carding agreements), so the play is similar to the deal in that the order of appearance of the cards is not material. However, there is information to be had from the appearance of a specific card.

Let's suppose declarer lays down the ace in the suit and LHO follows with card u. That tells us the LHO was not void in the suit. It also tells us that half of the combinations listed above have been eliminated, all those for which card u is held by RHO. Also, if the split is 3-1, LHO could have chosen any of three cards; if 2-2, either of two cards. If the split is 1-3, just one card can appear. The number of plausible choices is thus an important characteristic that distinguishes the splits. This is discussed further when we introduce Bayes' Theorem, in Chapter 7.

If the play continues with the RHO following with card x, then the possibilities are reduced to the following:

3 - 1	2 - 2	1 - 3
uwy - x	uw - xy	u - wxy
	uy - wx	

There are four combinations remaining, in the pattern of 1-2-1. The total number of plausible play permutations between LHO and RHO taken in tandem equals three for each of the 3-1 and 1-3 splits and equals four for the 2-2 split. This distinction is what makes probability during the play of the cards different from the probability of the deal of the cards.

There is one final point to be made here: saying that the defenders followed with two low cards is not the same as noting specifically that LHO followed with card u and RHO with card x. At the table, one sees which cards are played, and that allows for the specific reduction shown above.

Let's take a rest from all this theory and allow ourselves a brief vacation on an island in the South Pacific where combinations and permutations play a role in filling the vacant places in an establishment we shall call the Hôtel du Paradis.

Vacation at the Hôtel du Paradis

Early one morning as the sun rises above the Pacific to begin its relentless task of scorching the sands of the nearby beach, five bleary-eyed passengers emerge from a battered and dusty taxicab. Stiff-legged, they make their way in as straight a line as they can manage to the lobby of the Hôtel du Paradis. Awaiting them behind a formidable teakwood barrier stands the slight figure of bespectacled Assistant Manager Aristide-Maurice Laplace, whose intelligent features display a mixture of dignity, deference and bemusement.

Yes, he assures his prospective guests, he has their reservations for beachside accommodations, written down on three file cards which he holds before him and from which he proceeds to read their names: Mr. and Mrs. Henry Kraft of Kingston, Ontario; Mr. and Mrs. Barry Tulley of Boston, Mass.; and Brother Xavier of San Francisco, California. Unfortunately for the new arrivals, the thirteen rooms of Annex A and the thirteen rooms of Annex B are at present occupied; however, several vacancies will be forthcoming before noon. As soon as a vacancy occurs, he will assign that accommodation to one of the three parties before him. In the meantime, he is happy to be able to offer them complimentary Continental breakfasts under the palm trees in the open-air Tiki-Tiki Lounge and thereafter free use of the tennis courts until such time as rooms become available.

As they are leaving the lobby, Mrs Kraft draws aside her husband and says in a loud whisper, 'Henry, I can't stand the thought of spending two weeks in the same little Annex with those terrible Tulleys. Say something to the nice manager, will you?'

'Don't fuss, Zoe, the odds are against it,' reassures her husband wearily. To tell the truth, he favors the Tulleys as neighbors, being uneasy with the thought that his much-anticipated second honeymoon will be spent with Brother Xavier kneeling in silent prayer in the adjacent room.

As their third cups of strongly acidic French roast cool before them, Laplace arrives at their table and announces brightly that their accommodations are now available.

'Brother Xavier, I have you in Annex A,' he begins.

Now we interrupt our story and ask some questions.

QUESTION #1 How close was Henry Kraft to telling a fib when he said that the Tulleys probably would be assigned to a different Annex?

QUESTION #2 How does the fact that Brother Xavier has been assigned to Annex A affect the odds?

Monsieur Laplace continues, 'Mr and Mrs Tulley, you also are in Annex A.'

QUESTION #3 Now what are the odds that the Krafts will end up in Annex B? How much hope can Henry allow himself?

We shall answer these questions before proceeding further in our story by simply counting up the possible combinations. While we are taking a moment away from the narrative, it is worth drawing the reader's attention to the fact that each of our Annexes contains thirteen rooms. Be patient — eventually all of this will apply to bridge!

Perhaps the easiest way to think of the problem is to imagine M. Laplace at his counter. One party checks out; he assigns the vacated room to Brother Xavier. The next party checks out and he assigns their room to Mr and Mrs Tulley. After the third party checks out, his assignment is completed and he proceeds to the lounge with the good news.

Consider the first party to leave. There are thirteen possibilities in Annex A and thirteen possibilities in B, twenty-six in all. So the chance of the vacancy occurring in Annex A was 13 out of 26, and in Annex B, the same: 50% for each event.

Consider the second party to leave. As Brother Xavier is to occupy a place in Annex A, there were now only twelve possible new vacancies in A and still thirteen in B. So the odds that someone in A will be next to leave are reduced to 12/25 (48%), whereas the odds of someone leaving B are increased to 13/25 (52%).

Finally, after the Tulleys are also given accommodation in A, the odds of the next vacancy being in A are further reduced to 11/24 (46%) whereas the odds for B are now 13/24 (54%). So given this procedure and assuming the rooms are vacated in a purely random manner, we can write down the exact odds. To do this, we must consider all possible situations ('events' in probability terminology).

Annex A	Annex B	Odds for Occurrence	Normalized
KTX	—	(13/26) x (12/25) x (11/24)	11
TX	K	(13/26) x (12/25) x (13/24)	13
KX	T	(13/26) x (12/25) x (13/24)	13
KT	X	(13/26) x (12/25) x (13/24)	13

We can eliminate common factors in the 'Odds' column and arrive at the final column, which shows the relationship in terms of percentages. An 11 occurs if KTX are all assigned to the same annex, while the three 13s occur when both annexes receive new guests. This chart represents just half the events possible. Since it is equally likely that the first vacancy occurred in Annex B, our one 11 and three 13s must be doubled to account for the possibilities when A and B are exchanged. That leaves us with one 22 and three 26s, with the happy total of 100, a convenient coincidence, occurring in this case only, that facilitates the conversion to percentages.

Hold on, you might exclaim, all this is not really valid because the guests may not check out in a random sequence. Perhaps guests in adjacent rooms have arrived together and are leaving on the same flight, so their departure times are correlated to their spatial proximity. Yes, and the same is true of poorly shuffled cards. Cards get dealt in a non-random fashion because cards that were related in the play of the previous deal remain in that relationship due to poor shuffling. However, in the mathematical modeling of the process, one assumes that the shuffling is adequate and that the cards are dealt randomly.

Randomness in dealing means that the cards can be dealt in any sequence provided they are thoroughly shuffled. Randomness in play is another matter altogether. Although Laplace may select one reservation card over another in a random manner, the sequence of plays at bridge is governed by restrictions imposed by the rules of the game, such as having to follow suit. These rules impose order on chaos.

There is another way that Laplace might assign rooms. He could wait until three vacancies have occurred, then choose at random a card from his reservation file. He assigns that unknown party to the annex with more vacancies — it doesn't matter which annex he chooses, as the randomness of placement is a consequence of the shuffling of the reservation cards. As long as the deal is random, the mathematics is the same; only the implementation changes. So, one may think of dealing cards in several ways, but it is important to choose the implementation that best promotes understanding of a random process.

Do you remember the three questions we posed earlier? We are now ready to answer them by looking at the table above.

QUESTION #1 How close was Henry Kraft to telling a fib when he said that the Tulleys probably would be assigned to a different Annex?

ANSWER #1 K and T will occupy the same Annex 48 times out of 100, so Henry Kraft was on the correct side of his borderline claim by 52% to 48%.

QUESTION #2 How does the fact that Brother Xavier has been assigned to Annex A affect the odds?

ANSWER #2 The assignment of X to Annex A did not affect the odds of KT being together as the case of KT being together in Annex B was not ruled out. Thus the odds were still 24/50, or 48%. Another way of viewing this is as follows: Brother X could be assigned equally to either Annex A or Annex B. Whether it is B rather than A doesn't affect the number of cases where KT are together. This shows that information revealed may or may not be relevant to the question at hand. If the annexes had differing numbers of rooms, however, the initial placement of Brother X *would* affect the odds of KT being together in one annex.

QUESTION #3 Now that Xavier and the Tulleys are in Annex A, what are the odds that the Krafts will end up in Annex B?

ANSWER #3 There are thirteen occurrences where TX are together in Annex A and K is in Annex B, compared to eleven occurrences where all three are in Annex A. Therefore the odds of K being separated from the other two parties, and making both Mr. and Mrs. Kraft happy with the arrangements, are up to 54%. Henry breathes a little easier.

The astute Laplace has done his job well, as this indeed proves to be the placement. If he had overheard Zoe's loud whisper, he might have been subjected to what is known as a Restricted Choice. There are two vacancies in Annex A and one in Annex B. As the Krafts and Tulleys are best separated, the Krafts would be chosen first to go alone to Annex B and as Brother Xavier was an old customer, he would get the best room available in Annex A. Put another way, Laplace was limited to a single choice (Krafts in Annex B) in order to best suit the conditions. So the K card is played first, and the X card is played next.

When there is a basis for preference of one card over another, the placement of the guests is subject to restrictions and is not random. If Laplace announces first that the Krafts are in Annex B, the odds that the Tulleys are also in Annex B have been reduced, given that one is aware of the preference. Indeed, if the Tulleys are also in Annex B, Laplace might have announced that information first, which in itself reduces the odds of their sharing the same annex by half as there is no apparent reason why the Krafts should be announced first. This reasoning applies also to the play of cards at the bridge table. When one of two equivalent cards appears from a defender, the odds of the other equivalent card being in the same hand are reduced by the mere fact that the other equivalent card could have been played just as easily if it were in the same hand.

Back to Pascal's Triangle

The Hôtel du Paradis is just one of many analogies one might invent to make the mathematics plausible, but is it a valid approach? Not really — the real world is not meant to model mathematics, rather the other way around. The complexities of reality only serve to intrude upon the simplicity of numbers. Let's limit ourselves to cards and see how a mathematician might approach the problem of calculating the probability of a 2-1 split. Card combinations are the key and Pascal's Triangle the lock, so put the key in the lock, turn it and the doors of perception swing wide.

Let's return to the mathematical problem faced in the Hôtel du Paradis story but now think of cards rather than people. Suppose we wish to calculate for two hands (West and East) the probability of 3-0 and 2-1 splits for three known spades. To give the problem physicality, imagine that the spades are removed from the deck and three spades are chosen for relocation, the ♠K, the ♠10 and the ♠7. The cards in the remaining suits are dealt into three piles of thirteen and one pile is removed from further alteration. The two piles remaining will serve as the defender's hands. From these, three known cards are selected at random, say the ♡6, the ◊8 and the ♣2. These known cards are replaced in their piles and the twenty-six cards are shuffled and dealt into West and East hands.

The dealer now asks that West or East give him the ♡6. In return, he gives one of the three spades face down. The process is repeated until the three spades have all been placed with West or East. After this process is complete, what are the probabilities of a 2-1 split and a 3-0 split? This calculation can be made with reference to the non-spades. How many combinations can occur if the ♡6, the ◊8 and the ♣2 are all in the West hand? The answer is the number of ways in which ten cards can be chosen from twenty-three to fill the vacant places in the West hand. We know this answer is a big number: in fact it is 1,144,066. How many ways can eleven cards be chosen? A bigger number: 1,352,078.

What compels mathematicians to spring these huge numbers on the reader? Is this desire to impress any more commendable than a gorilla beating his chest? Perhaps by quoting a number, one conquers one's fear of it. At any rate, these numbers of combinations, impressive though they be, are of little use at the bridge table. However, help is on the way. Here, the purpose is to demonstrate the method by which these numbers are derived.

If one deals with ratios, the big numbers reduce to little numbers, in this case 11/13, which means that for every eleven times a 3-0 split occurs, there are thirteen occurrences of a 2-1 split. (Do these numbers sound familiar?) Double these numbers to account for the 0-3 and 1-2 splits. To get the total numbers of combinations, we must multiply by the number of combinations of the three spades to be substituted in the three vacant places. In a 3-0 split, there is only one way possible, but for a 2-1 split there are three possible singletons — so we have eleven 3-0 cases and 3 x 13 or thirty-nine 2-1 cases. So for every twenty-two combinations encompassing 0-3 or 3-0 splits, there are seventy-eight combinations involving 2-1 or 1-2 splits. In other words, the overall probability of a 2-1 split is 78%, and of a 3-0 split, 22%.

This result is the same as one obtains using the Hôtel du Paradis model and working from the other end of Pascal's Triangle, as it were. However, to imagine the guests exchanging rooms a million times during a short stay rather boggles the mind. It is better to get away from the hot beach and, under the umbrella of mathematics, coolly focus the mind on the ratio of the combinations, because that formulation can be applied without confusion to many different situations.

The Plot Thickens

When Henry says to Zoe that the odds are that they won't share an annex with the Tulleys, how sure can he be that he is not wiggling out of doing a husband's duty to ensure the contentment of a discriminating spouse? Perhaps he has found out more about the placement of the resident guests — in particular, whether there is an imbalance in the number of vacancies to be made available. It would be poor management if the assistant manager in charge had no idea how many of his guests would be departing on any given day, so the previous model, which assumes maximum ignorance in that regard, is not appropriate.

Let's look at how the odds change if some guests are known to be staying on so that Annex A has just seven possible vacancies to Annex B's five. We can construct a table of the number of possible combinations when fourteen of the twenty-six rooms will not become available.

Arrangements		If Annex A	If Annex B
KTX	—	21	6
TX	K	21	14
KX	T	21	14
KT	X	21	14

'If Annex A' means KTX are in A, etc. Here the total number of normalized occurrences is 132.

Let's revisit the same three questions under these new conditions.

QUESTION #1 How close is Henry Kraft to telling a fib when he says that the Tulleys assuredly will be assigned a different Annex? The number in which K and T don't appear together is 70. Therefore the chance of the Krafts and the Tulleys not sharing the same annex is now up to 53% (70/132).

The previous figure 52% applies when any room has an equal chance of being vacated. This is an *a priori* probability estimated in a complete state of uncertainty as far as Kraft is concerned. The figure 53% applies when Kraft knows something about the number of exclusions. The uncertainty is reduced by the additional knowledge, which gives a numerical advantage to one annex over the other. The reduction in the total and the imbalance of two in the numbers of vacancies have not had a large effect.

QUESTION #2 How did the fact that Brother Xavier was assigned to Annex A affect the odds of K and T being assigned the same annex?

The number of combinations where KT appear together is 35 (21 in Annex A with X and 14 in Annex B without X), so the odds of their being together is reduced to 35/77 or 45.5%. Because of the imbalance, the assignment of KT is not independent of that of X. (*With regard to bridge, one has to be careful not to accept arguments that have as their underlying assumption that the number of vacancies are balanced between two hands.*)

QUESTION #3 How did the fact that X and T were assigned to Annex A affect the odds that the Krafts would end up in Annex B?

The odds before assignment were five out of twelve or 42% as expected. With X and T assigned to Annex A, the vacancies in A and B became balanced at five in each, so the odds rise to 50%. This is a state of maximum uncertainty as to where the next vacancy will occur. (*When playing a bridge hand, declarer must keep track of the vacancies in order to keep track of the shifting probabilities that have a bearing on decisions to be made.*)

I hope this little story has both amused and informed. Calculating percentages is as easy as keeping track of combinations. In what follows, we shall be interested mainly in simple decision-making processes for which the key is which action addresses the greater number of combinations that represent success. Let's return to the bridge table and get back to work applying what we have learned about combinations and permutations.

Card Combinations

Card combinations in each suit are the building blocks of a bridge hand. One describes a hand as '5332', imparting the fact that the hand contains one suit of five-card length, two of three-card length, and one doubleton. To be specific, one writes 3=5=3=2 to indicate that the five-card suit was hearts and the doubleton, clubs.

The cards held jointly by defenders can be divided in several ways. It is the ratio of the number of cards held that is important with regard to probability. Let's start with a holding of three cards and build from there. There are four possible splits.

	3 - 0 split	2 - 1 split	1 - 2 split	0 - 3 split
Combinations	1	3	3	1

The number of combinations can be seen immediately to be those shown above. Four cards can be split in five ways:

Splits	4 - 0	3 - 1	2 - 2	1 - 3	4 - 0
Combinations	1	4	6	4	1

The numbers of combinations can be found in Pascal's Triangle, but there is a way to recall them conveniently at the bridge table. If one wishes to compare the number of combinations of a certain number of cards split between two hands, one need only align the splits with the larger number on the left starting with the most even split as follows:

	2 - 2	3 - 1	4 - 0	
Adjacent Ratios	1	2/3	1/4	
Full Ratios	1	2/3	1/6	(2/3)x(1/4) = 1/6
Combinations	6	4	1	

Read across the very top line in this table: the **adjacent ratio** is merely the ratio of the last number on the left to the first number on the right. So the 1 of 3-1 and the 4 of 4-0 give us the 1/4 adjacent ratio for the two splits. That gives the ratio of the two combinations involved. The full ratio with respect to the most even split is the product of the intervening adjacent ratios:

$$2/3 \times 1/4 = 2/12 = 1/6$$

The 4-0 split has just one possibility, so to obtain the numbers of combinations for each split, multiply the full ratios by the denominator, in this case 6, and voila! There are the coefficients of Pascal's Triangle: 1-4-6-4-1. Let's do two more for easy reference.

	3 - 2	4 - 1	5 - 0
Adjacent Ratios	1	1/2	1/5
Full Ratios	1	1/2	1/10
Combinations	10	5	1

The 2 from 3-2 and the 4 from 4-1 give us an adjacent ratio of 2/4 which is the same as 1/2. Similarly we have the 1 from 4-1 and the 5 from 5-0 giving us 1/5 in the last column. The product of these two is 1/10, which is the full ratio in the last column.

	3 - 3	4 - 2	5 - 1	6 - 0
Adjacent Ratios	1	3/4	2/5	1/6
Full Ratios	1	3/4	3/10	1/20
Combinations	20	15	6	1

In practice, we use the ratios more than the numbers of combinations. Why? Because probabilities are ratios of card combinations. That makes life simpler, but keep in mind that we are dealing with relative numbers of card combinations rather than some abstract quantity with magical properties we can take for granted.

Next let's look at the number of combinations for two suits, eight spades and six hearts. Suppose we know that LHO has eight cards in the majors, and RHO six. Which of the two cases below has the larger number of combinations?

	Condition I	**Condition II**
	♠ 5 - 3 (0.8)	♠ 4 - 4
	♡ 3 - 3	♡ 4 - 2 (0.75)
Ratios	0.8	0.75
Normalized	C	(15/16)C

The numbers of combinations in the two suits is the product of the numbers of combinations in each suit taken separately. The total number of combinations for Condition I (denoted by the capital letter C) is 1120 and for Condition II, 1050. The ratio of these two is 15/16. The ratio can be calculated directly from the ratios for the two suits taken individually, shown in brackets, so it is not necessary to calculate the total number of combinations.

Which condition is the more probable? That depends on the distribution of the minor suits. As it is known that the minor suits taken together are split 5-7 in both cases, Condition I is the more probable as it contributes the greater number of combinations.

Comparisons of Even and Odd Splits

The Gods love those of ordered mind.
- Sophocles (496-406 BC)

In decision making, one need only be concerned with the ratio of combinations for a given split relative to the maximum possible for a given number of cards in the suit. One must keep in mind that odd numbers and even numbers have different properties. Splits for odd numbers of cards have the greater rates of reduction, so the difference between the most probable split and the second-most is greater. Here are the results for some common splits and their adjacent splits.

Even Numbered Suits				Odd Numbered Suits			
Split	Next	Fraction	Decimal	Split	Next	Fraction	Decimal
5-5	6-4	5/6	0.83	5-4	6-3	4/6	0.67
4-4	5-3	4/5	0.80	4-3	5-2	3/5	0.60
3-3	4-2	3/4	0.75	3-2	4-1	2/4	0.50
2-2	3-1	2/3	0.67	2-1	3-0	1/3	0.33

The greatest reductions occur when an uneven split of an odd number of cards is made more uneven, for example a 3-2 split is changed to a 4-1 split (50% reduction in the number of combinations). Often a critical decision during the play is whether the defenders' six cards in a suit will divide 3-3 or 4-2. But these numbers cannot be viewed in isolation.

We saw above that when looking at two suits, one of eight cards and the other of six, there are more combinations with the shorter suit 3-3, because a 5-3 break in the longer suit is more probable than a 4-2 split in the shorter. However, if the longer suit held by the opposition is odd in number, then the lesser reduction is achieved by changing a 3-3 split to a 4-2 split (a reduction to 75%). This favors the assumption of a 4-2 split over a 3-3 split.

It is important to realize that suits encompassing an even number of cards must be treated differently from suits encompassing an odd number of cards. The familiar rule of 'Eight-Ever' holds universally, but the rule of 'Nine-Never' has conditions attached, as we shall discover in the next chapter. The differences are related directly to the fact that with 'Eight-Ever' the number of missing cards involved is five, an odd number, whereas with 'Nine-Never' the number of missing cards involved is four, an even number. With three or five cards held by the defenders, finessing for the missing honor always represents a better proposition than playing for the drop; however, with two, four, or six cards held by the defenders, the drop is preferred under some circumstances, depending on the number of vacant places available.

CHAPTER 5

A PRIORI ODDS AND VACANT PLACES

Happy the one who knows the reasons why.
- Virgil (70-19 BC)

The *a priori* odds and vacant place calculations of the odds have this in common: they both rely on the numbers of card combinations possible in suits that have not been played. In the former situation, no suit has been played, so all suits are involved. In the latter situation, some suits have been played, but some remain to be played. Of those that remain to be played, it is assumed there is an equal possibility of their cards having been dealt to either hand.

Most declarers have a working knowledge of the *a priori* odds concerning the most common splits. These odds appear in many books, but they are often misinterpreted as being the unalterable odds that govern the deal. A better interpretation is that these are the odds under the condition of maximum ignorance with regard to the deal about to be played. Once the condition of maximum ignorance is changed, the odds must necessarily change, but it is often the case that the changes are small in the early stages of the bidding and play. So the *a priori* odds remain a useful guide in a condition of high uncertainty where there doesn't appear to be evidence of an imbalance in the vacant places, a key attribute.

It is important to understand how the *a priori* odds are arrived at in order to comprehend what assumptions lie behind the probability figures. The reason this point comes up repeatedly in this book is that there has not in the past been enough emphasis put on the fact that the odds must be related to what is known at the time of decision. Let's now look at how one derives the *a priori* odds in order to understand how these are related to a state of maximum ignorance. We begin with the case of six cards held in one suit. Here are the commonly stated odds together with the numbers of card combinations as stated in Pascal's Triangle:

Card Split	6 - 0	5 - 1	4 - 2	3 - 3	2 - 4	1 - 5	0 - 6
Combinations	1	6	10	15	10	6	1
A Priori Odds (%)	0.75	7.3	24.2	35.5	24.2	7.3	0.75

We shall now show how to derive these figures from first principles, as we did in the story of the Hôtel du Paradis. Just like the problem facing our Assistant Manager, this involves consideration of **vacant places** — which is simply the number of slots in each hand whose occupancy is unknown. During the bidding and play, we discover something about the unseen hands, leaving fewer vacant places for cards whose locations we are attempting to guess.

Each hand contains thirteen cards. If it is specified that LHO holds six clubs, say, then RHO holds none. That leaves seven vacant places on the left and thirteen on the right to be filled with cards from the other suits. One may imagine taking twenty cards at random from a deck excluding clubs in order to fill the vacant places, dealing seven to the left and thirteen to the right. In fact, the number of possible combinations for these cards outside the clubs equals: $20! / (13! \times 7!)$[1]

If LHO holds three clubs and RHO holds three clubs, so that there are ten vacant spaces a side, the number of possible card combinations equals: $20! / (10! \times 10!)$. The relative probability of the two conditions is the ratio of the number of possible card combinations: in particular, the ratio of the 6-0 outside combinations to 3-3 combinations equals $(13! \times 7!)/ (10! \times 10!)$.

We call this proportion the outside card ratio. In order to get to probabilities, one must include the possible combinations within the club suit itself, which are given by Pascal's Triangle, 1 for 6-0 split and 20 for the 3-3 split. The resulting ratio of total combinations represents the relative probability of a 6-0 split to a 3-3 split.

The following table summarizes these results for all the possible splits of six cards:

		Club			
Split	Outside Card Ratio	Combinations	Full Ratio	Probability	Weights
3 - 3	1	20	1.0	0.355	44
4 - 2	10/11	15	0.682	0.242	30
2 - 4	10/11	15	0.682	0.242	30
5 - 1	(10x9) / (11x12)	6	0.205	0.073	9
1 - 5	(10x9) / (11x12)	6	0.205	0.073	9
6 - 0	(10x9x8) / (11x12x13)	1	0.021	0.007	1
0 - 6	(10x9x8) / (11x12x13)	1	0.021	0.007	1
		Sum	2.816	1.00	124

---

1. If you're reading this book at all, you must surely be familiar with the factorial notation, whereby $n! = n \times (n-1) \times (n-2) \times \ldots \times 2 \times 1$.

The sum of the full ratios representing relative probabilities (or weights) is not 1, whereas probabilities by definition must add to 1. This is easily rectified by dividing the former by their sum, 2.816. The resultant probabilities are what appear in tables of *a priori* odds.

In the analysis of some combinations, it is more satisfying to calculate using integers rather than fractions. Probabilities can be multiplied by a large number in order to achieve an integer representation of the relative strengths of the various combinations. Whether one employs the full ratio, the probabilities, or the integer weights is a matter of convenience. In the analysis of the following deal, the integer weights are used.

What does this tell us about the assumptions behind the *a priori* odds? We see that the missing cards in the other suits are treated equally. If one were in the position at the table of calculating odds based on the missing cards in suits which have not been played, one could imagine the remaining defenders' cards being collected, reshuffled, and redealt just as they were at the beginning. The process would be the same, a random deal of unknown cards, but the results could be much different. A reshuffle of the defenders' unknown cards may destroy an essential feature of the deal being played. Usually, but not always, there are inferences to be drawn from the bidding or play. Let's consider a 'pure' hand where the assumption of the *a priori* odds represents the best approach.

Old Hat Problem

> 'The matter is a perfectly trivial one' (he jerked his thumb in the direction of the old hat), 'but there are points in connection with it which are not entirely devoid of interest and even of instruction.'
> - Sherlock Holmes in *The Adventures of Sherlock Holmes* by Sir Arthur Conan Doyle (1859-1930)

In his excellent book for intermediate players, *Step by Step: Card Play in Suits*, Brian Senior lays down a procedure for declarer to follow once he has seen the opening lead and the dummy. Step 1 is 'Count your tricks'. Probability calculations enter as an afterthought if relevant to the deal. His Hand 57 is an instructive example.

♠ Q 10 9 7 6 3	♠ K J 8	1♠	2◇
♡ 7	♡ A K Q	2♠	4NT
◇ A J 3	◇ Q 7 6 2	5♠*	6♠
♣ A 5 2	♣ K 8 4	pass	

The lead is the ♡J and the reader is asked whether it is better to take the diamond finesse or to discard two diamonds on the hearts and try to ruff out the ◊K. An instant decision is required in order to maintain the entries in dummy necessary for two ruffs and a claim.

Senior states it is best to play to bring down the ◊K, so the recommended line is to discard two diamonds immediately on the ♡K and the ♡Q, cross to the ◊A, then play a trump to dummy. With three entries to dummy, one may hope to drop the ◊K by the third round of the suit, then use the ♣K as an entry to play the now-established ◊Q.

His argument relies on the *a priori* probabilities given in the table above. The drop succeeds on all 3-3 breaks (35.5%) and on one-third of the 4-2 or 2-4 breaks when the ◊K drops doubleton (16.2%). The total of these probabilities is 51.7%, which is better than the 50% for a finesse. The icing on the cake is an added 2.4% for the possibility of the ◊K falling singleton, giving an overall probability of 54%.

It is natural for an inexperienced declarer to grasp the one possibility staring him in the face, a diamond finesse. The point of Senior's instruction is to open the mind to the possibility of an indirect play, ruffing out the ◊K. Recognition is the key. In *The Adventure of the Blue Carbuncle*, upon looking at an old hat discarded at night in Goodge Street, Dr Watson sees little more than a felt hat that has seen better days, but Sherlock Holmes can deduce a lot about the unknown owner. Some of Holmes' assumptions are faulty — for example, he concludes that because the owner's hat size is large, he must be intellectual on the grounds that 'a man with so large a brain must have something within it.' He accuses Watson of being too timid in his inferences.

The good doctor is in the position of the declarer on this deal in that he assumes an attitude of maximum uncertainty. For example, what should one make of the lead of the ♡J? Is it from length or shortness? As a trump lead is perfectly safe, does the heart lead increase the chances that the opening leader holds the ◊K? What of the lack of bidding by the defenders? Does that indicate balanced hands? In answer to such questions, Watson would reply simply and correctly, 'I don't know.'

On this hand, it is not safe to attempt to gather information and give the defenders a second chance at defeating the contract, so a decision must be made in a state of maximum uncertainty as reflected in the *a priori* odds. Under that condition, the odds of a successful diamond finesse are 50%. Senior has given us the answer, but let's investigate the odds using the table of weights given above. The results below give the odds in favor of the drop when various splits are included in the calculation.

Splits Included	Sum of Weights	Drop
3-3	44	100%
3-3, 4-2	64	62%
3-3, 4-2, 5-1	67	55%
3-3, 4-2, 5-1, 6-0	67	54%

If only the 3-3 split is allowed, the drop of the $\Diamond$K in three rounds is assured. This is the single most likely occurrence. If in addition, a 4-2 and a 2-4 split are allowed, the percentage falls to 62%. If the 5-1 and 1-5 splits are included, the percentage falls to 55%. Finally, the drop is impossible on a 6-0 or 0-6 split, and the percentage of success falls slightly to 54%, the figure quoted by Senior on the basis of the *a priori* odds.

The *a priori* odds based on minimum knowledge allow for all splits. If one were to begin with what is most probable, namely the 3-3 split, playing for the drop is highly favored. As less likely conditions are allowed, the advantage for the drop decreases until one reaches the extremes of least probability where the drop has no chance whatsoever. To put this in reverse, declarer, like Sherlock Holmes, may in some cases deduce that extremes can be eliminated from consideration of the evidence. As extremes at the bottom of the table are eliminated from consideration, the more even splits remain, and as one progresses up the table, it becomes more and more likely that playing for the drop is correct.

Of perhaps greater importance is the assumption that the probability of success of the finesse remains at 50% throughout. If information could be gathered that indicated more diamonds were to be expected on the right of the $\Diamond$AJ tenace than on the left, then the probability of a successful finesse would increase above 50%. On the given deal, declarer suffers a disadvantage in not being able to draw trumps and safely explore the possibilities.

When declarer is facing a critical decision, he must attempt where possible to replace the *a priori* odds with those that reflect the current state of knowledge.

Vacant Places and Variable Odds

Sages and Fools never change their minds.
- Confucius (551-479 BC)

Each defender is dealt thirteen cards at the start, so before a bid is made there is a balance in the number of vacant places. The *a priori* odds are tied to this balance.

When the cards have been played out, there again is a balance of vacant places — now it is none to a side. During the play of the deal, vacant places vary, so the odds change.

Suppose a declarer has eight spades and must decide which defender to finesse for the missing trump queen. If in one room the defenders lead hearts to begin with and declarer discovers the suit splits 4-2, it is correct to finesse through the defender with fewer hearts. If in the other room the defenders lead clubs instead and declarer finds the suit divides 3-5, he should finesse through the defender with fewer clubs. Taking both plays into account, one sees that the clubs and hearts taken together are divided evenly, 7-7, so it is maximally uncertain which defender holds the ♠Q. Each declarer faced with a choice makes the best play based on the information that is available to him at the time: one way based on the club split; another on the heart split. Because we have the additional information of the splits in two suits, we reach a different conclusion.

Some argue that an opening lead must be made regardless, so the fact that one suit is chosen over the other shouldn't affect the odds on the placement of the trump queen. Bourke and Smith made the case for this in their book, *Countdown to Winning Bridge*. However, the choice of lead is based on bridge logic, so the choice contains information — information that is open to interpretation to be sure. Declarers mustn't ignore the reason behind the choice. If it affects the line of play, it must affect the probabilities as well.

There are two kinds of information, 'hard' and 'soft'. Hard information comes from sequence leads and from the count of the cards in a suit. Vacant places are hard information. Soft information requires interpretation in terms of motivation — active or passive, expected or unexpected. Regardless of the type, information is expressed optimally as a number. In Chapter 6, we shall investigate the idea of surprise, a characteristic related to probability — the greater the surprise, the less likely the occurrence.

An opponent should be assumed to make the lead that he feels is most likely to benefit his side's chances of a good score. *That is his bias.* The evidence he has to work with is the auction and the cards he can see in his own hand. Declarer has the auction as his guide, and once the opening lead is made, some working assumptions are in order. My approach is to suggest a tentative assumption and work from there. Of course, a flexible approach is best, but not to the extent that one ignores the implications of the opening lead and the information that dummy provides regarding the division of sides. So the question becomes, how much information is provided, and how reliable is it?

The problem in its simplest form is this: what evidence is there for an imbalance in the vacant places due to an uneven split in the suit led, and how much credence can be placed on such evidence?

Acting on the Information Available

Let's say on a given deal, on the lead of the ♠7 from West, the vacant places are shifted so that South judges the ◇Q to be more probably on the right with East. North is the declarer in the other room and receives the opening lead of the ♡7 from East. North judges the ◇Q to be more probably with West. Taking the *a priori* odds as a guide leads to the conclusion that either declarer has a 50-50 chance of being correct. Obviously both declarers won't get it right, but what other evidence is there on which to base the decision?

Both declarers can be 'right' in the sense that both are acting on the basis of the information that is currently available to them. Probabilities are a reflection of the state of partial knowledge in which one is operating. They vary with what is known and assumed. One player has seen a spade led, the other a heart led, so the evidence is clearly different and the probabilities merely reflect that difference.

There is a great deal of uncertainty if all one knows is that one player is probably longer in a certain suit than his partner. It is certain that the opening leader's partner, being shorter in the leader's suit, is longer in another suit, and that suit may not be diamonds. There's the rub. Ah, but it *could* be diamonds. Why should one assume it isn't? That's where the distribution of sides comes into play. Here is an example.

I		II		III	
♠	5 - 3	♠	5 - 3	♠	5 - 3	Case I hearts are unevenly split
♡	3 - 5	♡	4 - 4	♡	4 - 4	Case II clubs unevenly split
◇	2 - 2	◇	2 - 2	◇	1 - 3	Case III diamonds are unevenly split
♣	3 - 3	♣	2 - 4	♣	3 - 3	
	80		75		67	proportions of card combinations

Case I is the single most probable situation given that we know (or assume) spades are 5-3. It is most probable that the longest suit (hearts) is unevenly split rather than a shorter suit. It is least likely that the shortest suit (diamonds) is unevenly split. In other words, if a spade is the most likely lead from West, a heart is the most likely lead from East. Surprise! In either case, the diamonds should be assumed initially to be split 2-2 and the clubs 3-3, as this is the single most probable distribution.

In this example, then, Bourke and Smith are correct in stating that the major-suit leads from either side don't affect the odds on the placement of the ◇Q (or the ♣Q or any other club or diamond).

In practice, we don't know which case applies; we only know what is most probable under the circumstances where the division of sides is known. Declarer knows only the card led at his table. It is proper to work with that information and let the chips fall where they may. If declarer can safely gather more information before making a critical decision, he should do so. The principle is always the same: go with what you know. The probability one employs is called the conditional probability. The above example involves sides of 8-8-6-4, all even numbers. Let's look at the most common sides (8-7-6-5), which is a mix of odd and even numbers.

I	II	III	
♠ 5 - 3	♠ 5 - 3	♠ 5 - 3	Case I diamonds are evenly split
♡ 3 - 4	♡ 3 - 4	♡ 4 - 3	Case II 3 hearts left, 3 clubs left
♢ 3 - 3	♢ 2 - 4	♢ 2 - 4	Case III 4 hearts left, 2 clubs left
♣ 2 - 3	♣ 3 - 2	♣ 2 - 3	
100	75	75	proportions of card combinations

In this situation, the opening lead is again assumed to create two vacant places on the right. These can be filled readily by the naturally occurring uneven splits in the odd numbered suits, hearts and clubs, while the diamonds are split evenly (Case I). This requires that both hearts and clubs have an excess on the right.

Cases II and III feature a 2-4 split in diamonds, which by itself balances the vacant places created on opening lead. In these cases, the excess in hearts may be on the right or left with equal probability, and similarly for the clubs. They form a balanced set.

The number of combinations for a 2-4 diamond split add up to 150, half again as much as the combinations for a 3-3 split. So if we are wondering about the location of the ♢Q, the tendency is to assume a 2-4 split (a 4-2 split is highly unlikely).

Number of Combinations		
Hearts 3-4 175	Clubs 2-3 175	Diamonds 3-3 100
Hearts 4-3 75	Clubs 3-2 75	Diamonds 2-4 150

For each suit, there is most probably an excess of cards on the right where two vacant places need to be filled. Hearts and clubs have a higher degree of right-hand preference than diamonds.

Changing Circumstances

Naturally the more one knows the better, so part of declarer's plan should be to gather more information when it appears safe to do so. This involves risk. If the key finesse is in diamonds, one gathers information concerning another suit, usually the shortest suit held, here clubs. So if it can be done without risk, it is correct to play off some top clubs and see what happens. If the clubs split 2-3, there is still an imbalance of one vacant place on the right. It is most likely that the diamonds are 3-3 and hearts 3-4, their most even splits. If clubs split 3-2, the imbalance on the right is now three vacant places, and it is most likely that diamonds are split 2-4 and hearts 3-4 rather than 3-3 and 2-5.

Ideally, then, both North and South declarers should test the clubs before making a decision on diamonds. If it is judged not safe to do so, then each goes with what he has, and both can play 'correctly', even if one of them must be wrong.

The Evidence of the Bidding

Defenders who bid on nothing and end up defending give the eventual declarer a large edge. Here, if West has bid spades, the two hypothetical declarers will have the same evidence to work with. If West was silent in one room, more uncertainty exists there. So let's say West bid spades in one room and led a spade against South. The cases shown above apply, and declarer can go from there in the way indicated. In the other room, West was silent and East led a heart. North has an entirely different information base and one should not blame him for getting it wrong while South, with more information, gets it right. Under these circumstances, one readily sees that North was acting correctly given the evidence at hand. West, we may conclude, gave away too much information. There is really no problem with the idea that probabilities are different for North and South, and that only one of them will make the correct decision aided by the difference in the information available.

The Strength of the Evidence

If Bourke and Smith were to say simply that the evidence of the opening lead provides a weak basis for dealing with a missing honor in another, shorter, suit, one would agree; the information from leads can be deceptive at times. However, this is not how they phrase it. They take the view that 'the information that the opening leader has length in the suit he leads is not random, but biased, and therefore few if any inferences can be taken from it.'

The reference to bias is entirely wrong and misleading in the extreme. *The fact that the lead is not random is what provides the information!* Let's agree that the evidence is weak. But if you assume that the ♦Q is 50-50 to be on the right or left, you are assuming the opening lead provides no information that might sway declarer from the *a priori* assumption that the vacant places are balanced outside the diamond suit. The conclusion is that one may as well flip a coin as to draw any inferences whatsoever. On the other hand, analysts will often champion a line of play based on a small difference in the *a priori* odds. That's exactly the wrong way round: it doesn't make sense to make decisions on the basis of slim odds in highly uncertain circumstances. On the other hand, if you have a slight edge based on evidence, however weak, it is better to use what evidence you have than to flip a coin.

Examples with Tentative Conclusions

Consider the auction 1NT-3NT. Declarer can expect a major-suit lead. The ♠2 is led. What does it tells us? It says a lot if this is the fourth highest. There is no surprise, so the information content is rather low, but we should assume initially it is a true card and work from there. Yes, it could be from a short suit, but personally I have found this type of lead seldom works — my partners always return my suit and lose a tempo. So the probabilities favor this being a fourth-best lead and conclusions can be drawn as to the spade and heart holdings. In fact, the deal should play like a pianola.

Now suppose the opening lead is the ♦2. This lead can be highly informative, but should be treated with a certain degree of skepticism. There is a high degree of passivity, normal to some, suspicious in others. If it is a true card, the opening leader is marked with a flat hand, say 4-4 in the minors and 3-2 in the majors, or 3-3-4-3, and he also holds a fair proportion of the high cards held by the defenders, there having been no attempt to hit partner's major suit. Against a devious opponent, I would suspect a five-card diamond suit. If I play the hand on the assumption that the opening leader holds a four-card major suit just because the *a priori* odds favor that assumption, I am playing contrary to the evidence. Would I not justifiably be called to task by my teammates?

Recently, playing in 3NT, I received the ♦10 lead with ♦Qxx in dummy and ♦AJ8x in hand. The ♦Q was covered with the ♦K, taken by my ♦A. Later, after I had taken a wrong view of the position of the ♦9, it emerged that the opening lead was from ♦10x, and that my LHO was notorious in the club for this ploy. So now I know. This knowledge will be stored away for future use and become a factor in the estimation of the odds against this player, whose name seldom appears at the top of the scoring lists. Subjectivity is allowed in the mathematics. There is no need to give up on what we know about the tendency of our opponents. We incorporate the prior knowledge. Surely this is only common sense.

Final Example

Consider this false argument where a declarer must pick up the ◇Q from this combination:

◇K 10 8 6

◇A J 9 7

If he begins with the ◇A and finesses through the ◇K10, he has a good chance of success if the diamonds are split 3-2. If he begins with the ◇K and finesses through the ◇AJ, he has a good chance of success if the diamonds are 2-3. You might then conclude that his overall chance of success is 50%, because he may choose at random which way to start and 3-2 is as likely as 2-3. This is obviously a false argument, as something must be known about the distribution of the cards on this deal that makes one diamond split more likely than the other. Taking the finesse is always the correct play regardless, but one direction is better than the other given what is known from the bidding and the opening lead — for one thing, there was no diamond lead. The mathematics must reflect reality and common sense in order to bolster a good player's chances of success. Otherwise it becomes merely a sterile exercise of limited relevance. That translates into the use of conditional probabilities based on the evidence at hand, which includes the division of sides.

The Dog that Didn't Bark

'Is there any point to which you would wish to draw my attention?'
'To the curious incident of the dog in the night-time.'
'The dog did nothing in the night-time.'
'That was the curious incident,' remarked Sherlock Holmes.
- from *Silver Blaze* by Sir Arthur Conan Doyle (1859-1930)

Recently with regard to a trump combination of ♡K972 opposite ♡Q8654, I read in a Dec 2007 *Bridge Magazine* article, 'the chance of making four tricks is around 52.56%', the figure coming from the computer program *SuitPlay*. I find this statement misleading in two ways. First, those odds are only relevant when nothing is known of the cards outside the suit, but here the play in hearts was to be undertaken at Trick 4, so there was knowledge available about the defenders' hands. Second, four figures of significance greatly overstates the accuracy one can assume. The main factor in the play is from which side the first heart is to be played, low to the king or low to the queen, which pretty well accounts for the bulk of the odds in favor of the winning decision. The decision might be classified as 90% or better from the happy side and 10% or less from the sad side. Thus, the probability of success depends to a very great extent on what would be the basis for choosing the direction of the first lead, and that depends on what else has been discovered about the defenders' hands.

One of my favorite chapters from the pen of Terence Reese was given the poignant title "How Could I Tell?" (Chapter 1 of *The Expert Game*). Here is a deal illustrating the same theme which was played in the finals of the 2007 Spingold. Here the implication concerning the defenders' play provided a clue, as the analyst observed later.

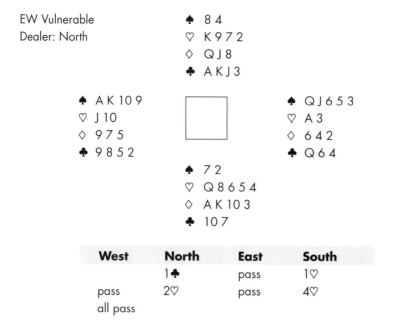

EW Vulnerable
Dealer: North

North
♠ 8 4
♡ K 9 7 2
◇ Q J 8
♣ A K J 3

West
♠ A K 10 9
♡ J 10
◇ 9 7 5
♣ 9 8 5 2

East
♠ Q J 6 5 3
♡ A 3
◇ 6 4 2
♣ Q 6 4

South
♠ 7 2
♡ Q 8 6 5 4
◇ A K 10 3
♣ 10 7

West	North	East	South
	1♣	pass	1♡
pass	2♡	pass	4♡
all pass			

West led the ♠K, which could have been from A-K or K-Q, then switched to a low diamond. Declarer tackled the trumps immediately by leading to the ♡K, losing to the ace. The ♠J was cashed, followed by a diamond exit to dummy. Declarer then took the 'theoretically correct' trump finesse, losing to the ♡10. Down one. How could he tell?

Although they held between them nine spades and 17 HCP, neither opponent had taken the opportunity to enter the auction at the one-level. This is a strong implication that their values were evenly divided and that neither opponent had distributional assets. When West showed a good spade suit on his opening lead, declarer might reason that he was unlikely to hold the ♡A and either length or shortage in the red suits. Based on the evidence, it appears the right play is to win the first diamond in dummy and lead towards the ♡Q. When the queen holds the trick, the rest is easy.

How might the observation that West didn't bid be expressed more precisely in numbers? Suppose declarer begins by leading towards the ♡K in dummy, as he did, losing to the ♡A. When he plays the second heart from dummy, he might pause to ask himself whether West would overcall with a good spade suit and a singleton heart. If he thinks that West would have bid 1♠ at least 50% of the time with a singleton and not bid with a doubleton, this would compensate for the reduced probability that West had played the ♡10 from a doubleton ♡J10 (the Principle of Restricted Choice). On this inference, declarer would play for the drop.

In the open room, Eric Rodwell as North opened the bidding with 1NT, so now it was more difficult for the opponents to enter the auction. The indications concerning the placement of the ♡A were not as strong here. East led the ♠Q and West overtook to cash the top spades. A club exit put declarer in his hand to make the winning play of a trump towards the ♡Q. The odds in favor of this play were much less than in the Closed Room because of the weaker inferences available to declarer — even holding the ♡A, West might not have had enough resources to merit an overcall at the two-level. Shutting out the opposition's bidding reduces the amount of information available to the eventual declarer.

Reese's Reading of the Much Maligned 3-3 Split

I grow old learning many things.
- Solon (640-558 BC)

A seven-card fit occurs in about two-thirds of the hands one is dealt. In about one in four of those hands, the longest fit is seven cards long. If one is playing in an eight-card or nine-card trump fit, very often the secondary fit of seven cards has to be broached, as it is rare that all one's losers can be discarded on outside winners. This brings to the fore the question of how the defenders' six cards are likely to be split.

For decades, bridge writers have warned declarers against playing for a 3-3 split. The basis of the argument was that the *a priori* odds favored a 4-2 split over a 3-3 by the margin of 48% to 36%. Consequently, when planning the play, declarers should keep this in mind and look to finesse in the seven-card suit rather than play for the drop. This is a false argument, as usually one can finesse only in one direction, so must play for either a 4-2 split or a 2-4 split, not both.

One of the most remarkable attacks on the misuse of *a priori* odds appears in *That Elusive Extra Trick* by Terence Reese and David Bird, with regard to the following hands.

♠ A Q J 8 6 4	♠ K 10 9 7		1♥
♥ 6 5	♥ A K 8 7 2	2♠	4♠
♦ A Q J	♦ 10 2	4NT	5♥*
♣ K J	♣ Q 10	6♠	pass

The ♣9 was led, won with the ♣A. The ◇6 was returned, and the question was asked, should declarer finesse in diamonds, a 50% proposition based on the *a priori* odds, or play for the hearts to break, only a 36% proposition? Reese, in his eighties at the time of publication (1994), had popularized the Principle of Restricted Choice forty years earlier. He had long been an advocate of a scientific approach to card play (well-matched to his dry style of presentation), so it was somewhat surprising that he would engage in a vigorous attack on what had become one of the mainstays of his fellow bridge analysts. He was, however, correct in doing so.

The argument made by Reese and Bird was that declarer should not finesse, as at this stage what was a 50% proposition before play had commenced had now been reduced by half to a 25% proposition, whereas the 3-3 split in hearts remained at the original 36%. The opening lead was the cause of the reduction, as it might just as easily have come from the diamond suit if North's holding in the suit were not headed by the ◇K.

This is a variation on the Restricted Choice argument. If a player takes an action, one assumes that action was not a choice from two equally likely possibilities. On the lead of a club, it may be assumed that a diamond lead was not an equal choice. That affords the assumption that the opening leader is more likely than initially expected to hold the ◇K.

The argument was rather loosely put in the limited space available, but worthy of expansion because of the far-reaching consequences. It is very close to the arguments underlying the use of Bob's Blind Rule. First let's check some likely division of sides.

	I	II	III	IV
	♠ 1 - 2	♠ 2 - 1	♠ 1 - 2	♠ 3 - 0
	♥ 3 - 3	♥ 3 - 3	♥ 4 - 2	♥ 2 - 4
	◇ 4 - 4	◇ 3 - 5	◇ 4 - 4	◇ 4 - 4
	♣ 5 - 4	♣ 5 - 4	♣ 4 - 5	♣ 4 - 5
Combinations	C	0.8C	0.75C	0.25C

The number of combinations in Case I, the most likely distribution, is denoted by C. The numbers of combinations for the other cases are given relative to that number. The six cards in hearts are less likely to split unevenly than the eight cards in diamonds. The presence of a void acts to decrease the number of combinations available, and hence the probability of occurrence, by a significant fraction.

The 3-3 heart split is represented in the two most likely sides and the club lead is favored by being from the longest suit. In these situations, declarer should play for the 3-3 heart split and spurn the diamond finesse.

In Cases III and IV, where the hearts are split 4-2, Reese's argument holds as the lead might have come equally from a topless diamond suit. In accordance with the Principle of Restricted Choice, this reduces the numbers of combinations by a factor of 1/2, so Case III in particular comes to represent a lesser choice. The Reese-Bird argument applies directly to this situation.

In Case III, a clever defender holding the ◊K might project the play and see that declarer could adopt the good line by drawing trumps and ruffing the third round of hearts. When the hearts are discovered not to split favorably, declarer has the diamond finesse in reserve, and that works. It is good defense to return a diamond at Trick 2, making declarer guess at the earliest stage. Of course, declarer doesn't known if RHO is being very clever. Rather than depend on the action of RHO, declarer should give more weight to LHO's opening lead, as that player had much less information on which to base his initial action and is more restricted in his choices.

Playdown in a Suit

Look and you will find it — what is unsought is unseen.
- Sophocles (496-406 BC)

Here is the classic decision when facing a possible finesse in a seven-card fit: should declarer finesse or play for the drop of the jack?

AKx ⬚ Q10xx

The standard answer to the problem is that declarer should play off the ace and king and lead towards the tenace. If LHO has followed throughout with low cards, the odds now favor playing for the drop of the jack, as the 3-3 split has become the more likely. However, this is not entirely correct; there are conditions to be met, as we shall show below.

By a playdown in a suit, we mean the process of playing off top cards in the suit so that the defenders must follow if they can with low cards. This is a process of gathering information. In our example, when declarer plays off the ace-king and leads a low card towards the Q-10, LHO has followed with three low cards, so the suit has been played down to the point where only the jack is outstanding.

There are two initial conditions still possible:

LHO	RHO		LHO	RHO
uvw	J*yz*		J*uvw*	*yz*

where *u,v,w,y*, and *z* represent low cards and J represents the jack. Let's run through the stages in detail, as this serves as an example for many playdowns to follow.

Card Split	6 - 0	5 - 1	4 - 2	3 - 3	2 - 4	1 - 5	0 - 6
Combinations	1	6	15	20	15	6	1

Round 1: after cards *u* and *y* appear, the remaining cards are four in number:

Card Split	4 - 0	3 - 1	2 - 2	1 - 3	0 - 4
Combinations	1	4	6	4	1

Round 2: after cards *v* and *z* have been played, the remaining cards are two in number:

Card Split	2 - 0	1 - 1	0 - 2
Combinations	1	2	1

When card *w* is played in Round 3, only one card remains to be played:

1 - 0	0 - 1
J - 0	0 - J

The playdown to this point has isolated two combinations, one from an original 4-2 split and the other from a 3-3 split. Which is the more probable initially will determine whether declarer should finesse or play for the drop. If the vacant places outside the suit are evenly distributed, then the 3-3 split is more probable, as it is under the *a priori* conditions. The classical advice of playing for the drop is based on this assumption. However, if there are more vacant places on the left, the 4-2 probability may be greater than the 3-3 probability to an extent that it overrides the initial advantage given to the even split. The rule applies also to the 2-2 split when the defenders hold four cards in a suit.

> With a vacant place difference of +2 or more on the left, take the finesse. With no vacant place imbalance, play for the drop. With a vacant place difference of +1 on the left, choose either.

This stands as an example of Kelsey's Rule, named after the late, great bridge author, Hugh Kelsey, which we shall present later in this chapter. First, though, we must clarify the concept of vacant places, something which has in the past caused some misunderstanding with regard to its translation into probabilities.

What Exactly Are Vacant Places?

One cannot present a science without simultaneously defining its terms.
- G. W. Leibnitz (1646-1716)

When one keeps track of where some cards are, one is keeping track simultaneously of where other cards aren't. The occupied places are the past; the vacant places represent the future. It is the latter which are the more important when planning one's next move. The occupied places represent the inflexible *yang* of the deal; the vacant places are the variable *yin*, which, like water, can flow freely to fill the empty spaces.

Vacant places are potential locations in the defenders' hands for the unknown cards. Declarer knows what cards are missing once the dummy appears; what is unknown is how the cards are divided between the defenders. The vacant places relate to the probability of the dealing of the cards and yield in their ratio the relative number of suit combinations available in the opponents' hands. They are a guide to the probable placement of the cards yet to be played.

We have written up to now of vacant places in a vague manner under the assumption that the reader is familiar with the concept. This is a dangerous procedure, however, and we have arrived at the point where we must provide better definitions. The specification of vacant places, like probability, is not unique, which has caused confusion. We employ three distinctions. The **inclusive** variety includes the suit about to be played and the **exclusive** variety excludes that suit. The **current** variety is the one encountered at the table as the cards are being played. With each card played, one takes a step in transition from the inclusive to the exclusive vacant places. As this step requires a defender to make a choice, the probability of a particular distribution of cards depends not only on the possible combinations of cards as dealt but also on the plausible permutations in the play. (How the probability can be computed exactly will be left until later in the book when we come to Bayes' Theorem.)

The best way to clarify these definitions is through demonstration. Consider the following situation in which the division of major suits is revealed through the bidding and early play. Declarer, South, must use the information provided to make a decision as to which defender is more likely to hold the queen of trumps.

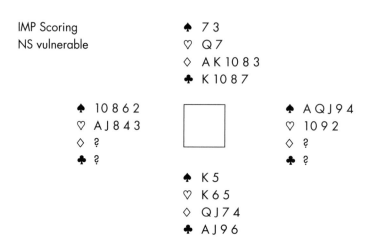

IMP Scoring
NS vulnerable

♠ 7 3
♡ Q 7
♢ A K 10 8 3
♣ K 10 8 7

♠ 10 8 6 2
♡ A J 8 4 3
♢ ?
♣ ?

♠ A Q J 9 4
♡ 10 9 2
♢ ?
♣ ?

♠ K 5
♡ K 6 5
♢ Q J 7 4
♣ A J 9 6

West	North	East	South
pass	1♢	1♠	dbl
2♡	dbl	3♡	3NT
4♠	pass	pass	5♣
all pass			

The free-style bidding indicates a double fit for both sides and in the end North-South are allowed to play at the five-level.

The play goes as follows: West leads a fourth-highest ♠2, East takes the ♠A and switches to the ♡10. West wins his ace and exits with the ♠8 to East's ♠J and South's ♠K. Declarer is about to undertake the task of drawing trumps. The vacant places in each hand are calculated as follows:

West has five hearts and four spades, so he has four inclusive vacant places (13 minus 9) to accommodate clubs and diamonds. East has five spades and three hearts, so he has five inclusive vacant places (13 minus 8) to accommodate the minors. As neither minor has been played, the odds when declarer obtains the lead are that the ♣Q lies with East in the ratio of 5:4. This ratio is based on the ratio of combinations containing the queen on the right and on the left, assuming the minor-suit cards were dealt at random. The exclusive vacant places accommodate only diamonds and total four in number. The split in diamonds will be known once the split in clubs has been determined.

Naturally South will play East for having the ♣Q, and so begins drawing trumps by playing to the ♣K in dummy. West and East follow with low cards, and declarer leads the ♣10 towards the hidden hand. East follows with another low card, so still missing at this stage are a low card and the ♣Q. How are the odds affected? The current vacant places now stand at three and three, and there are two clubs missing that could fill the vacant places. Has the location of the ♣Q become a 50-50 proposition? No. Here is a map of the entire process.

	West	East
Initial inclusive vacant places	4	5
First round West following	3	5
First round East follows	3	4
Second round East follows	3	3

At the beginning of the play in clubs, these were the possible combinations in the minors that could made up a 4-5 split in the vacant places.

♦ 4 - 0	♦ 3 - 1	♦ 2 - 2	♦ 1 - 3	♦ 0 - 4
♣ 0 - 5	♣ 1 - 4	♣ 2 - 3	♣ 3 - 2	♣ 4 - 1
(1/60)C	(1/3)C	C	(2/3)C	(1/12)C

The relative numbers of combinations are indicated at the bottom. Taking all combinations into account, the probability that the ♣Q was held on the right was exactly in the ratio of the vacant places, namely 5:4. Once a minor-suit card was played, the vacant places no longer provided an exact calculation. Why? Because the defenders could not play any club equally without cost — in particular, a defender must avoid playing the ♣Q.

Once West has played a low club and East has followed twice with low clubs, the two extremes involving voids have been eliminated, and the vacant places are equal at three in each direction.

♦ 3 - 1	♦ 2 - 2	♦ 1 - 3
♣ 0 - 2	♣ 1 - 1	♣ 2 - 0
(1/3)C	C	(1/3)C

With regard to card combinations, symmetry has been achieved, so it appears that the ♣Q could as easily be on the left as on the right. Let's suppose that the original missing clubs are designated as Q, u, w, x, and y. The two clubs remaining are the ♣Q and ♣x. Here are the possibilities:

I	II	III	IV
♦ 3 - 1	♦ 2 - 2	♦ 2 - 2	♦ 1 - 3
♣ 0 - Qx	♣ Q - x	♣ x - Q	♣ Qx - 0

However, the play in the club suit has not proceeded at random, so there is a question of 'restricted' choice to be considered. The effect is that Condition II is less likely than Condition III, and it is this effect that destroys the symmetry of the positions. As is shown in a later chapter, this fundamental result is a consequence of Bayes' Theorem, which in a general way takes into account the differences between the dealing of the cards and the playing of the cards. A full treatment is given in Chapter 7.

Finally, we consider the happy circumstance when West follows with the last remaining low card on the second round of clubs. Obviously, Condition III applies — the only trump still missing is the ♣Q and that sits in the East hand. This can be drawn with the ♣A, leaving the diamonds of necessity split 2-2. This is the most probable split of the four cards in that suit, the so-called exclusive vacant places. Taken in conjunction, the most probable split of the clubs and diamonds required to accommodate the initial four and five division of vacant places would have been clubs 2-3 and diamonds 2-2. This, then, is a demonstration of Bob's Blind Rule at work: given what one knows about the division of the major suits, one chooses at the start to play for the splits that give the greatest number of card combinations in the minor suits.

Vacant Places and Playing for the Drop

What would life be without arithmetic, but a scene of horrors?
- Rev. Sidney Smith (1771-1845)
at 64 years of age to a young lady contemplating marriage

Let's consider the situation where some suits have been played and one can determine their splits based on the bidding and play so far. There are still suits that have not been played, and the number of cards in those suits represents the number of vacant places. Suppose there are six missing cards in the critical suit, which declarer is about to breach, and those six cards occupy vacant places along with other cards in suits that have not been played. In total, these represent the **inclusive** vacant places. The cards outside the critical suit are the **exclusive** vacant places, as they exclude the suit about to be played. We need concern ourselves only with the 4-2 and 3-3 splits to determine whether to finesse or not.

With an even number of exclusive vacant places, the inclusive vacant places are either even or have a difference of 2. For balanced inclusive vacant places, the number of combinations in the outside suit(s) associated with 3-3 is greater, so play for the drop. For vacant places greater by 2 on one side, the number of combinations in the outside suit(s) associated with 4-2 is greater, so finesse.

With an odd number of exclusive vacant places, the inclusive vacant places have a difference of 1 or 3. For vacant places greater on one side by 1, the numbers of combinations in the outside suit(s) associated with 4-2 and 3-3 are the same, so take your pick of finesse or drop based on other factors. For vacant places greater by 3 on one side, the number of combinations in the outside suit(s) associated with 4-2 are greater, so finesse.

Next consider the case of four cards split either 3-1 or 2-2. The problem is whether to finesse or play for the drop of the queen in this situation:

KJxxx

Axxx

Declarer plays the ace and leads towards K-J-x-x-x.

Similar arguments apply. For vacant places greater by 1 on the left, the numbers of combinations in the outside suit(s) associated with 3-1 and 2-2 are the same, so take your choice of finesse or drop based on other factors.

And so on.

Kelsey's Rule

When all the insignificant cards in a suit have been played, but not before, these can be added to the known cards in the calculation of Vacant Places.

In this segment we look at vacant places as they were viewed by a master of the past. In his book *Bridge: The Mind of the Expert*, as elsewhere, the late Hugh Kelsey strongly advocated the count of vacant places as an exact calculation of probabilities. There were conditions to be met, things to watch out for. What cards can be included in the vacant place count? He did not distinguish between inclusive and exclusive vacant places. In his definition the exclusive vacant places were useable when, as noted above, all insignificant cards in the critical suit had been played.

Kelsey's approach was complicated by his desire to provide exact probabilities. What happens to the probabilities before all insignificant cards are played is not explained by Kelsey, which is to say he does not delve into Bayes' Theorem, although he appears to be aware of its consequences. Early in his writing career Kelsey expressed this opinion in his *Advanced Play at Bridge* (1968):

'If Bayes sounds to you like a manufacturer of aspirins, by all means continue in that happy belief.'

He goes on to suggest that the ordinary player need not know much in the way of mathematics, but that he should memorize the *a priori* odds of various splits to be used as guides in decision making. Of course, Kelsey himself knew better, but he was trying to be helpful to a mature readership that needed guidance in the logical aspects of the game. The difficulty with that approach is that it breaks down when put to a severe test.

Everything should be made as simple as possible, but not simpler.
- Albert Einstein (1879-1955)

Would bridge be a better game if it were simpler, if all one needed to do was memorize tables of *a priori* odds? No. As we shall demonstrate in a later chapter, the experienced player can easily enough grasp the basic principle behind Bayes' Theorem. Then he or she knows the reason why. Understanding replaces blind adherence.Here is an example where Kelsey's Rule kicks in unexpectedly. The defenders begin with five trumps, so the permutations in play will not reach a neutral state through directly drawing trumps. However, one trump is eliminated when a defender is able to obtain an early ruff, leaving the defenders with just four trumps remaining when declarer begins the trump extraction process. This is very significant, as one may now apply the rules derived above for even cards missing with regard to the ratio of vacant places to obtain exact estimates of the probability of success at the time of decision.

West		**East**
♠ A J 8 7		♠ K 10 5 3
♡ 8 7 5		♡ Q 9 4
◇ K 9 6		◇ A Q 5
♣ A J 8		♣ K Q 9

West	**North**	**East**	**South**
			2♡
pass	pass	dbl	pass
4♠	all pass		

South overtakes North's lead of the ♡J with the ♡K and continues with the ♡A, on which North discards the ♣7. The third heart, the ♡6, is ruffed by North with the ♠6, who then exits with the ◇2.

When declarer wins in hand to play the ♠A and then leads towards the ♠K105 in dummy, North follows with the last low spade. Here is the situation covered by Kelsey's Rule, as there is just one trump outstanding. The question is, what are the vacant places at this point in the play? Kelsey argues as follows: South has shown six hearts and a spade, so the number of vacant places in that hand is six. North has shown three spades and one heart, so the number of vacant places in that hand is nine. The odds are then 3:2 that North holds the ♠Q. This supposes that one can ignore the play in diamonds.

Another way to view this situation is to look for the combinations of cards in the defenders' hands. The cards may be distributed between North and South as follows:

Condition I				Condition II	
Spades	3 - 2			Spades	4 - 1 (0.5)
Hearts	1 - 6			Hearts	1 - 6
Diamonds	3 - 3			Diamonds	4 - 2 (0.75)
Clubs	6 - 2 (0.4)			Clubs	4 - 4

At the beginning of play, the division on the left is the more probable by the narrow margin of 16:15. Condition I has one uneven split outside hearts, whereas Condition II requires uneven splits in spades and diamonds. By the time declarer reaches the critical point in the play of the trumps, the effect of the spade combinations has become neutralized so that only the splits in the minors are the determining factor. The number of combinations in the minors is greater for an 8-6 split than for a 9-5 split in the ratio of 9:6, exactly the same odds predicted by Kelsey's Rule. Thus those odds refer to the initial conditions in the minor suits as dealt, the exclusive vacant places in particular.

However, there is that one round of diamonds that in theory cannot be ignored. At the time of the critical play in trumps the South hand has five current vacant places, not six, and the North hand has eight, not nine. Thus the current vacant place ratio is 8:5, still very much in favor of the finesse. The difficulty arises from the fact that the round of diamonds initiated by a defender cannot be thought of as being a random occurrence in the strictest sense. As both defenders have followed to the first round of diamonds, there has been no surprise forthcoming from a play that appears to be routine, but it is unreasonable to assume that no change has occurred as a result of some diamond combinations having been removed from consideration. So the odds in favor of North's holding the trump queen lie somewhere between 9:6 and 8:5. The exact ratio is not important, as both odds greatly favor taking the finesse. It's the decision that's important, not the estimation of how wide the margin.

> When the opponents have used up one of their five trumps for a ruff, there are four trumps remaining. After a round of trumps is drawn successfully, the current vacant places can be used as a guide as to whether to finesse for the queen or play for the drop.

CHAPTER 6

INFORMATION THEORY AND DECLARER PLAY

Plans are the dreams of the reasonable.
- Ernest von Feuchtersleben (1806-1849)

We have seen that when the defenders follow with low cards, declarers should play according to Jaynes' Principle and assume even splits throughout in the absence of information to the contrary. This led to Bob's Blind Rule: Gather as much information as you safely can, then play for suits to split as evenly as possible under the circumstances. We termed this rule 'blind', because it takes no account of the relevance of the spot cards played. But of course, in real life the spot cards are relevant, which leads us to:

ADJUNCT TO BOB'S BLIND RULE: if you can see a better play, make it.

Because it is based on the interchangeability of the spot cards, Bob's Blind Rule discounts the finer points of play. If declarer discerns a difference due to rank that is important, he should make use of the implications; however, if he is unaware of a significant difference due to rank, then the odds favor an even split over an uneven split. He should pay special attention to the nine in a key suit as it may be a significant card, substituting for the ten or guarding against the ten held by the opposition. We'll discuss an example later in this chapter.

Basically the advice is this: if the situation is so complex that you cannot see a solution, then simplify and solve the simpler problem. If you are lucky, the solution to the simple problem applies also to the unsolvable problem which it resembles.

The *A Priori* Odds and Suit Splits

The most important thing to know is how your suits are going to break.
- Hugh Kelsey in *Advanced Play at Bridge*

When the dummy comes down, declarer sees how the defenders' cards are divided between the suits. Although he would like to gather information concerning how the suits are going to break, there are occasions when a decision must be made before the process can be undertaken with safety. Kelsey's advice is to rely on the *a priori* odds, which, as we know, operate in a state of maximum uncertainty. An alternative approach is to apply Jaynes' Principle, using the distribution of the suits that has become known when the dummy appears. Of course, discretion must be observed. Here is an example from the book quoted above that can be used to illustrate the alternative approaches.

West		East
♠ A 5		♠ K 8 7 6 2
♡ 3		♡ A 9 7 4 2
♢ A K Q J 10 6 4		♢ 3
♣ A 8 4		♣ K 5

West	North	East	South
2♢	pass	2♠	pass
4♢	pass	4♡	pass
4NT	pass	5♢	pass
5NT	pass	6♡	pass
7♢	all pass		

The bidding is old-fashioned but effective and a grand slam is reached in which twelve tricks are assured off the top. North leads the ♣7 and Kelsey asks the question, how should declarer develop a thirteenth trick? One way is to ruff a club in dummy. This requires clubs to be split no worse than 5-3. A second way is to draw trumps immediately and establish a spade trick through ruffs, which requires spades to split no worse than 4-2. The *a priori* odds for the first play are 79% and for the second, 84%. Knowing these odds enables declarer to make the correct choice.

An alternative approach is to consider the various common splits in the context of the full deal. Nothing is known of the distribution of the suits in the defenders' hands apart from the division of sides, which is 6-7-5-8. The question is this: is it more likely that the clubs split 6-2 or the spades split 5-1? We saw in the previous chapter that taken in isolation it is more likely that the clubs split 6-2. Thus it is more dangerous to try to ruff a club than it is to play on spades.

Here are five common conditions in order of probability:

I	II	III	IV	V
♠ 3 - 3	♠ 4 - 2	♠ 4 - 2 (0.75)	♠ 4 - 2 (0.75)	♠ 5 - 1 (0.3)
♡ 4 - 3	♡ 3 - 4	♡ 4 - 3	♡ 4 - 3	♡ 3 - 4
♢ 2 - 3	♢ 2 - 3	♢ 2 - 3	♢ 3 - 2	♢ 2 - 3
♣ 4 - 4	♣ 4 - 4	♣ 3 - 5 (0.8)	♣ 2 - 6 (0.4)	♣ 3 - 5 (0.8)
C	0.75 C	0.6 C	0.3 C	0.24 C

Conditions I, II and III	both lines of play succeed
Condition IV	establish the spades, don't attempt a club ruff
Condition V	ruff a club

The distinction between ruffing a club and ruffing a spade comes only when considering Conditions IV and V. Condition IV represents the greater number of combinations, hence is the more probable, so declarer should win the club lead in hand, draw trumps and attempt to establish the spades.

Odds and Evens

The *a priori* odds incorporate all splits at once, whereas the five common conditions obviously do not. It is worthwhile to see if there is a more reliable way to assess the probabilities at the table. Note that the red suits are composed of odd numbers of cards. There are two ways that these can combine with maximum uncertainty, one way providing no imbalance of vacant places and the other creating an imbalance of 2.

No imbalance	♡ 4 - 3	Imbalance of 2	♡ 4 - 3	♡ 3 - 4
	♢ 2 - 3		♢ 3 - 2	♢ 2 - 3
Total	6 - 6		7 - 5	5 - 7

Now consider the splits in the black suits, which are critical in the decision.

Balanced at 7 - 7

♠ 1 - 5	♠ 2 - 4	♠ 3 - 3	♠ 4 - 2	♠ 5 - 1
♣ 6 - 2	♣ 5 - 3	♣ 4 - 4	♣ 3 - 5	♣ 2 - 6

Unbalanced at 6 - 8

I	II	III	IV	V
♠ 1 - 5	♠ 2 - 4	♠ 3 - 3	♠ 4 - 2	♠ 5 - 1
♣ 5 - 3	♣ 4 - 4	♣ 3 - 5	♣ 2 - 6	♣ 1 - 7

When the vacant places are balanced, there is no preference between ruffing clubs or ruffing spades; they succeed or fail together, so it matters not which line declarer selects. However, with an imbalance of 2, the spade ruff succeeds where the club ruff fails under Condition IV, whereas the club ruff succeeds and the spade ruff fails under Condition I. As Condition IV is the more probable in the ratio of 5:4, the indication is that declarer should play for the spade ruff.

Bob's Blind Rule and Vacant Places

Bob's Blind Rule is based on the numbers of combinations in the suits that are to be played; so is the use of vacant places to estimate probabilities. Although they are not equivalent, the two methods share common ground and have similarities. To illustrate this point, here is a simple example in which the declarer is pushed by vigorous preemption to a grand slam he would not otherwise have bid. An early decision is required in the trump suit.

West		East
♠ —		♠ A 9 7
♡ 9 4		♡ A 10 8
◇ K Q 8 5		◇ A 7 6
♣ A 10 9 8 7 6 4		♣ Q J 5 3

West	North	East	South
pass	2♠	dbl	4♠
5♣	pass	6♣	6♠
dbl*	pass	7♣	all pass

West's double was of the upside-down variety, showing interest in bidding the grand slam if partner had controls, which he did have. South's bidding is the kind often encountered in bridge clubs, and he could be a hero if declarer doesn't find the ♣K.

The lead is the expected ♠K. West wins the ♠A, discarding a losing heart from hand, and leads the ♣Q, to which South follows with the ♣2. To finesse or not to finesse: that is the question. Let's go through the process of estimating the probabilities using vacant places.

It is reasonable to assume North holds six spades to South's four. This leaves seven vacant places in the North hand and nine vacant places in the South hand. The full vacant places analysis goes as follows.

	NS Vacant Places			On the Play		
Inclusive VP	7 9		7 9	Initial	7	9
Clubs	0 2		1 1	S follows	?	8
Exclusive VP	7 7		6 8			

Outside the club suit, the fourteen vacant places in hearts and diamonds can be split 7-7 or 6-8. The related numbers of combinations imply a ratio of 8:7 in favor of the even split in the red suits and these are the odds in favor of finessing South for the ♣K. Kelsey's Rule applies, since there is one remaining outstanding card and that card is an honor.

Let's examine the situation with regard to the division of sides.

Condition I	Condition II	Condition III	Condition IV
♠ 6 - 4	♠ 6 - 4	♠ 6 - 4	♠ 6 - 4
♡ 4 - 4	♡ 4 - 4	♡ 3 - 5 (0.8)	♡ 3 - 5 (0.8)
◊ 2 - 4 (0.75)	◊ 3 - 3	◊ 3 - 3	◊ 4 - 2 (0.75)
♣ 1 - 1	♣ 0 - 2 (0.5)	♣ 1 - 1	♣ 0 - 2 (0.5)

Given that spades are split 6-4, Condition I represents the most likely division of sides. The red suits are split 8-6. Condition II represents the most likely division when the clubs are split 0-2, as the red suits are evenly divided at 7-7. Condition I is more probable in the ratio of 8:5. That is the situation before a club is played and South follows with the ♣2. Once that occurs, one of the 1-1 splits has been eliminated from Condition I, making the 1-1 split and the 0-2 splits equally populated, ♣K on the right or ♣K on the left, respectively. It has become a question of the ratio of card combinations in the red suits, and the odds favor taking the finesse in clubs.

However, there is more information available that must be taken into account, namely that North has opened a weak two in spades so probably does not hold four hearts. This rules out Conditions I and II, and leaves Conditions III and IV as the most likely distributions of sides given the bidding. In these cases, the imbalance in spades is neutralized by the imbalance in hearts. The 1-1 club split is reduced by half when the ♣2 appears, but the greater weight is still given to Condition III, because of the even split in diamonds. Condition III has become the favorite by a margin of 4:3, so based on Bob's Blind Rule, declarer's decision should be to play for the drop.

If we return to the vacant place analysis where the inclusive vacant places were assumed to be seven and nine, we see that this assumption did not take into account the restriction that North wouldn't hold four hearts. A heart split of 3-5 fills the vacant places created by the spade preempt, and with the vacant places adjusted to a balanced condition, declarer should play for the drop. You can see that the vacant places argument has become questionable because of the uncertainty of how to define the vacant places, that is, whether or not hearts should be included. Comparison of the most likely distributions, Conditions III and IV, resolves any such difficulty.

There are other possible combinations that would be needed to calculate the exact probabilities involved; however, a 2-6 heart split would only serve to create a greater imbalance in the vacant places and would favor that play even more. The advantage of using the most likely candidates is that one must take into account the splits in all suits, so that the condition in the heart suit is more likely to be recognized in the heat of the battle. As well, this avoids the tricky question of how to incorporate partial knowledge in the vacant place analysis, which is at the same time both too simple and too complex.

The Division of Sides

In the beginner's mind there are many possibilities, but in the expert's mind there are few.
- Shunryu Suzuki (1905-1971)

When you sort your bridge hand into suits, a pattern emerges which you characterize by the number of cards in each suit. As a declarer counts the cards in each suit held jointly by himself and the dummy, he automatically has a count of the cards held in each suit by the defenders: the 'sides'. Once this has been observed and recorded, the possibilities for the defenders' hands are greatly reduced in number. The division of sides is a most important and neglected characteristic with regard to card play and is discussed in detail below, but first let's look at hand patterns, something with which everyone is familiar.

Hand Patterns

One may divide hand patterns into two categories: notrump hands and suit-oriented hands, the former containing hands with at least two cards in each suit. Here are the most common patterns with their probabilities of being dealt to you (PD).

Notrump	PD(%)	Distributional	PD(%)
4432	21.6	5431	12.9
5332	15.5	6421	4.7
4333	10.5	6331	3.4
6322	5.6	4441	3.0
5422[1]	5.3	5422[1]	5.3
Total	58.5	Total	28.3

The Holistic Approach to the Division of Sides

Holism: the tendency in nature to produce whole organisms from ordered groups of unit structures, a concept eminently applicable to bridge hands.

---

1.   5422 hands vary in their suitability for notrump contracts and suit contracts, so this pattern has been divided equally between the two categories. From the above table we can see that 4432, 4333 and 5332 constitute nearly half the hands one is dealt. The most common pattern with a singleton is 5431, occurring about once in every eight deals. The implications of this with regard to bidding systems are discussed in a subsequent chapter.

The distribution of the twenty-six cards controlled by the declarer determines the distribution of the cards held by the defenders. If declarer and the dummy have between them eight spades, seven hearts, six diamonds and five clubs, the defenders must hold five spades, six hearts, seven diamonds and eight clubs: both sides have a distribution denoted as 8765. If declarer's cards are divided 7775 (all odd numbers), the defenders cards are divided 8666 (all even).

Two hands with 4432 patterns don't necessarily combine to produce a flat distribution of the thirteen cards: 8864 is a possibility, as is 7766. The trump total in the former is seventeen and in the latter fourteen, indicating a vast difference in trick-taking potential. Similarly, two 5422 hands can produce a distribution of 10664 whereas a different mix might also result in 7766.

How are the defenders' suits expected to split? The greater the number of related card combinations possible, the greater the probability that a particular set of splits will occur. This condition is met, as usual, when the suits are as evenly divided as possible. Let's take as an example the 8-7-6-5 sides where the defenders have length in the majors.

I	II	III	IV	Combinations
♠ 4 - 4	♠ 5 - 3	♠ 3 - 5	♠ 6 - 2	4 - 4 (70)
♡ 3 - 4	♡ 3 - 4	♡ 5 - 2	♡ 3 - 4	4 - 3 (35)
◇ 3 - 3	◇ 3 - 3	◇ 3 - 3	◇ 2 - 4	3 - 3 (20)
♣ 3 - 2	♣ 2 - 3	♣ 2 - 3	♣ 2 - 3	3 - 2 (10)
C	0.8 C	0.48 C	0.3 C	C = 490,000

The greatest number of card combinations (C) for 8765 is related to the splits that are closest to even as possible (Condition I). This, then, is the most probable situation. The number of card combinations for a hand in which known splits occur is the product of the number of combinations in each suit taken separately. These numbers are shown on the right. A simple multiplication yields the result that there are 490,000 ways in which Condition I can be dealt, not a number anyone wishes to carry around in one's head for future reference. However, there is no need to work with such large numbers, since probabilities are ratios expressed in numbers that run from 0 to 1. So without loss of generality, when comparing cases, you can use the ratios of the numbers of combinations to obtain relative probabilities.

If the spade suit is found during the early play to split 5-3 instead of 4-4, there is an imbalance of two cards within the suit that must be accommodated by the placement in the other three suits. This can be achieved most efficiently by rotating the combinations in an odd-numbered suit (Condition II). The other suits retain their best splits, but the club suit has three cards on the right instead of on the left. The number of card combinations is reduced by a factor of 0.8 from the maximum represented by Condition I.

In Condition III, an imbalance of 3 exists in the heart suit, and now rotating an odd-numbered suit cannot fully accommodate that difference. The other suits can no longer retain their optimal splits, and one of the suits is forced to split more unevenly. The imbalance is made up most efficiently by changing the 4-4 split to a 3-5 split. The resulting number of card combinations is reduced to 0.48 of the maximum available for the 8-7-6-5 sides.

If the spades are split 6-2 (imagine that West has opened a weak two in spades), the imbalance in the suit is four cards and the number of card combinations is reduced by a factor of 0.3 (Condition IV). The diamonds are more likely to divide 2-4, with four on the right, than 3-3, against the expectation of the *a priori* odds, so declarer should plan accordingly.

We note at this time that for the all-even sides, 8666, if one suit is found to be split unevenly, another suit must also be split unevenly. If the eight cards are split 5-3, then most probably one suit of six cards is split 4-2. It is also possible that all three suits have such a split, but the odds are reduced by a factor of 0.56, another example of why a simple assumption is usually the best assumption.

We have seen how to calculate the proportion of suit combinations easily at the table. The main point I wish to make is that the split in one suit affects the split in another suit. Declarers should take this into account and not treat each suit as independent. The bidding, the opening lead, the play of a few rounds of cards, all provide information and to a greater or lesser extent act to invalidate the *a priori* estimates made in a state of maximum uncertainty.

Vacant Places Ratios Can Still Apply

A variance in the number of cards held in different suits does not invalidate the use of vacant places ratios in the determination of probabilities. Let's take the example of ten vacant places to be filled by six diamonds and four clubs, each suit missing the queen. On a vacant places argument, the odds of either queen being in the hand with six vacancies as opposed to that with four vacancies are 6:4, the number of diamonds and clubs involved having no effect on the odds assigned. Here is the breakdown for this situation.

Diamonds Split	6 - 0	5 - 1	4 - 2	3 - 3	2 - 4	
◇ Combinations	1	6	15	20	15	
Clubs Split	0 - 4	1 - 3	2 - 2	3 - 1	4 - 0	
♣ Combinations	1	4	6	4	1	
Total Combinations	1	24	90	80	15	Total of 210

The total numbers of card combinations for which the $\diamond$Q is on the left or on the right are:

$\diamond$Q on left	1	20	60	40	5	Total of 126
$\diamond$Q on the right	0	4	30	40	10	Total of 84

The ratio of card combinations is 6:4 as predicted by the vacant place ratio.

The total numbers of card combinations for which the $\clubsuit$Q is on the left or on the right are:

$\clubsuit$Q on left	0	6	45	60	15	Total of 126
$\clubsuit$Q on the right	1	18	45	20	0	Total of 84

Although the numbers of clubs and diamonds are different, in total there is no distinction between the $\diamond$Q and the $\clubsuit$Q with regard to the number of combinations on the left and on the right. The ratio of 6:4 applies equally to any specific minor-suit card, be it an honor or a low card. The probability of the deal does not make any distinction according to rank.

The Distribution of Sides

Well begun is half done.
- Aristotle (384-322 BC)

Bridge teachers are forever advising students that as declarers they should take a minute to think before playing to the first trick. Our advice is slightly different: count first, then think. Think, yes, but of what? It is counterproductive to dwell overly long on the inadequacies of the dummy. After all, a cold contract gets you no glory — it is the tricky one that allows you to excel. So a simple 'Thank you, partner' is all that is required to express your gratitude for once more being dumped in the soup.

In order to make full use of Probability Theory, declarer's first task is to record mentally the sides, that is, the numbers of cards held by the opponents in each suit. Those numbers, unlike high card points, are real, not an invention. They are the elevations of the territory in which you must operate, be it as flat as a plain, or as shapely as a mountain range. Moreover, they are a reminder that there are a finite number of cards for each player and that the situation in one suit must necessarily impact upon the situation in another.

Here are three common distributions that make up roughly 40% of all possible deals along with the probability that your side would be dealt that distribution.

Your Side	Their Side	Probability	Total Trumps
8765	8765	23.6%	16
7766	7766	10.5%	14
7775	8666	5.2%	15

The first two sides listed have two even and two odd numbered suits. The opposition side has the same distribution and the total number of trumps is an even number. The third side is all even on one side and all odd on the other. The result is that the number of total trumps is an odd number. The trick-taking potential of one side will therefore be greater than the other.

The 8765 side is the most common by far. Both North-South and East-West have an eight-card fit. This represents what many have come to think of as a normal situation. Generally the feeling is akin to that when holding a 4432 hand pattern. The *a priori* probability that neither opponent has a singleton or void is 54%, so the alarm bells are not ringing early.

The 7766 side is the equivalent of a 4333 hand. In the absence of bidding, you expect flat hands around the table. The probability of no singleton or void in the opponents' hands is 64%. This gives declarer timing. The approach to the play with this shape is *not* to race towards a quick resolution of the contract, but rather to maneuver the opponents into breaking new suits. Declarer will duck tricks and think about setting up endplays.

With a nine-card major-suit fit, one tends to play in a suit contract and the probability of shortages is greater. With a nine-card minor, one expects a competitive auction.

Your Side	Their Side	Probability	Total Trumps
9764	9764	7.3%	18
9665	8774	6.6%	17

It may be surprising to some that reciprocal nine-card fits are so frequent. This favors the bold bidders. The 8774 is an intriguing side, as in this case the two sides are not matched. Which distribution of sides would you prefer to hold? This shows that one side's holding a nine-card fit does not guarantee that the other side also holds a nine-card fit.

Your Side	Their Side	Probability	Total Trumps
9755	8864	4.9%	17
9854	9854	4.1%	18
8855	8855	3.3%	16

It isn't until one reaches eighth place in frequency of occurrence that one again encounters a pair of sides without a nine-card fit. Although both contain sixteen total trumps, 8855 is more than a minor variation on the much more common 8765. In his book *To Bid or Not to Bid*, Larry Cohen comments that hands with double eight-card fits play well, the reason being that a declarer may develop tricks in either long suit.

The 8765 Distribution of Sides

Recall the past, diagnose the present, foretell the future.
- Hippocrates (460-377 BC)

This is the most common division of sides, so it deserves special attention. Declarers and defenders have the same distribution of sides, but generally not the same division. In fact, there is no special relationship between the division on one side to the division on the other when the hands are dealt randomly. *Shortage doesn't attract shortage.* The most interesting aspect is the relationship with a side between the majority even numbers (eight and six) and the minority odd numbers (seven and five). Here are the five most common divisions for 8=5=7=6 with the relative numbers of combinations.

	W E	W E	W E	W E	W E
♠	4 - 4 (1.0)	5 - 3 (0.8)	4 - 4 (1.0)	5 - 3 (0.8)	5 - 3 (0.8)
♡	3 - 2 (1.0)	2 - 3 (1.0)	2 - 3 (1.0)	2 - 3 (1.0)	3 - 2 (1.0)
♢	3 - 4 (1.0)	3 - 4 (1.0)	3 - 4 (1.0)	4 - 3 (1.0)	2 - 5 (0.6)
♣	3 - 3 (1.0)	3 - 3 (1.0)	4 - 2 (0.75)	2 - 4 (0.75)	3 - 3 (1.0)
	C	0.8C	0.75C	0.6C	0.48C

The most probable division of sides is made up of 4432 and 4333. That division and the next most likely both encompass a 3-3 split in the six-card suit, clubs. Let's compare the 3-3 with the 4-2 division of clubs:

Combinations for clubs 3-3:   C + 0.8C + 0.48C   = 2.28C
Combinations for clubs 4-2:   0.75C + 0.6C   = 1.35C

The combinations with a 3-3 split outnumber those with 4-2 split by a fair margin. Without interference during the bidding, declarer might favor the 3-3 split during the play. Note that clubs represent the lowest number of even cards (6).

The 5431 Hand

As we noted previously, 5431 is the most frequent shape containing a singleton (12.9% *a priori*), and the frequency of occurrence varies with the distribution of sides. With an 8765 distribution, it is reduced to 12.2%. Here are some common combinations.

	W E	W E	W E	W E	W E
♠	5 - 3 (0.8)	4 - 4 (1.0)	5 - 3 (0.8)	5 - 3 (0.8)	3 - 5 (0.8)
♥	1 - 4 (0.5)	1 - 4 (0.5)	1 - 4 (0.5)	3 - 2 (1.0)	1 - 4 (0.5)
♦	4 - 3 (1.0)	5 - 2 (0.6)	3 - 4 (1.0)	4 - 3 (1.0)	5 - 2 (0.6)
♣	3 - 3 (1.0)	3 - 3 (1.0)	4 - 2 (0.75)	1 - 5 (0.3)	4 - 2 (0.75)
	0.40C	0.30C	0.30C	0.24C	0.18C

Combinations with ♣ 3-3 total 0.7C.   Combinations with ♣ 4-2 total 0.48C.

There are certain combinations that are not allowed. For example, with 5431 a player can't be matched with a partner also holding 5431 and still form a side of 8765. This affects the probabilities of the occurrence of a 5431 hand for a given distribution of sides.

If the defenders have entered the bidding, they have given away information on the division of sides, information that should be incorporated into your decision making. If they have passed throughout, that also provides information, but it is of a less certain kind. As a result, you should welcome intervention that provides information on distribution without promising enough strength to compete further. Those who overcall on minimal values without removing bidding space, and without being able to convince a partner that it is worthwhile to push higher, are benefactors whose generosity should not be refused.

Going with the Odds

Science and Opinion: the first begets progress, the second, ignorance.
 - Hippocrates (460-377 BC)

The Internet is a wonderful medium for the exchange of opinions. Bridge Base Online is a facility for dropping in on contests between experts commented upon by experts — long may it continue. Some analysts are especially insightful — Bart Bramley, Michael Rosenberg and Larry Cohen come to mind, the latter gracefully taking on the role of a teacher. My favorite appearance is that of Debbie Rosenberg, whose wry comments on her husband's methods are most entertaining.

But — always the 'but' — and I think Hippocrates if he were still around would agree with me on this one — there is too often too much opinion and not enough science. Regularly we are fed preconceived ideas about probability that mislead the masses about the advisability of bidding slams that are not obviously iron-clad. In particular, some commentators seem to have access to calculators designed for the purpose of giving out the *a priori* odds, when it is the conditional probabilities that apply. Here is my take on how it might come across with an 8765 slam where there is no acknowledgement that there has occurred a large change in probabilities due, of course, to a large amount of information being made available by an opponent during the auction.

North
- ♠ A
- ♡ A K 7 4
- ◇ A Q J 3
- ♣ J 7 6 4

West
- ♠ K Q J 9 7 4
- ♡ 6
- ◇ 8 5 2
- ♣ 10 9 3

East
- ♠ 6 5
- ♡ 10 9 3 2
- ◇ 10 9 7 4
- ♣ K Q 2

South
- ♠ 10 8 3 2
- ♡ Q J 8 5
- ◇ K 6
- ♣ A 8 5

West	North	East	South
		pass	pass
2♠	dbl	pass	3♡
pass	4NT*	pass	5♣*
pass	5◇*	pass	6♡
all pass			

The lead is the ♠K. The bidding was bad, but a makeable slam was reached, the type of action that annoys commentators sitting on the sidelines while some lucky ones get to misplay the hands. Here is how the BBO broadcast might come across.

[East's pass] - Greetings, all. This morning we are coming to you from somewhere in the middle of the vast continent of China, Round 51 of the national championships.
- is it morning in China?

[South's pass]- would you open a weak NT?
- not me, not with two four-card majors

[2♠]   - Jason H would have opened 3♠, puts on the pressure
        - I would
        - me 2

[dbl]   - ten tricks off the top in 3NT to tie the board
        - agree: 4441 plays poorly as there are bad splits about
        - a coffee hand: anyone want me to bring some?

[3♡]   - I wld bid 3NT. 10xxx is a stopper versus nonvul
        - but 3NT denies a stopper
        - does any bid means what it says these days?
        - so 3NT is right either way LOL

[4NT]   - never bidding a bad slam means you never have to say you're
          sorry

[5♣]   - don't play 1430, do they? surely not with hearts as trumps
        - everyone in America does
        - I do
        - I don't

[5◇]   - looking for the queen
        - was it Oscar Wilde who said I can resist anything but
          temptation?
        - if he didn't he should have
        - they don't put you in jail for bridge misdemeanors
        - sentenced to a year of yarboroughs

[6♡]   - queen and jack as well, but is it enough?
        - I remember when we used to count points. Bridge was fun in
          those days.
        - slam needs diamonds 4-3 and the long heart with the long
          diamond. I make it a 14.09% chance, just above Roger's
          Plimsoll Line of 12.93%.
        - I've been in worse jams on several continents
        - South has to get it just right
        - slams

[♠K led] - I lead a club as they are prepared for a spade
         - a trump
         - LOL   gotta go ♡♡♡
         - who was that?

And so it goes. At least one gets encouraging insights as to what one's opponents may be thinking at the table.

Looking at all four hands, even the spectators, supposedly a lower life form than the commentators, can spot a winning line. There are eleven tricks to be had in straightforward play, so declarer has to create one more winner. This can come from ruffing two spades in the dummy, the second ruff requiring a top honor. So the play goes: the ♡A and a heart to the ♡Q; ruff a spade low, a club to the ace, play on diamonds to this position:

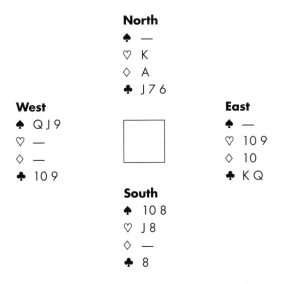

On the ◇A, a club is discarded from the South hand, then a club ruff, a spade ruff and a club from dummy ruffed with the ♡J. Note that if the ♡J and the ♡10 were exchanged, this line would still work as a coup *en passant* where East can't profitably ruff with the master trump.

This seems remarkably easy, but declarer must formulate his plan at the start. First relaxing, counting tricks, envisioning the distribution of sides that works in favor of the contract's being achieved. It is reasonable to assume the spades are split 6-2, so the most probable distributions at this point are the ones given below.

I	II	III	IV	V	VI
♠ 6 - 2	♠ 6 - 2	♠ 6 - 2	♠ 6 - 2	♠ 6 - 2	♠ 6 - 2
♡ 2 - 3	♡ 2 - 3	♡ 1 - 4	♡ 3 - 2	♡ 1 - 4	♡ 2 - 3
◇ 3 - 4	◇ 2 - 5	◇ 3 - 4	◇ 2 - 5	◇ 4 - 3	◇ 4 - 3
♣ 2 - 4	♣ 3 - 3	♣ 3 - 3	♣ 2 - 4	♣ 2 - 4	♣ 1 - 5

Ruffing two spades in dummy will succeed against any lead in all these most probable cases except Case V, and even then there are some chances. This evaluation is a far cry from the 14% estimated from a superficial appeal to *a priori* odds. All that has been assumed is that West holds six spades for his preempt.

Suppose that instead of making a lengthy analysis a declarer were simply to follow Bob's Blind Rule, choosing to consider only the most likely estimate for the distribution of sides, that being the one with the most even splits (Case I). The winning play would be much easier to envision, and that player might proceed with some degree of confidence of success, even on the shocking revelation of a bad trump split (Case III).

The 7766 Division

Playing for even splits combines likelihood with optimism.

The 7766 is to a side what 4333 is to a hand, namely, an occasion for caution in the bidding and in the play. This is one of the rare (one-in-ten) occasions where the pessimist triumphs and the optimist finally gets his comeuppance. The table below contains some common divisions of sides with the numbers of combinations noted. Instead of the full numbers of combinations, we shall note only the ratio of the given split to the maximum possible for the given distribution of sides, denoted by the letter C. The numbers in brackets are the relative number of combinations for a given number of cards within a suit.

	W E	W E	W E	W E	W E
♠	4 - 3 (1.0)	4 - 3 (1.0)	4 - 3 (1.0)	5 - 2 (0.6)	4 - 3 (1.0)
♡	3 - 4 (1.0)	3 - 4 (1.0)	3 - 4 (1.0)	3 - 4 (1.0)	4 - 3 (1.0)
♢	3 - 3 (1.0)	2 - 4 (0.75)	4 - 2 (0.75)	3 - 3 (1.0)	4 - 2 (1.0)
♣	3 - 3 (1.0)	4 - 2 (0.75)	2 - 4 (0.75)	2 - 4 (0.75)	1 - 5 (0.3)
	C	0.56C	0.56C	0.45C	0.30C

Not all possibilities are shown, but enough to show that the configuration of 4333 opposite 4333 is a very stable one. The next closest configuration of 4432 opposite 4432 provides only 9/16 of the combinations, so is less probable in that ratio. The most common configuration with a singleton is shown on the far right. The probability of this is less than 1/3 that of the most likely configuration, which is shown on the extreme left. It would be a surprise if this were the actual situation.

When a declarer recognizes his side is 7766, it should register automatically that the opponents are also 7766. Table 50 in *The Mathematical Theory of Bridge* by E. Borel and A. Cheron informs us that a specified defender will hold a 4432 pattern 29% of the time, a 4333 pattern 16% of the time and a 5431 pattern 11% of the time. The *a priori* odds of a particular player being dealt a hand where the longest suit is of four-card length is 35%, but within a 7766 pattern, the probability is close to 50%. The differences from the *a priori* odds are significant and should be taken into account by a declarer.

Let's take a break from theory and watch a fictitious declarer in action, one who thrives on 7766.

Emeritus Jones's 7766 Disaster in the Dining Hall

See how the world its veterans rewards!
A youth of frolics, an old age of cards
- Alexander Pope (1688-1744)

Gentleman Whose Name Escapes Me
- ♠ K 9 2
- ♡ 4 3 2
- ◇ A Q 7 6
- ♣ Q 5 3

Peterson
- ♠ Q J 7 5
- ♡ A 8 7
- ◇ 10 4 2
- ♣ 9 7 6

Smith of Organic Chemistry
- ♠ 10 6 4
- ♡ Q J 10 9
- ◇ J 9 8
- ♣ J 8 2

Jones
- ♠ A 8 3
- ♡ K 6 5
- ◇ K 5 3
- ♣ A K 10 4

'Thank you so much, partner,' said Professor Emeritus M. L. Jones, affectionately known about campus as 'Maximum Likelihood Jones', as he noted with satisfaction that the proffered dummy produced cards that made up his favorite distribution of sides. For some, the appearance of a 7766 is a gathering of storm clouds, but to Jones it is a harbinger of April showers that bring May flowers.

The contract, as so often the case with Jones, was 3NT, the opponents having remained silent throughout the short auction. The event was the annual Faculty-and-Friends Duplicate Challenge in which an academic was paired with a potential benefactor — the size of whose contribution, human nature being what it is, had been found by the Department of Computer Sciences to correlate highly to the place of finish. Jones felt that a good result in this, his specialty contract, was a necessity to his returning next year to the prestigious circle of the Millionaires' Selects. Noting the lead of the ♠5, he considered, as was his wont, the most likely divisions of the opponents' cards.

	I		II		III	
	West	East	West	East	West	East
Spades	4	3	4	3	4	3
Hearts	3	4	3	4	3	4
Diamonds	3	3	4	2	2	4
Clubs	3	3	2	4	4	2

Many players think along the lines that 4432 hands are twice as frequent as 4333 hands, so would dismiss the latter possibility. Jones thought otherwise. A 3-3 split produces twenty combinations whereas as a 4-2 split produces only fifteen. Case I, in which both minors are split 3-3, presented the most possible card combinations, so it was clearly the maximum likelihood division of cards on a spade lead.

The combinations associated with 4-2 minor splits each represented just 9/16 of the maximum number. A construction in which the majors are 4-4 in West's hand is half as likely because according to the Principle of Restricted Choice the opening lead might as easily have been a heart, a hypothesis strengthened by the fact that the defenders' hearts were stronger than their spades. However, before accepting Case I as the true situation, it would be easy enough to test for 4-2 minor splits using the cards he saw before him.

Jones' plan was to test one minor for a 3-3 split by giving the opponents a chance to tell him whether this was the case. To cloud the situation in the spade suit, he played the ♠9 from dummy, covered with the ♠10 and won by the ♠A. A low diamond towards ◊AQ drew the ◊2 from West. The ♣Q from the dummy drew the ♣2 from the East.

Having confirmed to his satisfaction that the maximum likelihood combination was now even more likely than at the start of play, he tried to construct a deal in which he might make eleven tricks when others were making only ten. He was reluctant to follow the field by taking his ten sure tricks and then lead at the end towards the ♡K, hoping for the ♡A to be onside.

Jones cashed the diamonds first and then the clubs, reaching a five-card position with the ♣10 about to be cashed. Smith had discarded the ♡Q to inform his hard-to-please partner of the situation in that suit, impeccably count, attitude, and top-of-a-sequence all in one.

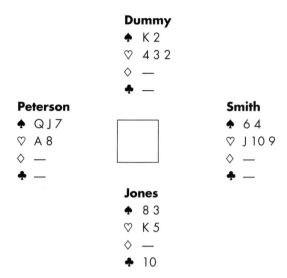

Dummy
♠ K 2
♡ 4 3 2
◇ —
♣ —

Peterson
♠ Q J 7
♡ A 8
◇ —
♣ —

Smith
♠ 6 4
♡ J 10 9
◇ —
♣ —

Jones
♠ 8 3
♡ K 5
◇ —
♣ 10

Peterson of Peterson Petroleum, a potentially generous patron, had a tough discard on the ♣10. Thanks to Smith's informative signal, he knew from a count of high cards that Jones held the ♡K, so baring the ♡A was obviously a bad move. On the other hand, if his partner held the ♠8, unblocking the top spades would force an entry for East to lead through the ♡K, with unpleasant consequences for the declarer.

Peterson had not made a fortune in recycled engine oil by accepting the fate of a humble upbringing that necessitated wearing his brother's hand-me-downs and he was not now about to submit to being held to two defensive tricks when he might get three. He unblocked the ♠Q on the ♣10 and Smith gave out the bad news by contributing an apologetic ♠6. Jones then played spades from the top, forcing an apoplectic Peterson to give him the last trick in hearts, eleven tricks in all and a top score.

The next day over lunch at the Faculty Club, Smith took another sip of mulligatawny soup and commented, 'Unfortunate that, Emeritus Jones giving Peterson fits with his endplay in 3NT. Nothing I could do'.

'I heard about it,' replied the Bursar sourly. 'It's a pity that with old age what we say becomes wiser, but what we do, more foolish. I was hoping for a new Zamboni, but all we got was a stained glass window in memory of his mother.'

'Gentlemen, Gentlemen, a beautiful day despite the wind and the snow.' It was Emeritus Jones rubbing his hands and making so as to join them. 'My partner, I've forgotten his name, was so pleased with our first-place finish that at my not-so-subtle suggestion he has donated most generously to the classical languages section of the library. Some of those editions of Virgil and Homer are quite dog-eared. Sorry now I didn't try for a snowplow. I am quite looking forward to next year, aren't you?'

CHAPTER 7

INFORMATION AND SURPRISE ON THE OPENING LEAD

Dame Fortune is the arbiter of half of our actions,
leaving it to us to direct the other half.
- Niccolo Machiavelli (1469-1527)

It may come as a surprise to some readers that the opening lead comes under the governance of probability. Intent as we are as defenders on finding the killing lead by logic, we may not consider the matter as a random process. We are happy to lead the top of an honor sequence or our 'fourth highest', confident everyone will do the same. That is not always the situation. Mike Lawrence, in his book *Opening Leads*, suggests that about 50% of leads represent a universal choice. That leaves 50% of deals with a variety of choices that from the outside may appear to be part of a random process. In some bridge magazines, there are entertaining quizzes for experts on opening leads in which often it is revealed that the killing lead is not the most frequent expert choice. Many a disgruntled panelist will argue that although his lead was not successful, it was the most probable means of defeating the contract based on what was known at the time.

From declarer's point of view, some suits are more likely to be led than others, based on what he sees in dummy and the information transmitted by the auction. This is where surprise enters the picture. If the lead is a surprise, the affected declarers must sift through the evidence with care looking for clues. The inferences drawn from the opening lead are an important consideration in the planning of the play; the stronger the inferences, the more one may be drawn to depart from reliance on the *a priori* odds.

Information scientists have tried to personalize the mathematics by adopting familiar expressions for some of the quantities that appear in their governing equations. Some have invented new words like 'surprisal' to overcome prejudice while at the same time attempting to utilize it. Surprise is an emotion, thus the term surprisal adds subjectivity to an otherwise abstract quantity. In the 50% of situations where the lead is 'automatic', the probability of a given suit being led is nearly 1 and the probabilities of other leads are negligible. If we bid three suits and end up in notrump, it is highly likely that a card from the fourth suit will hit the table first. There is no surprise when the action is very much what one expects. On the other hand, if a particular lead is strange, its occurrence occasions a great deal of surprise in any but the most fervent of pessimists.

Surprise is a measure of the degree of departure from the expected, so surprise is therefore related to the associated amount of information. Mathematically, they share the same equation. The greater the surprise, the greater the amount of information the disclosure reveals. It would be difficult for a declarer to assign a numerical probability to any given opening lead; nonetheless, declarers should be aware there is a connection with information and should take pains to extract it.

It is worthwhile to dwell for a moment on the surprise factor, as it will arise again when we come to discuss the opening bid. You would be surprised to find in a dictionary under the letter Q a word that did not have 'u' as its second letter. If you were to choose blindfolded a word from the Q-section, the probability that your finger would rest upon a word for which 'q' is followed by 'u' is very nearly 1, but if your finger rested upon Qatar, a non-democratic but oil-rich state on the Persian Gulf, you might be greatly surprised — not by the presence of the word in the dictionary, but by its selection in a random process. The surprise would be less if instead of a dictionary you were choosing from a gazetteer of the Middle East, a region notorious for bad spellers, where you might expect to encounter, in addition to Qatar, such place names as Qazvin, Qarzshi or Qom.

In the next few pages, we shall explore how the fundamental principle of information theory, which links information to probability, applies to the opening lead. As we have seen, that principle is expressed by the equation

$$\text{Information} = \text{-log (Probability)}$$

Our analysis will be based on the number of possible card combinations after a low-card lead against a notrump contract.

Here are the basic conclusions:

1) The less probable an opening lead, the more information it provides
   and
2) The greater the amount of information in the opening lead, the fewer the number of card combinations that remain to be considered.

These conclusions are simple enough and amount to common sense when one thinks about it, provided always that one has thought about it. Nonetheless, it would be nice to produce some evidence for them without extensive computer simulation (the results of which may not convince the skeptical mind), so we'll need some simplifying assumptions. The major assumption we make is that the lead is a low card from the defender's longest suit. Not always true, of course, but true a lot of the time, and for the great majority of cases where it is true, the results follow like clockwork.

Here are the bridge rules that arise from this analysis:

1) If the opening lead is in the shortest suit jointly held by declarer's side, the information content is relatively low, and many distributions of sides remain as possibilities;

2) If the opening lead is in the longest suit jointly held by declarer's side, the information content is relatively high, and relatively few possible distributions of sides remain;

3) The difference between the information in one suit relative to that in another increases with the difference in the number of cards held in the suits.

There is some confusion even amongst expert players as to how probability fits in with the opening lead. One hang-up we have encountered in the bridge literature is that an opening lead is not a random choice but a conscious choice. The conclusion appears to be that this excludes it from the realm of probability, which refers to random events, not deterministic events. This confusion goes back to the time of the Greek philosophers. It is more useful to think of probability merely as a reflection of uncertainty and to consider its use in making decisions when in a state of partial knowledge. Information and probability are linked mathematically.

To illustrate these concepts, we shall work through an example with simple, but realistic, assumptions. The purpose is to get players thinking within the correct framework of modern information theory. First, however, we shall digress briefly to look at how probability applies to situations where a non-random choice is being made.

Predicting an Obama Win

We are all familiar with the opinion surveys that were so often quoted on the news during the 2008 US presidential election. Many of the polls predicted a very close race when it seemed intuitively obvious that McCain had no chance at all against Obama. One of the questions raised at the time was, 'Who is getting polled?' If the pollsters were asking only registered voters, as was often the case, then the predictions were biased as there would be many previously unregistered voters who would be taking part and voting for Obama. If one asked a registered Republican whom he was voting for, the answer was probably McCain, and if one asked a registered Democrat the same question, the answer was probably Obama, so in the end such a poll was doing little more than predicting the outcome of the previous election. Consequently it was disastrous for McCain not to lead in the polls. He had lost even before the Wall Street collapse.

What's that got to do with bridge? When a citizen enters the voters' booth, he makes a conscious choice between two alternatives. It is not (usually) a matter of flipping a coin at the last moment and placing the 'X' accordingly. Nonetheless, valid predictions can be made with regard to the eventual outcome over a wide population of committed voters. There is previous knowledge concerning past tendencies in some states (Texas for McCain, New York for Obama, etc.), yet probabilities are still valid when we come to make predictions since uncertainty still exists to a greater or lesser degree. The same is true of opening leads. We know that in certain situations some leads are more likely than others. We know the opening leader is trying hard to make the best lead possible. We may even predict the lead on the basis of the bidding, but we can't be certain. Probability still plays a role in declarer's predictions and the opening lead is a fine piece of evidence that needs to be taken into account. Determinism is a red herring.

The City Council's Secret Ballot

Suppose you are keen to predict the outcome of a critical vote of your city council on a controversial issue that divides two major factions; the Reds are against it, the Blues are for it. There are thirteen councilors: six Reds, six Blues, and one independent Green. As they arrive for the closed-door meeting, you have the opportunity to ask just one of the councilors how he is going to vote. It is tricky to predict the outcome of thirteen votes from a sample of one, but if you had to make such a choice, which one would you ask? As the Green member represents the swing vote, it is pretty obvious that you should choose to ask her. There is much more relevant information to be had from the exceptional case than from the common case. Sure, some Reds might vote Yes and some Blues might vote No, but individual preferences will be rare and may tend to balance themselves out. So the Green vote is the best single predictor.

If you can ask only one councilor, but have no choice about whom to ask, you expect a Red to say No and a Blue to say Yes; that does not represent a good predictor as it is the expected response. Similarly, a low card selected at random from a large number of low cards is not going to tell you much about the deal as a whole. However, if you happen to ask the leader of the Reds and he says that on his daughter's urging he is changing his vote to Yes, that is a major development. Something that occurs against the odds, such as receiving a highly unusual opening lead, is very informative. Another way of putting it is this: the greater the surprise, the greater the information.

Next, suppose there are five Reds, five Blues and three Greens on the council. Naturally one again chooses to question a Green, but the Greens are a diverse lot. If a randomly chosen Green is voting Yes, the other two Greens may vote No, but the odds favor 2-1 for Yes. The answer is still more significant than a Yes from a Blue.

If we consider the opening lead in the same manner, a passive lead that conforms to expectations doesn't provide much information. That is the principal argument for choosing such a lead. Declarer may be lulled into assuming that the probability of an exceptional card distribution is low. If one leads a singleton, declarer may well read the situation immediately.

A Mathematical Model for Opening Leads

We shall consider a simple model for a simple problem in order to illustrate how the information in an opening lead gets transformed in probability and vice versa. The bidding has gone 1NT-3NT and the opening lead is a low spade. Not a surprise. The normal lead is the fourth highest from the longest and strongest suit, but before we draw inferences, let's look at the cards in dummy and form the distribution of sides to see if, indeed, the spade lead is what we should expect. Our dummy is such that we can calculate that the defenders hold eight spades, seven hearts, six diamonds, and five clubs, thus a sides of 8-7-6-5 and, indeed, spades is their most plentiful suit. Spades weren't necessarily LHO's longest suit, but it is comforting nonetheless to find our expectations are realized and normality confirmed. On consideration of the deal alone, the most likely distributions of the cards left and right when a spade is led from length are as follows:

	I	II	III	IV	V
♠	4 - 4	♠ 4 - 4	♠ 5 - 3	♠ 4 - 4	♠ 5 - 3
♡	4 - 3	♡ 3 - 4	♡ 3 - 4	♡ 4 - 3	♡ 3 - 4
◊	3 - 3	◊ 3 - 3	◊ 3 - 3	◊ 2 - 4	◊ 2 - 4
♣	2 - 3	♣ 3 - 2	♣ 2 - 3	♣ 3 - 2	♣ 3 - 2
Weights	100	100	80	75	60

The weights reflect the relative number of card combinations for each condition. The most even splits are the most likely. The weights for Conditions I and IV must be reduced, as in those cases a heart might have been led as easily as a spade. So, the situation appears at first glance to be rather mundane. However, what if the lead is not a spade? On the basis of what was written above, one expects a lead in a less plentiful suit to be more informative. The following section demonstrates how this translates into bridge logic.

Probability Linked to Information

Declarer notes the lead of a low card and calculates that the division of sides is 8-7-6-5. The greatest expectation is that a spade will be led, but there will be times when that does not occur. Declarer will also have formed, consciously or unconsciously, a set of prior probabilities for leads in the various suits. Let's assume on a tentative basis the following set for the sake of illustration: $P(\spadesuit) = 0.50$, $P(\heartsuit) = 0.35$, $P(\diamondsuit) = 0.10$, and $P(\clubsuit) = 0.05$.

When a low card is led in this situation, it is likely to be a spade half the time. A club lead would be unusual, occurring just once in twenty occasions. A heart is expected once in three occasions, and a diamond once in ten. The numbers could be the subject of a test using computer simulations, but let's assume these are close enough for now. Next we consider the most likely distributions, assuming that the lead was from West's longest suit.

Lead	$\spadesuit$	$\heartsuit$	$\diamondsuit$	$\clubsuit$	$\clubsuit$
	$\spadesuit$ 4 - 4	$\spadesuit$ 3 - 5	$\spadesuit$ 3 - 5	$\spadesuit$ 3 - 5	$\spadesuit$ 3 - 5
	$\heartsuit$ 3 - 4	$\heartsuit$ 4 - 3	$\heartsuit$ 3 - 4	$\heartsuit$ 3 - 4	$\heartsuit$ 3 - 4
	$\diamondsuit$ 3 - 3	$\diamondsuit$ 3 - 3	$\diamondsuit$ 4 - 2	$\diamondsuit$ 3 - 3	$\diamondsuit$ 2 - 4
	$\clubsuit$ 3 - 2	$\clubsuit$ 3 - 2	$\clubsuit$ 3 - 2	$\clubsuit$ 4 - 1	$\clubsuit$ 5 - 0
Weights	100	80	60	40	6

As the number of cards available to the defenders decreases from spades to clubs, the number of combinations for the most likely distribution decreases. Overall there will as well be fewer combinations available in each category. The possibilities are reduced as the number of available cards in the suit led is reduced. The fewer the possibilities, the greater the information, and the more severe the restrictions on the hidden hand.

The last two columns are the two most frequent cases where a club is led. Of low probability, the last column will be quickly eliminated when RHO follows suit. So we may conclude that a club lead on the first round establishes the full distribution of the defenders' cards. Very impressive! A spade lead is less restrictive and many possibilities exist apart from the most probable. The same is true to lesser degree for a heart.

The mathematical connection between probability and information is simply stated: the amount of information in an opening lead is minus the logarithm of the probability of that lead having been chosen. If the information from a specific suit being led is denoted by I(suit), then using log to the base 10 we find: $I(\spadesuit) = 0.30$, $I(\heartsuit) = 0.46$, $I(\diamondsuit) = 1.00$, and $I(\clubsuit) = 1.30$. Thus, given our prior assumptions, the amount of information in a low club lead should be more than four times the information in a low spade lead. However, that estimate seems low, so perhaps we overestimated the chance of a club lead. Perhaps 1 out of a

100 is a better guess. Let's have a look at the situation after a diamond lead, when it is assumed diamonds is West's longest suit. Here are the six most frequent distributions with their relative weights:

	I	II	III	IV	V	VI
♠	3 - 5	3 - 5	4 - 4	3 - 5	3 - 5	2 - 6
♡	3 - 4	3 - 4	2 - 5	2 - 5	4 - 3	3 - 4
◇	4 - 2	5 - 1	5 - 1	5 - 1	5 - 1	5 - 1
♣	3 - 2	2 - 3	2 - 3	3 - 2	1 - 4	3 - 2
Weights	60	24	18	14	12	12

The total number of combinations for all six possibilities shown (140) is less than for the two most frequent distributions after a spade lead. Many combinations have been eliminated and few remain. The best way of thinking about this result is that a diamond lead is much more informative than a spade lead, but less informative than a club lead, roughly by a factor of 3. Because probability and information are linked, this reduction in possibilities should be reflected in the relative frequencies of the respective leads, a subject for future research requiring extensive computer simulation.

The Random Element

The choice of an opening lead is not random, it is deterministic. That applies as the opening leader ponders his choice, looking at his thirteen cards. Declarer is looking from the outside. He sees the result of the deliberations, but can only guess why a particular lead was chosen. There must have been a reason, and therein lies the information. It is not exact knowledge he gains, merely information subject to uncertainty. If the lead has no good reason behind it, declarer is not well informed; that is why it is more difficult to play against a bad, erratic player than a good, dependable one. The more predictable an opponent, the fewer his possible choices, and however sound a player he may be, the easier it will be to draw conclusions from his actions and peek into his hand mentally.

The randomness in the opening lead comes largely from the dealing of the cards. Usually a rational choice of a lead is limited to at most three possibilities, but there are a myriad of card combinations for a given division of sides. Declarer, looking from the outside, doesn't know which cards the opening leader has been dealt, but he can make a shrewd initial guess based on the opening lead. His deductions are based on assumptions that fit the circumstances. Those assumptions are the key ingredient. The opening lead has begun a prediction process during which assumptions and deductions should be tested continually as the play progresses and more information is obtained.

I believe bridge authors have been reluctant to employ Bayes' Theorem, and the concept of vacant places during the playdown of a suit, because until a player shows out of a suit, information can be tainted. Showing out allows no deception. Many rely too much on the *a priori* odds as being the only reliable information available — everything else may be a sham. This is a rather unproductive attitude.

Edith Kemp Was Surprised at First

We never do anything well until we cease to
think about the manner of doing it.
- William Hazlitt (1778-1830)

Here is an outstanding example of information extraction reported by Derek Rimington in his book *Learn Bridge from the Experts* in which the great American player, Edith Kemp, turned initial surprise into a useful inference.

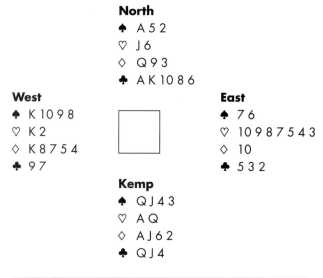

North
♠ A 5 2
♡ J 6
♢ Q 9 3
♣ A K 10 8 6

West
♠ K 10 9 8
♡ K 2
♢ K 8 7 5 4
♣ 9 7

East
♠ 7 6
♡ 10 9 8 7 5 4 3
♢ 10
♣ 5 3 2

Kemp
♠ Q J 4 3
♡ A Q
♢ A J 6 2
♣ Q J 4

West	North	East	South
	1♣	3♡	3♠
pass	4♠	pass	4NT
pass	5♡	pass	6NT
all pass			

Kemp had to gather information over the 3♡ preempt, so she bid a minimal 3♠ to keep the auction going. As is often the case, Blackwood 4NT propped up a shaky auction and 6NT ended the affair with very little achieved in the way clarification. The opening lead was a most passive ♣9.

In Rimington's view, the non-lead of a heart was a big surprise. Kemp deduced that West held the ♡K; otherwise why not lead the suit? Concluding thus, Kemp won in hand and led the ♠Q, which was covered. After winning in dummy, she finessed in diamonds, losing to the ♢K. Another club was led by West. Staying with her original evaluation, declarer placed West with the ♡K and length in spades, so cashed her winners and successfully played to squeeze him in the majors.

Looking back over the years, one might conjecture to what extent the declarer was surprised by the lead. The fact that she played for the unusual ending indicates she believed West was reliable and would certainly have led his partner's suit unless there was good reason not to. Taking that into account, Kemp's plan was based on the highly informative nature of the opening lead.

Silence Is Golden

Be valiant but not too venturesome.
- John Lyly (1554-1606)

The modern game has become increasingly one of venturesome bidding that seldom gets the punishment it deserves. The losses incurred are often indirect and so less noticeable by those whose bids escape the axe. Declarers should take into account these preemptive proclivities of overly active opponents. In the final segment of the high-scoring 2005 World's Open Teams Championship, Italy's lead over the USA was insurmountable when Jeff Meckstroth in one room and Bob Hamman in the other combined to gain 12 IMPs in a lost cause on the following slam hand. (Hands rotated for convenience.)

Meckstroth		Rodwell
♠ K 8 7 4 3		♠ 6
♡ Q		♡ A K 10 4
♢ K 6		♢ A 9 4 2
♣ A K Q 6 2		♣ 10 9 7 5

Meckstroth	North	Rodwell	South
1♣*	1♡	1NT	pass
2♣	pass	2NT	pass
3♣	pass	4♣	pass
6♣	all pass		

Meckstroth began with an artificial 1♣, giving North the opportunity to advertise a heart suit consisting of J-9-8-5-3. Against 6♣, North led from his paltry heart suit. Rodwell's surprising holding of three heart honors must have prompted Meckstroth to wonder what on earth North was bidding on. Meckstroth began the spade suit by playing low towards the dummy, South winning. The ◊J was returned to the ◊K and a spade was ruffed.

Without interference a declarer might be forgiven a careless slip, but once the defenders have disclosed some shape, a declarer should be alert to possible bad breaks. Meckstroth drew just one round of trumps, felling the jack, and proceeded to ruff another spade in dummy. He could claim at this point, as the ♡A and the ♡K provided discards for the losing spades in his hand.

Doing things the right way seems so simple that it is easy to overlook what can go wrong. The thought occurs that simple is usually best. On the other hand, it must be remembered that what information is available is critical to the analysis. Here is the full deal.

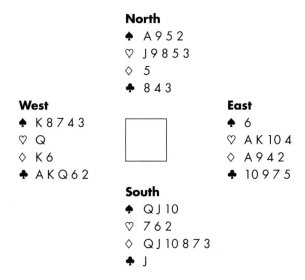

North
- ♠ A 9 5 2
- ♡ J 9 8 5 3
- ◊ 5
- ♣ 8 4 3

West
- ♠ K 8 7 4 3
- ♡ Q
- ◊ K 6
- ♣ A K Q 6 2

East
- ♠ 6
- ♡ A K 10 4
- ◊ A 9 4 2
- ♣ 10 9 7 5

South
- ♠ Q J 10
- ♡ 7 6 2
- ◊ Q J 10 8 7 3
- ♣ J

At the other table, the bidding was natural, and North was deprived of the opportunity for fruitless interference. Not to worry, South was able to make some noise on the auction by doubling a diamond cuebid as East-West bid to 6♣.

With East as declarer, the lead was a normal ◊Q, won with the ◊A, and again spades were started at Trick 2, North winning the ♠K with the ♠A. Hamman is known to think a bit deeper than most; his trump return was won in dummy with the ♣A and another spade was ruffed. The Italian declarer did not take the bidding into full account, perhaps lulled by the trump return at Trick 3. A defender hoping for a ruff seldom leads a trump himself. Carelessly declarer tried to return to dummy with a second diamond rather than with a heart ruff. Down one.

One cannot help but feel that declarer discounted too greatly the information that had been presented to him by South free of charge. A double of diamonds at the three-level needs something behind it and here that something has to be length. Or has it become a matter among old rivals that the unusual is now the ordinary?

The Heart Lead Against 3NT

'I had,' he said, 'come to an entirely erroneous conclusion
which shows, my dear Watson, how dangerous it
always is to reason from insufficient data.'
- Sherlock Holmes in *The Adventure of the Speckled Band*

As we said earlier, declarer takes inference at his own risk. How often is the opening lead against 3NT the advertised fourth highest from the longest and strongest? Here is an amusing example from the 2006 Spingold Final, where the Nickell team faced old rivals from Italy, in which neither defender led from his longest suit!

Lauria	Rodwell	Meckstroth
♠ J 6 5	1◇	1♠
♡ Q 10 5	2♣	2♡*
◇ Q 8 5	2NT	3NT
♣ K 7 4 3	pass	

Rodwell opened the bidding on Lauria's left with a nebulous 1◇ bid that didn't promise more than two diamonds. He had, in fact, opened on a shapely 10 HCP, and his 2NT bid was somewhat discouraging. The unbid suit was hearts, so Lauria began with the ♡5, an attitude lead. Dummy played low from ♡AJxx, Versace put in the ♡K from ♡K92 when the ♡9 was the right choice, and the Nickell team emerged triumphant. It appears the ♡5 was not sufficiently informative for Versace. Rodwell later was able to take advantage of the 3-3 heart position and scored ten tricks.

The amusing aspect of the deal is that the late Paul Soloway, who was particularly fond of short-suit heart leads against 3NT, chose the ♡2 from the other side, ostensibly 'fourth highest'. Here is the full deal with hands rotated.

Fantoni
- ♠ 10
- ♡ 8 7 3
- ◇ A K J 9 6
- ♣ Q 10 9 5

Soloway
- ♠ A 9 3 2
- ♡ K 9 2
- ◇ 10 4 3
- ♣ J 8 6

Hamman
- ♠ J 6 5
- ♡ Q 10 5
- ◇ Q 8 5
- ♣ K 7 4 3

Nunes
- ♠ K Q 8 7 4
- ♡ A J 6 4
- ◇ 7 2
- ♣ A 2

Soloway	Fantoni	Hamman	Nunes
pass	2◇	pass	2♡
pass	3♣	pass	3NT
all pass			

South's 2♡ was an artificial enquiry, and the 3♣ rebid described North's hand pattern in the minors. Soloway reasoned that declarer was well prepared for a spade lead, so he chose to lead from his heart holding. Hamman provided the needed ♡Q. Despite the existence of a 7766 sides, Nunes impatiently made a precipitate move by winning the ♡A and leading the ♣2 towards dummy, putting in the ♣10 and drawing Hamman's ♣K. The ♡10 return was covered and won by Soloway, who withheld the winning ♡9 for now. There was no rush, so Soloway switched to the spade suit. When Nunes was forced to try the losing diamond finesse, the defenders were able to score two spades, two hearts, a diamond and a club. That prodigious pas-de-deux made it a difference of three tricks, and this deal provided the winning margin in the match.

Prelude to Bayes' Theorem — The Journey So Far

If you want to master military science, don't stop partway. Study and
practice until you reach the inner secrets, thereafter to return to your
original simplicity. If, however, you spend your days pursuing half-baked
notions without reaching the inner secrets, thereby losing the way back
to your original simplicity, you will remain frustrated and demoralized,
which is most regrettable.
- Taira Shigesuke, samurai strategist (1639-1730)

At the beginning, we invited the reader on a journey of discovery through the Forest of Probability. Now we have reached a clearing where we can rest and profitably look back with some pride on our accomplishments. There is just one more hill to climb and we shall have reached the Summit of Wider Vision.

These are the major concepts we have discussed.

1) Pascal's Triangle can help us calculate card combinations;
2) Probabilities are ratios of card combinations;
3) Probability is equivalent to information;
4) A priori odds express a state of maximum ignorance;
5) Uncertainty is reduced through an increase in information;
6) A bridge deal is a finite world in which conditions in one suit affect the conditions in the other suits;
7) Vacant places are a convenient way of expressing suit interdependence;
8) Within the restrictions of current partial knowledge, the most even splits are the most probable splits.

In the probabilistic analysis of declarer play, we have reached the stage where declarer gets to see the dummy. The amount of surprise on the opening lead has been registered and inferences drawn. As declarers, we have got our emotions under control by subduing the Ancestral Voices, have weighed the implications of the auction, have noted the sides and decided upon the most likely distributions given what we know. Our plans are beginning to take shape.

Sooner or later, a declarer gains the lead and is in a position to initialize play in a suit of his choosing. Usually his choice is a suit in which he controls seven, eight, or nine cards. At this point, his plan of action is formulated in detail. The information obtained from the defensive moves is incorporated into a revised estimation of the most likely distribution of sides. Any imbalance of vacant places is a major factor in the prediction of the existing conditions.

There are two conditions that can apply to a suit about to be played:

1) There are no significant cards that need to be withheld by a defender, and
2) There are significant cards that would be withheld by a defender except to win a trick or promote a trick for his partner.

Under Condition 1, we have seen that in a playdown of a suit to which the defenders follow at random with insignificant cards, the relative probabilities of the most even splits remain unchanged. As each card from a defender's hand appears, a vacant place is filled and overall probabilities change. With just two splits remaining as possibilities, the more probable case at the start is still the more probable at the end, and the ratio of the most probable to the next most probable is what it was at the beginning of play. This is what we have learned so far.

Now we come to Condition 2, where a defender is restricted in his choice of cards so that the sequence of plays cannot be considered to be random. The major problem in bridge play is to locate missing honors that defenders will guard as best they can. How does one estimate the probabilities under these circumstances? Vacant places can be used as a rough guide as they represent combinations and the larger the number of combinations, the more likely a given honor card lies in that mix. However, that is not exact; it is in fact possible to calculate the probabilities exactly with each card played, given the assumptions made on the basis of partial knowledge.

How is this done? What follows answers this vital question by describing the application of a fundamental law of Probability Theory known as Bayes' Theorem. This applies equally under Condition 1 and Condition 2, so we have a general procedure that applies to all plays of the cards. It unlocks all the hidden secrets, and encompasses all that we have learned so far about card play.

CHAPTER 8

APPLYING BAYES' THEOREM

> *The probability of an event is the ratio between the value at which*
> *an expectation depending on the happening of the event ought to be*
> *computed, and the value of the thing expected upon its happening.*
> - Thomas Bayes (1702-1761)

Words, words, words, but what we want are numbers, numbers, numbers. As one can judge from the above definition, Thomas Bayes was a man of many, many words that spread confusion, perhaps a result of his profession: he was a non-conformist preacher. Like Pascal before him and Florence Nightingale after, he mixed Probability with Religion, not realizing that mixing the two benefits neither.

However, it is Bayes' equation rather than his words that has caught the fancy of latter-day statisticians. It is very simply stated, as we shall see. Although Bayes published just two articles during his lifetime, he gained a reputation great enough to allow his acceptance as a Fellow of the Royal Society in 1742. There was a period when his contributions were misunderstood, especially in the English-speaking world, and his name fell into obscurity. Today his influence grows as computers are increasingly being used to describe the present and predict the future using very large databases. In the 20th century, money was collected to honor Bayes' memory by restoring his tomb in Bunhill Fields, the Dissenters' burial grounds not far from London's Liverpool Street Station. This is the inscription that appears on the cover of the vault:

> In recognition of Thomas Bayes' important work on probability this vault was restored in 1969 with contributions received from statisticians throughout the world.

Further restoration took place in 2006 thanks to a donation from an American company located in Hoboken NJ, Bayesian Efficient Strategic Trading, LLC, and The International Society for Bayesian Analysis takes responsibility for maintenance of the site. Now on to the equation that prompted these generous acts.

In keeping with its origins in the 17th century — the consideration of a game of dice — the theory of probability received its most wide-spread public exposure three centuries later through another game of chance, the popular television program 'Let's Make a Deal' hosted by Monty Hall. The circumstances are well described by Jeffrey S. Rosenthal in his entertaining and instructive book *Struck by Lightning: The Curious World of Probabilities*.

The controversial discussion revolved around Bayes' Theorem. The basic idea is that one should make one's probability estimates based on what one has observed. This can be done even if the observations are not complete and therefore any uncertainty is not entirely resolved. In the context of card play, the Bayesian approach is to estimate probabilities based on one's observations rather than relying totally on the *a priori* odds. This is the basis for the Principle of Restricted Choice at the bridge table. Because the concept is still misunderstood even in the 21st century, it is worthwhile to go back to the discussion of the Monty Hall problem, since it served to enlighten the general public as to the essential features involved.

Monty, Marilyn and the Theorem of Bayes

What is real is reasonable.
- G. W. F. Hegel (1770-1831)

The game that Monty Hall conducted worked as follows. On the studio stage were placed three doors — let's call them Door A, Door B, and Door C — behind one of which was hidden a new car. A contestant was invited to choose one of the doors (we'll suppose he picked Door A), and if he chose happily, the gas guzzler would be his prize. Obviously there is a 1 in 3 chance of choosing the right door, so the initial odds on guessing right were 2:1 against.

With regard to bridge, the *a priori* odds are those associated with the deal before any action is taken by the players. Once a player takes an action, the initial odds no longer apply and should be adjusted accordingly. In the game show, the MC, who knew where the car was located, would now open one of the two remaining doors, say Door C, revealing there was no car hidden there. The contestant was now given the option of changing his mind and switching his choice to the remaining closed door. To the bulk of the audience, this was an amusing situation in which the psychological aspect was paramount. It appeared that the odds were 50-50 as to whether one should stick to the original choice or not.

The fun in such a game was reduced significantly by a popular author and acknowledged 'brain', Marilyn vos Savant, who in her magazine column, *Ask*

Marilyn, revealed that it was no contest regarding switching to Door B: it was twice as likely to succeed as sticking with one's original choice. Terence Reese would nod in agreement, but many American readers were outraged. Apparently losing confidence in one's initial action, a sign of weakness of will, was unduly rewarded, a result very much against the American spirit of 'stay the course no matter what'.

Marilyn's column stirred up controversy, with thousands of letters sent in pointing out that her logic was entirely false. Even university mathematicians claimed the initial odds remained intact to the extent that the two remaining doors were equally likely to hide the prize. The prize was put in place before the studio lights went up, so what had physically changed? This is the same argument one often sees in the bridge literature. 'Probabilities don't change' is a common false theme. True enough, if by probabilities one means only *initial* probabilities which don't take into account what one has learned subsequently. Naturally, when making decisions, *all* evidence should be included.

It always helps to lay out the possibilities in a diagram and work from there. You don't have to be a genius like Marilyn vos Savant or Benito Garozzo; you just have to be an orderly investigator who lays out the options systematically. There are three equally likely prior configurations as shown below.

	Door A	**Door B**	**Door C**	**Probability**
Condition #1	Car	No Car	No Car	1/3
Condition #2	No Car	Car	No Car	1/3
Condition #3	No Car	No Car	Car	1/3

Door A denotes the contestant's initial guess. Doors B and C are placed in clockwise order.

The Probability Argument

The probability of the car being behind the contestant's initial choice, Door A, is 1/3. The MC can always choose to open another door behind which there is no car, so the fact that he does so does not add any information with regard to the presence or absence of the car behind Door A, which remains at 1/3 probability. However, only one of the other doors remains a possibility. As probabilities must add to 1 at every stage, the probability that the car lies behind the remaining door must now be 2/3. The odds therefore now favor switching from Door A to the remaining door by 2:1. In this argument, the only restriction on the MC's choice is that he must open a door without a car behind it, which doesn't restrict his choice under Condition #1, but does so under Conditions #2 and #3.

An Idealized Experiment

In answer to her critics, vos Savant suggested that teachers undertake Monty Hall experiments in their classrooms to see what happens in practice. Some did, confirming in practice what can be proved in theory. Let's see how Monty's bias would be reflected in a 'perfect' experiment of 300 trials, 100 for each of the equally probable conditions.

		Number of Choices	
	Door A	Door B	Door C
Condition #1	Car	50	50
Condition #2	No Car	0	100
Condition #3	No Car	100	0
Totals		150	150

In all 100 cases under Condition #2, Door C must be chosen. In all the cases under Condition #3, Door B must be chosen. Under Condition #1, let's assume half of the MCs would choose Door B and half would choose Door C. The argument now proceeds: if Door B is chosen, there are 100 incidents under Condition #3, only 50 under Condition #1, so the odds are 2:1 that the contestant should switch. Similarly for the choice of Door C.

When the results from the schoolchildren's games came in with overwhelming support for Marilyn's assertion, the dissenting professors had to admit they were wrong. So Thomas Bayes at long last gained public acceptance by those with an open mind.

It is comforting to note that the odds are 2:1 no matter which door is chosen. To assume no bias in the choice of doors is to assume a state of maximum uncertainty concerning the circumstances, but suppose studio considerations required that, where possible, the MC prefer Door C, the door not clockwise adjacent to Door A, say in the ratio of 3:1. Such a bias would be reflected in an idealized trial as follows.

		Number of Choices Observed	
	Door A	Door B	Door C
Condition #1	Car	25	75
Condition #2	No Car	0	100
Condition #3	No Car	100	0
Totals		125	175

In all 100 cases under Condition #2, Door C must be chosen. In all the cases under Condition #3, Door B must be chosen. Under Condition #1, Door C is chosen more often than Door B, but there are still 200 cases where it pays to switch door selection and 100 where it doesn't, so the 2:1 odds are preserved.

The Principle of Restricted Choice in card play has the very same basis in probability theory. As Terence Reese pointed out long ago, a defender following suit should be assumed not to have had a choice rather than to have exercised a choice in a certain way. Using the same principle, the contestant should have assumed that Monty Hall chose a door out of necessity, because the car lay behind the other choice, the true situation two times out of three.

Bayes' Theorem Applied to Card Play

> *It is a law, that every event depends on the same law.*
> - John Stuart Mill (1806-1873)

Let's look at the more complex problem presented by Reese, more complex because the alternatives don't have equal *a priori* probabilities. Declarer faces the problem of play in this combination:

A 9 7 3

K Q 5

Upon the play of the king and queen, RHO follows with a low card and then the ten. The probability of success of the subsequent finesse for the jack has risen to 2:1, claims Reese. Let's see how he reached such a conclusion.

Suppose P(3-3) and P(4-2) represent the probabilities of particular 3-3 and 4-2 splits respectively just prior to a card being played in the suit. Here are the possible splits given that RHO has followed with an honor on the second round with this situation remaining:

A 9

5

and the lead in declarer's hand.

Relative Probability Weights*

Holdings	RHO Plays J	RHO Plays 10	Overall
xxx – J10x	0.5 x P(3-3)	0.5 x P(3-3)	P(3-3)
10xxx - Jx	P(4-2)	—	P(4-2)
Jxxx - 10x	—	P(4-2)	P(4-2)

* At any stage the probabilities must be normalized
so as to add to 1.

The appearance of either honor on the second round from the RHO affords the assumption that the honors are split in the ratio of P(4-2) to half of P(3-3). This is not the same as the 2:1 ratio in the Monty Hall problem, where each condition had the same initial probability. Reese expresses the result rather loosely. The actual ratio of P(4-2) to P(3-3) depends on the ratio of vacant places before the declarer breaks the suit.

What if East doesn't simply play randomly from the jack-ten[1]? If it can be assumed that the RHO will tend to play the jack three times as often as the ten in an attempt to give the wrong impression, there is a distinction between the jack and the ten. If one observes the play of the ten on the second round, the chance of the jack being in the same hand is much reduced. The following table now applies:

Relative Probability Weights*

Holdings	RHO Plays J	RHO Plays 10	Overall
xxx – J10x	0.75 x P(3-3)	0.25 x P(3-3)	P(3-3)
10xxx - Jx	P(4-2)	—	P(4-2)
Jxxx - 10x	—	P(4-2)	P(4-2)

* At any stage the probabilities must be normalized
so as to add to 1.

The ratio of relative weights, which began as P(4-2) divided by P(3-3), has been increased fourfold, that value making it much more likely the jack is on the left. If the jack appears, the increase in the odds for the 3-3 split against the 4-2 split with the ten on the left is less drastic at 4:3, so there is greater uncertainty as a result and there are situations where playing for the drop is correct. However, the overall odds in favor of finessing if one sees an honor drop from East are unchanged.

---

1.   This is analogous to the situation described by Frank Vine in 'How I Abolished the Rule of Restricted Choice', *North of the Master Solvers' Club,* Master Point Press, 2008.

Probabilities are affected by the situation at the table, possibly by prior knowledge of an opponent's proclivities. This introduces a subjective element to the calculation, which is welcomed as it allows the theory to model more closely the real world. Unashamedly make use of what you know, keeping in mind that generally it is better to assume a defender is not playing a deep game, for to do so gives added weight to a rare occurrence.

The Bayes Equation

The power of mathematics rests on its evasion of all unnecessary thought.
- Ernst Mach (1838-1916)

All the fuss about the Monty Hall Problem could have been avoided if dissenters had accepted the power of the Bayes equation. Sometimes it is difficult to express good ideas clearly in words; emotional connections distort the meaning. Bayes himself experienced just such a difficulty, which delayed the acceptance of his basic result. Mathematics was invented for just such a purpose. Equations begin as exact expressions of common sense, but they can carry us far beyond the familiar tangled undergrowth of triviality until we get lost in the complex cloudy kingdom of the abstract. We have already seen how confusion arose in the Monty Hall problem and was resolved by considering the evidence. Here we are going to develop Bayes' idea in two easy steps, after which as a demonstration we shall extend the application to a card play situation.

Suppose the dealt cards give rise to two possible conditions, which we can denote as Condition A and Condition B, and the probabilities associated with these two conditions add to 1. (This says simply that A and B cover all possibilities. A probability of 1 represents certainty.) Let's put this in concrete terms. When the dummy comes into view and declarer, South, sees his side doesn't possess the ♣Q, Condition A can be the presence of the ♣Q in West's hand while Condition B involves East having the ♣Q. When the cards are dealt, the probabilities associated with these conditions can be assumed to be 0.5 each, but immediately after the opening lead is registered, these numbers change. If one goes up, the other goes down by the same amount. If West leads the ♡2, say, this causes a change if only because a club wasn't led. The probability of A goes down and that of B goes up, because at this point West has twelve unknown cards and East thirteen. Remember the cards exist within a limited, interdependent environment so what happens in one suit has repercussions for another. There are still many cards to be played and the probabilities will change continuously. Play on.

Next we assume that the club suit is not played until declarer breaks the suit and, when it is, the defenders follow with low clubs. The probability of seeing any specific sequence of low cards is the sum of the probabilities that the sequence would arise from Condition A or from Condition B. These numbers are not hard to produce:

> Probability of the sequence arising from Condition A is proportional to the Probability that A exists multiplied by the chance of seeing this sequence if A does in fact exist.

Let's suppose that there is a 60% chance the sequence arose from Condition A and a 40% chance it arose from Condition B. Once that sequence is observed, it is reasonable to assume that Condition A has a 60% chance of being the actual condition. Similarly we would estimate that there is a 40% chance that Condition B exists. This very simple idea of proportionality is fundamental to probability theory, and we have essentially arrived at Bayes' theorem.

This idea can be extended to any number of conditions. Suppose we add a third condition, C. If a specific sequence would arise 50% from A, 40% from B, and 10% from C, then having observed the sequence, one would surmise that the probability of the originating condition was 50% for A, 40% for B, and 10% from C.

The importance of this relationship lies in its reciprocity: one can estimate the probability of competing conditions on the basis of an observation and the known properties of those conditions. One is not forever stuck with the initial guess represented by the *a priori* odds. Having arrived at the basis for determining probabilities of various conditions from observations at the table, one may carry this one step further by noting that it is the proportions that are important, not the actual numbers of card combinations involved — which can be huge. The ratio of the probabilities of Conditions A and B under certain circumstances can be expressed as a ratio of vacant places at the time of initiation of play in the club suit.

Monty's Messages

> *Information is the resolution of uncertainty.*
> - Claude Shannon (1916-1998)

It is worthwhile to maintain a link with the concepts of Information Theory. The action of the MC in the Monty Hall scenario is to send one of two messages: Message B meaning 'the car is not behind Door B', and Message C meaning 'the car is not behind Door C'. The amount of information in a message is determined exactly by the probability that the message will be chosen to describe the current situation. The average amount of information transmitted will be greatest if the two messages can be chosen equally. The system is then described as possessing maximum uncertainty or maximum entropy. The uncertainty relates to the choice of messages.

The Bayes approach is to consider the information contained in a given message. If Message B is less frequent than Message C, then there is more to be learned from the former than from the latter once it has been received. The application of information theory to bidding systems at bridge is discussed in a later chapter.

Bayes' Theorem and Random Discards

It seems to me that one of the principle criteria to be applied to successful science is that its results are almost always obvious retrospectively.
Russell Ackoff (1919-)

Concerning discards, Frank Stewart noted in his 1988 book *The Bridge Player's Comprehensive Guide to Defense* that 'the literature on the subject is relatively lean... Discarding is not an easy subject to write about systematically.' It is surprising that this neglect has not been addressed in the following decades as discarding is a fascinating aspect of defensive play where even expert partnerships playing for a world's championship can come up embarrassingly short.

Here we are concerned primarily with the information content of discards, which can be of two kinds, 'hard' information giving count or 'soft' information giving attitude. A Vinje discard gives both: 'a discard from a suit we don't want led giving count in that suit.' Of course, a defender may not see an advantage to passing information around the table, so even descriptive discards may be made with deception in mind. Recently I held ♡Kxx under the ♡AQx in dummy. In the endgame of a 3NT contract, declarer had to decide whether or not to finesse for an extra overtrick after my partner had made a revealing discard of the ♡J. When asked the significance of that card, I replied without fear of contradiction that it was an upside-down attitude discard which denied the ♡K but promised the ♡10. Her subsequent refusal to take the finesse, despite my admission, I consider to be the apex of my career as a deceptive defender.

As defensive signals must be considered largely on a case-by-case basis, it is difficult to generalize and place them in a mathematical context. However, there is one situation where Bayes' theorem can be applied, that situation being when a defender can be assumed to discard randomly from a selection of insignificant cards in two or more suits. Random discarding is the means used to transmit the least information. The first few discards may convey little, but, as in a squeeze situation, the accumulated effect of many choices gradually comes to bear in the form of a restricted choice.

Let's look at how a pattern of discards can be interpreted in such a way as to affect the probabilities of various splits in the side suits. The question is this: what is the significance of a sequence of discards when the expectation is that the discards would be chosen at random from two suits? The longer the sequence, the more significance can be placed upon it. Here is a modest example for the purposes of illumination.

Consider a division of sides where the defenders hold 8-5-8-5 and the contract is being played in notrump. The defenders take the first four tricks in spades before switching to hearts. West is found to hold four hearts, so East must find three discards, which turn out to be three diamonds. The question to be asked is: how does that affect the probabilities of the various minor-suit splits? Does it imply that East holds many more diamonds than expected initially? Here are the possible splits with their relative weights, given that the major-suit splits are known, with West having five vacant places and East eight.

Diamonds	0 - 8	1 - 7	2 - 6	3 - 5	4 - 4	5 - 3	
Clubs	5 - 0	4 - 1	3 - 2	2 - 3	1 - 4	0 - 5	
Weights	1	40	280	560	350	56	Total 1287
Probability	~0	3%	22%	44%	27%	4%	

Bayes' Theorem takes effect when East discards three diamonds at random. What are the probabilities no club will be chosen given the six possible splits shown above?

Probability of a split given no club has been played, denoted by P(split | no ♣), is related to P(no ♣ | a specific split) multiplied by P(split in the first place). To illustrate here is how to calculate P(no ♣ | a specific split) for the case of East holding six diamonds and two clubs:

Probability of no club on round 1:	6/8
Probability of no club on round 2, if no club was played before:	5/7
Probability of no club on round 3, if no club was played before:	4/6

Probability of no club being played on three rounds is the product of these three numbers, which is 5/14. Here is the relevant table of weights from which the conditional probability is derived.

◇ Split	Initial Wt	Discard Wt	Overall Wt	P(split | no ♣)
0 - 8	1	56	56	0.4%
1 - 7	40	35	1400	10%
2 - 6	280	20	5600	40%
3 - 5	560	10	5600	40%
4 - 4	350	4	1400	10%
5 - 3	56	1	56	0.4%
		Total	14112	

Before a discard was made, the probability of a 3-5 split in diamonds was twice that of a 2-6 split. After three presumably random diamonds were discarded, the two splits had the same probability. The chances of a 4-4 split were greatly reduced, and are now the same as that for an uneven 1-7 split. In terms of vacant places, the imbalance due to the major suit splits was three. The three diamond discards served to achieve a balance in the current vacant places, and the 3-2 and 2-3 club splits became equally probable. This is a commonsense result.

We can carry the analysis a step further. How are the conditional probabilities affected if the discards are two diamonds and one club, one diamond and two clubs, or three clubs? Here are the results for all possible sequences, where P(start) denotes the conditional probability given that one knows the major-suit splits. The notation P(split | 3◇) denotes the probability of the split existing given that three diamonds have been discarded (ignoring the order of the discards). The probability of this occurring is shown along the bottom of the table.

◇ Split	P(start)	P(split | 3◇)	P(split | 2◇ 1♣)	P(split | 1◇ 2♣)	P(split | 3♣)
0 - 8	~0	0.6%	—	—	—
1 - 7	3%	14%	3%	—	—
2 - 6	22%	43%	28%	10%	—
3 - 5	44%	36%	47%	44%	25%
4 - 4	27%	7%	20%	39%	55%
5 - 3	4%	0.6%	2%	7%	19%
Occurrence		27%	33%	27%	13%

Before a discard is made, the most probable split is 3-5 in diamonds and 2-3 in clubs. This distribution remains one of the more likely candidates except when three clubs are discarded, an unusual circumstance with so many diamonds available. If three diamonds are discarded, it is natural to assume an excess of diamonds in the East hand, and the figures show that a 2-6 split is more likely than a 3-5 split. If the vacant places are filled with two diamonds and one club, the most likely combination is that for which East holds five diamonds. The observation of three club discards makes the 1-4 split in clubs almost twice as likely as it was at the start. These are common-sense results, and the numbers merely back them up.

Next let's look at the case where the eight missing diamonds contain one significant card, say the ◇K, and seven insignificant cards. The odds at the beginning that the ◇K lies in the East hand are in the ratio of inclusive vacant places, 8:5. It may be surprising at first to learn that the three discards do not alter the odds, which remain at 8:5 for all four cases shown above. Why is that so? In the Monty Hall problem, the MC was always able to open a door behind which there was no prize. This action had no effect on the initial probability that a prize lay behind the door chosen by the contestant. Did he open Door B or

Door C? It is not specified. East may choose to discard any insignificant card, be it a club or a diamond, without affecting the probability that he was dealt the ◇K. His action is neutral in that regard as long as he has complete freedom of choice. Which diamonds or which clubs are chosen, and in what order, is immaterial to the argument. Furthermore, the same applies if the diamonds contain two significant cards, the ◇K and the ◇Q: it is still 8:5 that East holds the ◇K.

> A discard changes the current number of vacant places, but might not change the odds of finding a particular card in a particular location.

The Role of Card Play Sequences

The sequences of plays observed at the table may be considered to be messages transmitting information to the players. The observed sequence includes the cards played by both defenders. If the message is unique, certainty follows: one possible play, one possible combination. This would be the situation when one player fails to follow suit. If the message is one of many possible messages, that is, if there are many plausible alternative plays, the information content is lower.

In the above situation, the sequence of plays by West as he follows in the heart suit is determined, so is not subject to uncertainty. East, who has to discard, has a free choice of random sequences involving a large number of insignificant cards. The sequence in which he chooses to discard is more or less independent of the distribution of clubs and diamonds. The appearance of one, two, or three clubs eliminates some possible splits in the diamond suit, but does so without changing the probability of the location of the ◇K, since a given observed sequence is equally probable from whatever splits remain.

The situation is different when one considers a playdown in a suit where both defenders are obliged to follow suit. Now the order of play should be taken into account and the cards played are specified by their rank, not just as 'an insignificant card'. This is a fundamental difference from discarding with a freedom of choice in two suits.

Let's apply this idea to a simple example. Suppose the club suit has not been played up to the three-card end position where both defenders are known to hold three clubs. The question is, how does the probability that West holds the ♣Q change as clubs are played down?

North
♣ K J 3

South
♣ A 10 2

	West	**East**	**Combinations**
Condition A	Quv	wxy	10
Condition B	uvy	Qwx	10

The missing low cards are denoted u, v, w, x, and y. The probability of Condition A before clubs are played, P(A), equals the initial probability of Condition B, P(B), and the number of vacant places is three on each side. Because any sequence of low cards is as likely as another, the probability of any particular sequence being played relates to the total number of possible sequences at each stage of the play. So if there were six plausible sequences available up to a given point, the chance of having observed any particular sequence at that point is 1 in 6. Let's go through the play step by step.

Under Condition A on the first round, West can follow with two equal choices, card u or card v. East has three equal choices. Together on the first round they can choose their first cards in six different ways. In other words, there are six plausible permutations, six plausible sequences. On the second round, West has only one choice, the low card he didn't choose initially, and East has two choices. Now there is a distinction between West and East due to a restriction in choice. Let's put this into a chart and consider both conditions.

Plausible Permutations

	♣A Played from South			♣K Played from North		
Card sequence	u	u - w	u - w ; v	w	w - u	w - u ; x
Condition A	2	6	6	3	6	12
Condition B	3	6	12	2	6	6
P(A)	60%	50%	67%	40%	50%	33%

West and East have followed with specific low cards, so the sequence is defined exactly. It can be seen that the probability of Condition A is 67% after the sequence u followed by w followed by v. The results of this table some would find disturbing. They might argue that East and West will always follow with low cards up to the critical moment, so the fact that they do so should have no bearing on the probabilities. That would be the case of random discards, but here West and East are under restriction.

Although it's obvious that initially the ♣Q could be placed equally with East or West, the probabilities based on the play differ depending on a random choice of whether play is begun from North or from South. The difference is obvious and due to the restriction of choice that the ♣Q cannot be played plausibly without loss. This is akin to the restriction that Monty Hall cannot open a door with a prize behind it. Without such a restriction, the two options would produce the same number of sequences. The restriction arises not from the dealing process, but from the rules of the game, which affect how the cards are played.

There is another aspect of this chart worth noting: the probabilities on the left are the complements of the probabilities on the right. At the bridge table, one can choose one start or the other, not both. Overall, given that half the time the ♣A is played first and half the time the ♣K, the overall probability of success is 50% at each stage of the play. At the table, one must choose, for better or worse, but having chosen, the odds will vary favorably for your choice. Once both defenders follow with low cards, balance is achieved and the conditional odds are back to 50-50.

If you are a fan of science fiction, you may like to think of the right-hand side of the chart and the left-hand side as representing two equally probable parallel universes. You act within the left universe and your doppelganger does just the opposite on the right. So if you choose to lead the ♣A first, he will choose to lead the ♣K. Where you fail, he succeeds.

There is a related case that can be fitted into the mathematical framework. Suppose the hidden hand, South, contains ♣A109, and the play begins with the ♣J from the dummy, not the ♣K. The East player may see a reason to cover with the ♣Q; after all, East cannot see that South holds the fillers. As Zia said, 'If they don't cover, they don't have it.' Here one might reassign probabilities under Condition B as follows: card w or card x, probability 0.25; card ♣Q, 0.5. So when card w appears, P(A) is favored by the odds 4:3 and it makes sense to overtake with the ♣A and run the ♣10 back the other way.

The Effect of a Partial Playdown

> Scientific progress is the discovery of a more and
> more comprehensive simplicity.
> - George Lemaître (1894-1966)

The application of Bayes' Theorem to a partial playdown in a suit requires a certain amount of mathematical manipulation, but in the end, the result is quite simply stated:

> When the defenders hold only insignificant cards, their following in a suit acts
> to eliminate the extreme splits while the relative probabilities of the remaining
> splits are unchanged from their original values.

In an informative sense, the only purpose to playing out a long suit is to discover whether the suit is unevenly split. That is useful in evaluating vacant places; it is unnecessary for determining which of the remaining splits is most likely, as one knows that from the beginning. Here is an example of how this works in an 8-6-4-8 distribution of sides. Assume spades are known to split 6-2, and hearts

2-4. The question is: are clubs more likely to split 3-5 or 4-4? Here are the five possibilities.

	A	B	C	D	E
♠	6 - 2	6 - 2	6 - 2	6 - 2	6 - 2
♡	2 - 4	2 - 4	2 - 4	2 - 4	2 - 4
◇	4 - 0	3 - 1	2 - 2	1 - 3	0 - 4
♣	1 - 7	2 - 6	3 - 5	4 - 4	5 - 3
Weights	1	14	42	35	7
Probabilities	1%	14%	42%	35%	7%

The weights are derived from the numbers of combinations in the minors, no cards having yet been played in those suits. Initially, the probability of Condition C, P(C), is greater than that for Condition D, P(D), in the ratio 6 to 5. Suppose now that a round of diamonds is played, with both defenders following. The effect of this is to eliminate Conditions A and E while leaving the proportions of the weights of B, C and D unchanged. So P(C) and P(D) are affected but their ratio remains unchanged. Before diamonds are played, weights produce the probabilities shown above, and after one round, these become 0%, 15%, 46%, 38%, and 0% respectively. Let's look at the arrangement of weights where the club weights are not changed due to play in the suit.

Diamonds	3 - 1	2 - 2	1 - 3	
Weights	4	6	4	
Clubs	2 - 6	3 - 5	4 - 4	
♣ Weights	28	56	70	
Total Weights	112	336	280	Sum = 728
Probability	15%	46%	38%	

When the suit played contains significant cards that would not be played normally, the appearance of a significant card affords the assumption that the card was played of necessity. There is a strong possibility then that the suit is splitting unevenly. If both defenders follow with insignificant cards, the indication is that the suit is splitting more evenly than would be expected if all cards were of equal significance. A special circumstance occurs when the plausible plays reach equality for the remaining combinations.

> When the defenders hold significant cards in a suit, their following with insignificant cards increases the chance of an even split in the suit. With one honor missing, if the numbers of plausible plays reach equality for the remaining combinations, the relative probabilities are the same as would be calculated from the current vacant places.

The simplest case to consider is that where four cards that include the queen are missing, denoted by Q, u, w, and x. After the defenders follow to the first round with low cards, u and x, the following combinations remain.

4 - 0	3 - 1	2 - 2	1 - 3	0 - 4
none	Qw - 0	Q - w	0 - Qw	none
		w - Q		
Plausible plays	2	2	2	

There are two cards outstanding, so the appropriate Pascal arrangement is 1-2-1.

In the above example, the numbers of combinations in diamonds and clubs are now given by this arrangement of weights derived from the Pascal Triangle.

Diamonds	3 - 1	2 - 2	1 - 3	
Weights	1	2	1	
Clubs	2 - 6	3 - 5	4 - 4	
♣ Weights	28	56	70	
Total Weights	28	112	70	Sum = 210
Probability	13%	53%	33%	

If the number of vacant places for the minors were split five on the left and seven on the right, the odds of the queen on the right would be 7:5 before a diamond or club was played. If one round of diamonds is played without incident, the current vacant places are reduced to four on the left and six on the right, and the odds of the queen on the right are 6:4. This can be verified by counting the weights.

Queen on the left	28 + 56	Queen on the right	56 + 70
	(21 × 4)		(21 × 6)

If diamonds are continued and the LHO follows with the last remaining low card, card w, only the queen remains at large and one has reached the situation referred to in Kelsey's Rule (when all the insignificant cards in a suit have been played, these can be added to the known cards in the calculation of Vacant Places).

There are just two conditions remaining, an original 2-2 split or a 3-1 split, and the number of plausible plays remains at two for each combination. The club weights are 56 and 28 respectively, so the odds are 2:1 in favor of the queen being on the right. The number of current vacant places is three on the left and six on the right, so the ratio of current vacant places gives the correct odds as predicted by Kelsey's Rule.

By applying Bayes Theorem to a sequence of plays, one arrives at a generalization of Kelsey's Rule that holds when there are more than two possible conditions remaining.

When the playdown in a suit reaches a point where the plausible plays are equal for all remaining combinations, the relative probabilities of those remaining conditions are in their original proportions.

Plausible Plays with the Queen-Jack Missing

The interdependence of the splits in different suits is a concept that should be emphasized, especially as it is often ignored in discussions of the best play in a suit taken in isolation. Here's yet another example of how the play in one suit yields information concerning the split in another and how vacant places are involved. If the suit being played down contains both significant and insignificant cards, then plausible plays must also be taken into account. Bayes' Theorem is the general approach that applies to all situations.

Suppose seven diamonds and five clubs are outstanding, and these suits have yet to be played. If the vacant places are even at six and six, here are the possible splits and their number of combinations.

	7-0	6-1	5-2	4-3	3-4	2-5	1-6	0-7	
Diamonds	7-0	6-1	5-2	4-3	3-4	2-5	1-6	0-7	
Clubs		0-5	1-4	2-3	3-2	4-1	5-0		
◇ Weights	1	7	21	35	35	21	7	1	
♣ Weights	0	1	5	10	10	5	1	0	
Total Weights	0	7	105	350	350	105	7	0	Sum = 924

If the diamonds are found subsequently to split evenly, then the clubs must also do so, but if the diamonds split unevenly, so must the clubs in such a way as to compensate for the imbalance. As the diamonds are played down with both defenders following with low cards, the even splits become more probable, even more so if there are significant cards lurking about that haven't appeared.

Next consider the situation where the vacant places are seven on the right and five on the left. The possibilities are given below.

	7-0	6-1	5-2	4-3	3-4	2-5	1-6	0-7	
Diamonds	7-0	6-1	5-2	4-3	3-4	2-5	1-6	0-7	
Clubs	0-5	1-4	2-3	3-2	4-1	5-0			
◇ Weights	1	7	21	35	35	21	7	1	
♣ Weights	1	5	10	10	5	1	0	0	
Total Weights	1	35	210	350	175	21	0	0	Sum = 792

The total weights are reduced from 924 to 792, the ratio being 7:6 as expected from a comparison of the number of combinations available from a 6-6 split and a 7-5 split in the minors taken together before a play is made in either suit. This is the probability of the deal. After three rounds of diamonds are played without incident, the only possibilities remaining are either a 4-3 or a 3-4 split. The diamond weights remain equal. Consequently, when the vacant places are in balance, the clubs can split either 2-3 or 3-2 with equal probability. However, when the exclusive vacant places are seven and five, the clubs cannot split 2-3 and are more likely to split 3-2 than 4-1 in the ratio of 2:1. This is in agreement with the ratio of the current vacant places reduced from 7-5 to 4-2.

A mixture of significant and insignificant cards affects the number of plausible plays, which are then no longer equal across the board. As the playdown progresses and both defenders continue to follow with low cards, the tendency is towards an even greater probability of an even split in the diamonds. If an honor appears, the alarm bells go off, the indication being for an uneven split because a restricted choice has been forced upon a defender.

Suppose now that the missing diamonds contain the queen and the jack. An exact calculation is easy when the LHO has followed with the queen on the third round of diamonds. There are just two initial conditions remaining.

	QJ*uw* opposite *xyz*	Q*uw* opposite J*xyz*
Plausible Plays	24	12

Again we have a restricted choice situation, essentially making our two intial conditions equally likely. The consequence of this is that when the vacant places were 6-6 initially, the weights are 2:1 in favor of a 3-2 split in clubs. If the vacant places were 7-5 initially, there is now an equal chance that the clubs are split 3-2 or 4-1.

NINE-NEVER, EIGHT-EVER, AND BEYOND

By doubting we come to enquiry,
and by enquiry we come to truth.
- Peter Abelard (1079-1142)

In this section we are going to look at cases where the defenders hold an even number of cards including a queen (four cards) or a jack (six-seven cards). We shall see that the 'Nine-Never' slogan applies only when the vacant places are unfavorable to the finesse.

♠ 8 6		♠ J 10 4
♡ A 10 8 7 3		♡ K J 9 5
◇ A K 3		◇ Q 7 6
♣ K J 4		♣ A 7 2

West	North	East	South
		1◇	1♠
dbl	pass	1NT	pass
3♡	pass	4♡	all pass

East begins with a weak and nebulous 1◇ opening bid, which allows South to enter the auction cheaply. North leads the ♠A and continues spades. On the third round of spades, West ruffs with the ♡10 and North follows with (presumably) his last spade. Declarer cashes the ♡A and leads towards the ♡KJ tenace in the dummy, North following twice and South once so far. What is the probability the heart finesse will succeed?

First let's look within the heart suit to see what combinations could have been dealt and how they might be played. We will denote the missing hearts as

Q, *u*, *w*, and *x*. Suppose LHO has followed to the first two hearts with cards *u* and *w*, and RHO with card *x*. Here are the original possibilities and what remains:

Splits	3 - 1	2 - 2
Initial	Q*uw* - *x*	*uw* - Q*x*
Plausible Plays	2	2
Remnants	Q - 0	0 - Q

To get from the original condition resulting from the deal to the current condition with just the queen missing, the number of cards held by the defenders was reduced from 4 to 1. For each split remaining, there were two plausible paths from the initial state to the current state, namely *u* then *x* then *w* (*u-x-w*) or *w* then *x* then *u* (*w-x-u*). The probability of each path being chosen by the defenders is the same for the two splits, so there is no distinction in that regard. The only distinction remaining is the initial number of exclusive vacant places. Normally the 3-1 split will be of lesser probability, but not if there is an imbalance favoring the left-hand side, in which case it is more probable that the queen lies on the left, just as it was before a card in the suit was played. As Kelsey's Rule states, the vacant place ratios determine whether or not to play for the drop.

Consider the most likely divisions of sides that could have been dealt under the stated circumstances. The current vacant places are shown on the right as cards are played.

Defenders	N S	N S	N S	Vacant Places as	
Spades	3 - 5	3 - 5	3 - 5	hearts are played	
Hearts	3 - 1	2 - 2	1 - 3	10	8
Minors	7 - 7	8 - 6	9 - 5	9	7
Minors Weights	24	21	14	8	?

The imbalance in the vacant places due to the uneven split in spades requires that the even split in the minors becomes matched with the 3-1 split in hearts to allow for thirteen cards to be dealt to each defender.

The weights for the heart suit after one round are shown below. The splits are divided into subgroups — queen on the left or queen on the right.

Subgroups	I	II	III	IV
Generic	Q*uw* - *x*	Q*u* - *wx*	*uw* - Q*x*	*u* - Q*wx*
Number	3	3	3	3
Paths	2	2	2	2
Remnants	1	1	1	1
♡ Weights	1	1	1	1
Minors	24	21	21	14
Probabilities	30%	26%	26%	18%
Remnants	Q*w* - 0	Q - *w*	*w* - Q	0 - Q*w*

After a full round of hearts, the plausible paths from sixteen combinations to four are the same for each subgroup, so that has no bearing on the relative probabilities. The probability of the queen on the left is 56% and the probability the drop will succeed is 26%. When North follows to the second round with card w, only two possibilities remain, Q-0 with a weight of 24 and 0-Q with a weight of 21. The odds favor the finesse in the ratio of 8:7, the ratio of the current vacant places. This is in accordance with Kelsey's Rule.

Now let's assume that, without the overcall, spades were led and found to split 4-4.

Defenders	N S	N S	N S	Vacant Places	
Spades	4 - 4	4 - 4	4 - 4	9	9
Hearts	3 - 1	2 - 2	1 - 3	8	8
Minors	6 - 8	7 - 7	8 - 6	7	?
Minors Weights	21	24	21		

Subgroups	I	II	III	IV
Generic	Quw - x	Qu - wx	uw - Qx	u - Qwx
Number	3	3	3	3
Paths	2	2	2	2
Remnants	1	1	1	1
♡ Weights	1	1	1	1
Minors	21	24	24	21
Probabilities	23%	27%	27%	23%

After one round of hearts, the location of the queen is a 50-50 proposition. When North follows to the second round with card w, the odds favor the queen being on the right rather than on the left in the ratio of 8:7, again in full agreement with the ratio of current vacant places.

In general, after the sequence u-x-w, the proportions are as follows:

Remnants	Q - 0	0 - Q
Weights	W(3-1)	W(2-2)

where W represents a relative weight that may be based on the situation after cards have been led in the minor suits. However, for the sake of simplicity we shall stick with the assumption that play in the outside suits has not significantly changed the ratio of weights from the ratio of vacant places.

> When there are four cards missing to the queen, plan to finesse if the imbalance of inclusive vacant places is 2 or more to the left. If the imbalance to the left is 1, play for the drop or the finesse as desired. Otherwise, play for the drop.

This result holds when the plausible plays for each condition have attained equality. That is the key requirement. This is generally the case when the defenders hold an even number of cards including a single honor. It is not generally true when the defenders hold an odd number of cards including a single honor, in which situation the numbers of plausible plays do not reach equality until all insignificant cards have been played.

Missing Four to the Queen-Jack

A little inaccuracy sometimes saves tons of explanation.
- Saki (H.H. Munro) (1870-1916)

Common sense demands that when a decision is to be made, one should take into account all information available at the time. Mathematically, this translates into the use of *a posteriori* odds obtained from an application of Bayes' Theorem. Advice on how to play suit combinations is too often based on the *a priori* odds without giving due regard to how current conditions have altered the odds significantly. Let's now consider such a case, which was addressed by humorist Frank Vine in his article 'How I Abolished the Rule of Restricted Choice' (*North of the Master Solvers' Club*, Master Point Press, 2008).

Vine describes a trump suit combination in which he held ♠98762 opposite ♠AK105, so the defenders held Q-J-4-3. He played the ♠A, dropping the ♠Q from the RHO. Returning to hand, he played towards the tenace in dummy and LHO followed with the remaining low spade. Should he finesse for the ♠J or play for the drop? This is not an example of the Nine-Never Rule, which applies to the situation where only one honor is missing.

Let's look at the situation at the point where Vine must decide to play the ♠10 or the ♠K. If we represent the missing cards as Q, J, *u*, and *w*, and note that the sequence of plays was *u* followed by Q followed by *w*, we have these two possibilities remaining.

Probabilities	P(3-1)	P(2-2)	
Combination	J*uw* opposite Q	*uw* opposite QJ	
Plausible Plays	*u* - Q - *w*	*u* - Q - *w*	*u* - J - *w*
	w - Q - *u*	*w* - Q - *u*	*w* - J - *u*
Card Remaining	J opposite void	void opposite J	
Number of Plausible Plays	2	4	

Declarer has observed the sequence *u*-Q-*w*, which is one of two plausible choices for a 3-1 split and one of four plausible choices for a 2-2 split. The probability of choosing the given observed sequence is 1/2 that of a 3-1 split plus 1/4 that of a 2-2 split.

The relative probabilities of the jack on the left (JL) and the jack on the right (JR) are proportional to these quantities:

JL = 1/2 x P(3-1) and JR = 1/4 x P(2-2), so that
JL/JR = 2 x P(3-1)/P(2-2)

If this ratio is greater than 1, declarer should finesse; the jack is more likely to be on the left.

So now we need to consider the values of P(3-1) and P(2-2), the probabilities of the individual 3-1 and 2-2 combinations before the spade suit is played. In fact, all that is needed is their ratio. This depends on the ratio of vacant places, which is not the ratio of the *a priori* odds, because significant cards have been played outside the spade suit. However, if the information is scant and the vacant places are in balance, one may assume that the *a priori* odds represent a fair approximation. As P(3-1) and P(2-2) represent the probabilities of a particular combination and the *a priori* odds refer to the total numbers of combinations possible, one must divide the *a priori* odds by the number of possible combinations for each split. Thus,

P(2-2) = 0.407/6 and P(3-1) = 0.2485/4, or more exactly,
2 x P(3-1)/ P(2-2) = (11/9) x (6/4) = 11/6

Without much information on how the outside suits are split, declarer is justified in taking the finesse. It is not quite a two-to-one proposition, but it is close enough to that for the purpose of determining the better play.

When *A Priori* Doesn't Work

'It is a capital mistake to theorize before one has data. Insensibly one begins to twist facts to suit theories, instead of theories to suit facts.'
Sherlock Holmes in A Scandal in Bohemia
Sir Arthur Conan Doyle(1859-1930)

Once some cards have been played, the values of P(3-1) and P(2-2) are different from their *a priori* values, but the differences in their ratios may not be great enough to affect the decision as to whether or not to finesse. For example, suppose it is known that the hearts have split 4-4, so the number of vacant places has been reduced from the initial twenty-two to a current fourteen. In that case, it can be shown that

$$2 \times P(3\text{-}1)/P(2\text{-}2) = (12/7) \times (6/4) = 18/7$$

The change of the ratio from 11/6 to 18/7 does not affect the decision to finesse. What does change are the probabilities, the more even split being more likely as outside cards are placed equally between the two defenders. More significant changes in the ratio are due to imbalances in the vacant places, and these may affect the decision. Suppose that from the early play the hearts are known to split 6-2, resulting in an imbalance of four vacant places in favor of the RHO. The *a priori* odds no longer provide a valid approximation to $P(3\text{-}1)/P(2\text{-}2)$ at the time of decision, and playing for the drop becomes (mathematically) an equally attractive proposition. Let's look at a specific occurrence.

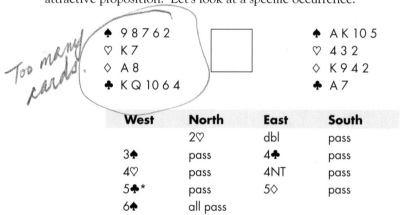

Too many cards.

	♠ 9 8 7 6 2		♠ A K 10 5
	♡ K 7		♡ 4 3 2
	◇ A 8		◇ K 9 4 2
	♣ K Q 10 6 4		♣ A 7

West	North	East	South
	2♡	dbl	pass
3♠	pass	4♣	pass
4♡	pass	4NT	pass
5♣*	pass	5◇	pass
6♠	all pass		

North leads the ♡A and continues with the ♡Q, won with the ♡K. Declarer plays to the ♠A, under which South plays the ♠Q. Declarer returns without incident to the ◇A in order to lead a second round of trumps towards the ♠K105. North follows to both spades with low cards. What are the odds that South holds the ♠J? Here are the remaining possibilities.

	♠ 3 - 1	♠ 2 - 2
	♡ 6 - 2	♡ 6 - 2
Minors	4 - 10	5 - 9

The minor-suit card combinations are in the ratio of 2 to 1, so our key ratio is 1, and at the point of decision, it is equally likely that the jack lies with North or with South. Should declarer finesse?

The decision is not quite reduced to a coin toss, because one also has the opening lead to consider. North holds the ♡AQ. Is it more likely that he would lead the ♡A when holding ♠J43 or when holding ♠43? With the former holding, he might well have hopes for a trump trick in his own hand and so cash the ♡A rather than bank on declarer needing a trick from his presumed ♡K. However, if North had led the ◇Q, declarer might take the view that he is more likely to hold ♠43 and doesn't want to abandon the hope of two tricks in the red suits.

If the imbalance in the vacant places is 5 or more, the odds favor playing for the drop, a result noted in Roudinesco's *Dictionary of Suit Combinations*. This is a rare, but not negligible, possibility. Here is an example where North preempts with a seven-card suit.

♠ 9 8 7 6 2	♠ A K 10 5
♡ K 7	♡ 4 3
◇ A 8	◇ K 9 4 2
♣ K Q 10 6 4	♣ A 7 3

West	North	East	South
1♠	3♡	4♡	pass
4♠	pass	4NT*	pass
5♣	pass	5◇	pass
6♠	all pass		

North leads the ♡A and play proceeds as before. At the point of decision, the relevant distributions of the minors are as shown below.

	♠ 3 - 1	♠ 2 - 2
	♡ 7 - 2	♡ 7 - 2
Minors	3 - 10	4 - 9

Now $2 \times P(3\text{-}1)/P(2\text{-}2) = 4/5$ which is less than 1, so there is a strong indication that the jack lies in the South hand. Declarer should reject guidance based only on the *a priori* odds and play for the drop.

> When there are four cards missing including the queen-jack and an honor falls on the first round from the RHO, plan to finesse on the second round unless there is an excess of four or more vacant places on the right. With an excess of five or more, play for the drop. If there is an excess of four, play for the drop or finesse according to other information received.

The Eight-Ever Rule

> *Eight-Ever Rule: When the defenders hold four insignificant cards and the queen in a critical suit, finesse for the queen rather than play for the drop. If possible, finesse through the hand with the greater number of vacant places.*

We now come to a rule of thumb for finessing that a declarer can take to the bank. Unlike the 'Nine-Never' rule, the finesse is unconditionally the better percentage play, even when it must be taken against the grain, as it were. What happens to the odds when the queen is accompanied by a second, or third, significant card? Any initial conditions can be accommodated by the application of Bayes' Theorem, the rule behind the rules, so that will be our approach in this chapter. It will be seen that the key factor is the number of insignificant cards that can be played freely: four with Q-x-x-x-x, three with Q-x-x-x or Q-10-x-x-x, and so on. This number determines the number of plausible permutations available when a suit is played down and the defenders follow with low cards. We begin with a three-card situation.

Missing Three to the King

Consider the play when declarer leads towards dummy's tenace when holding ten cards in the suit missing the king:

♠ A Q J 5 4

♠ 10 9 8 7 6

Suppose the LHO follows with the ♠2. Why is the finesse always better than playing for the drop? Isn't it worse than a 50-50 proposition with two cards missing when the RHO has a greater number of vacant places remaining? Well, that's not the correct way of thinking about it. The question is not whether the finesse wins or loses, but whether it is better than the drop. Here is the situation after the ♠2 is played, where P represents the probability of a given split before the suit is played.

Split	3 - 0	2 - 1	2 - 1	1 - 2
Probability	P(3-0)	P(2-1)	P(2-1)	P(1-2)
Cards	K32 - 0	K2 - 3	32 - K	2 - K3
Plausible Plays	2	1	2	1
Weights	P(3-0)	2 x P(2-1)	P(2-1)	2 x P(1-2)

The weights are the factors that must be applied to the remaining card combinations in order to arrive at the correct conditional probabilities. They depend on the ratio of the initial probabilities of the split and the number of plausible plays. The former depends on the observed conditions outside the suit, the latter on observed conditions within the suit. The weights are proportions, so can be expressed in a convenient form involving integers instead of fractions.

The proportion of the card combinations for which the finesse wins is denoted by FW, and the proportion for which the drop wins is denoted by DW.

$$FW = P(3\text{-}0) + 2 \times P(2\text{-}1) \quad \text{and} \quad DW = P(2\text{-}1), \text{ so}$$
$$FW - DW = P(3\text{-}0) + P(2\text{-}1) > 0$$

Once the low card appears from the LHO, there are always more card combinations that favor the finesse than favor the drop. The determining factor is the imbalance in the numbers of plausible plays within the 2-1 split, the conditional probability of one candidate being halved relative to the other.

If FL represents the proportion for which the finesse loses, then

$$FL - FW = 2 \times P(1\text{-}2) + P(2\text{-}1) - 2 \times P(2\text{-}1) - P(3\text{-}0) > 0$$

If the vacant places are balanced, the finesse is less than 50% successful.

Missing Three to the King-Jack

Now let's look at the situation when declarer leads the three towards dummy's tenace when holding ten cards in the suit missing the king-jack:

♠ A Q 10 9 8

☐

♠ 7 6 5 4 3

Suppose the LHO follows with the ♠2. When should declarer play the ♠10 instead of the ♠Q? This problem can be solved using the Bayes approach as presented above, the difference being that at the point of decision the number of plausible plays is the same for all candidates.

Split	3 - 0	2 - 1	2 - 1	1 - 2
Probability	P(3-0)	P(2-1)	P(2-1)	P(1-2)
Cards	KJ2 - 0	K2 - J	J2 - K	2 - KJ
Plausible Plays	1	1	1	1
Weights	P(3-0)	P(2-1)	P(2-1)	P(1-2)

Playing the ♠10 caters for a 3-0 split, whereas to play the ♠Q caters for a 2-1 split with the jack offside. One should play the ♠10 if P(3-0) > P(2-1), which requires an imbalance in the exclusive vacant places of at least three on the left.

Missing Three to the King-Ten

The same process can be applied to the case where the king-ten are held by the defenders. Until recently, I had assumed every experienced player knew to finesse in these conditions.

North
♠ A 6
♡ J 8 7 5
◇ A Q 7 3
♣ K Q J

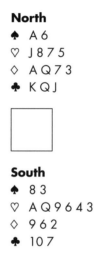

South
♠ 8 3
♡ A Q 9 6 4 3
◇ 9 6 2
♣ 10 7

West	North	East	South
1♣	1NT	2♠	3♡
4♠	5♡	all pass	

The bidding was unsound but normal for a Friday night at the local duplicate. Despite the crudities of the auction, 5♡ was reasonable and eleven tricks were within reach. The opening lead was normal, the ♠9, signifying 0 or 2 higher honors. Declarer won the ♠A in dummy and attacked hearts. In fact, he followed the habit of decades by leading an unsupported jack hoping for a cover. When East followed smoothly with the ♡2, declarer studied the card intently for some time. Muttering what sounded like, 'If this doesn't work, blame Zia', declarer went up with the ace and awaited the fate of the contract.

We are in a position to estimate the success of finessing versus playing for the drop after East follows with the ♡2.

Split	3 - 0	2 - 1	1 - 2	0 - 3
Cards	K102 - 0	K10 - 2	2 - K10	0 - K102
		K2 - 10	10 - K2	
		102 - K	K - 102	
After ♡2	K10 - 0	K - 10	10 - K	0 - K10
Plausible Plays	1	1	1	1
Weights	P(3-0)	P(2-1)	P(2-1)	P(1-2)

The bidding and play have not been helpful as there is still a great deal of uncertainty involved. It is reasonable as a first step to assume the *a priori* odds represent a fair approximation of the existing conditions, so one is in a position to evaluate the options numerically. The *a priori* odds for each individual combination within the possible splits are as follows:

3 - 0	2 - 1	1 - 2	0 - 3
11%	13%	13%	11%

Because East has length in spades, it appears more likely that the hearts are split 2-1 rather than 1-2 and that West must hold the ♡K to justify his opening bid. The situation seems nearly hopeless. Confusion may arise if one has to ponder the imponderables: the more pondering, the more confusion. Some players, noting that the jack was not covered, will try to drop the king rather than finesse for it. This is incorrect reasoning. The decision should be based not on where the king is more probably located, but which play works more often. One can easily show that the finesse wins more than the drop, regardless of the number of vacant places. Suppose FW represents the sum of weights for which the finesse wins and DW the sum of weights for which the drop wins. Now,

FW = P(3-0) + P(2-1), and DW = P(2-1), so that
FW - DW = P(3-0) >0

Nothing could be simpler.

Post Mortem Analysis After all the cards are disclosed, it is easy enough for kibitzers to find reasonable arguments to support the winning play whatever it happens to be. Here an assumption necessary for the success of the contract is that the ◇K lies with West to the left of the tenace. Given that assumption, West doesn't require the ♡K for his opening bid and it becomes likely that East holds the ♡K in order to justify the free bid of 2♠. However, it is easy enough to construct hands where the ♡K lies with West and the ♠K with East, whose free bid is justified by the quality of the suit.

Missing Five to the Queen

Now we come to the most famous and successful rule for declarer play, the Eight-Ever Rule. This is of great interest because an eight-card trump fit is very common, and the queen is often enough held by the opponents. The problem is how to play this combination:

$$A \; 10 \; 8 \; 6 \qquad\qquad\qquad K \; J \; 9 \; 7$$

The first consideration is from which hand to begin with a top honor. Starting with the jack may tempt a cover from the RHO. To make the problem more difficult, let's change the configuration to remove the temptation to cover.

$$A \; 10 \; 5 \; 4 \qquad\qquad\qquad K \; J \; 7 \; 6$$

Let's suppose that declarer starts with the ace on the assumption that the LHO is more likely to hold the queen, then plays towards the KJ, the defenders following with low cards all the way. Here is the situation at the time of decision after the sequence of low cards, u - y; w.

Split	4 - 1	3 - 2	3 - 2	2 - 3
Probability	P(4-1)	P(3-2)	P(3-2)	P(2-3)
Cards	Quwx - y	Quw -xy	uwx - Qy	uw - Qxy
Remainders	Qx - 0	Q - x	x - Q	0 - Qx
Plausible Plays	6	4	6	4
Weights	2P(4-1)	3P(3-2)	2P(3-2)	3P(2-3)

The situation has been reduced to the case discussed above with an honor card and an insignificant card still outstanding and three possible splits involved. The weights are adjusted to account for the current set of plausible plays. We can easily show that

$$FW - DW = 2 \times P(4\text{-}1) + P(3\text{-}2) > 0,$$

so the finesse is always a better proposition than the drop.

$$FW - FL = 2 \times P(4\text{-}1) + P(3\text{-}2) - 3 \times P(2\text{-}3)$$

so the finesse is less than 50% successful when there is a balance in the inclusive vacant places. If there is an imbalance of 1 or more in favor of the LHO, the finesse is better than 50%.

The Vacant Place Approximation

We have now come to the problem of estimating probabilities of a successful finesse when there are an uneven number of cards missing in a suit and freedom of choice has not been completely eliminated by the play. The defenders hold five trumps (hearts) including the queen, denoted by Q, u, w, x, and y. Assume eight spades are known cards from the opponents' hands and declarer has decided to play the ace and finesse for the queen in the situation ♡A987 opposite ♡KJ106. A known split in the spade suit will play a part in determining the probability of success, as that will determine the number of vacant places to be filled by hearts and the minors.

First, assume spades are divided 4-4. Declarer cashes the ♡A, to which both defenders follow with low cards, and LHO follows with a low card when declarer leads a heart towards the dummy. Here are the remaining possibilities in the heart suit together with the plausible permutations in the play after the sequence u-y; w:

Split	4 - 1	3 - 2	3 - 2	2 - 3
Spades	4 - 4	4 - 4	4 - 4	4 - 4
Hearts	Quwx - y	Quw - xy	uwx - Qy	uw - Qxy
Permutations	6	4	6	4
Probability	15.8%	31.6%	21.0%	31.6%

The finesse will succeed when the ♡Q is on the left, a probability of 47.4%, down from the initial 50% before a heart was played. The decrease is due to the fact that two favorable conditions have been removed, the queen singleton or doubleton on the left. Playing for the drop is much worse at 21%.

The vacant place ratio depends on the imbalance in the number of spades held by the opponents. The following table shows the ratio of the probability of the queen on the right to the probability of the queen on the left after the sequence u-y; w in comparison to the ratio of the current vacant places (CVP) under the same circumstances.

Conditions	4 - 1	3(Q) - 2	3 - 2(Q)	2 - 3	CVP	Ratio
Spades 3-5	22%	32%	22%	24%	1.14	1.18
Spades 3-4	19%	32%	21%	28%	1.00	1.03
A Priori	17%	31%	21%	31%	0.92	0.93
Spades 4-4	16%	32%	21%	32%	0.88	0.90
Spades 4-3	14%	31%	20%	35%	0.78	0.80
Spades 5-3	11%	30%	20%	40%	0.67	0.69

As the imbalance in the spades increases from -2 to 2, the difference between the extremes of the 4-1 split and the 2-3 split increases. The difference in the probabilities in the middle change but little. The current vacant place ratio is slightly lower than the actual ratio between the probability of the queen on the left and the probability of the queen on the right. Nonetheless, the CVP ratio tracks the variations so as to give a fair approximation. The odds based on the assumption that spades are not known (the *a priori* case) gives a good approximation to the situation where there is a balance in the vacant places with spades split 4-4.

This result shows that at the table one can rely on the current vacant place ratio as a guide to the rate of success of the finesse, to which a declarer is nevertheless committed. This result shows that the vacant place ratio remains a practical approximation when adjusted for the appearance of low cards in the suit being played down.

Eight-Ever Success Rate The current vacant place ratio is a practical approximation to the ratio of the probability of the queen onside to the probability of the queen offside at the time when a defender follows to the second round with a low card. When the ratio is less than 1, the finesse has less than a 50% chance of success, but remains a better proposition than playing for the drop.

The Play Missing Five Cards to the Queen-Ten

We now come to the problem of the best play for the situation below where there are five cards held by the defenders: the queen accompanied by the ten and three insignificant cards:

K 9 4 2   ☐—————☐   A J 8 3

The reader may anticipate that, because there are an odd number of insignificant cards, the number of plausible plays on a playdown of the suit will reach equality after a round and a half, so that only the Q-10 remain to be played. Let's suppose that declarer starts with the king on the assumption that the LHO is more likely to hold the queen, then plays towards the A-J, the defenders following with low cards all the way. Here is the situation at the time of decision after the sequence of low cards, u - y; w.

Split	4 - 1	3 - 2	3 - 2	2 - 3
Probability	P(4-1)	P(3-2)	P(3-2)	P(2-3)
Cards	Q10uw - y	Quw -10y	10uw - Qy	uw - Q10y
Remainders	Q10 - 0	Q - 10	10 - Q	0 - Q10
Plausible Plays	2	2	2	2
Weights	P(4-1)	P(3-2)	P(3-2)	P(2-3)

The presence of the ten makes the number of plausible plays equal to 2 for all combinations, assuming the ten will not be played unless forced by a restricted choice. It follows that

$$FW - DW = P(4-1) > 0,$$

so the finesse is always a better proposition than the drop.

$$FW - FL = P(4-1) - P(2-3)$$

which is greater than 0 if there is an imbalance in vacant places of 1 or more on the left.

The analysis above is just another simple application of Bayes' Theorem; however, there is more to this problem than a straightforward play based on a superficial reading of the situation. Declarer must anticipate that two leads are required to pick up the two missing honor cards, so an optimum strategy must be planned over two plays, not just the one, as in the case of 'Eight-Ever' where the queen is the only significant card to be finessed. The initial play of the king destroys a tenace against the ten lying on the right. On the other hand, if an immediate finesse for the queen is taken, a tenace against the ten remains intact in both hands, so appropriate action against the ten can be taken on the second round in either direction.

The optimum strategy depends upon the number of tricks required. At matchpoints, one might wish to take as many tricks as possible, so the first-round finesse of the jack is the marked play. At IMP scoring, one of the most beloved of safety plays is initially to cash the ace behind the presumed longer holding on the left in order to neutralize the ten on the third round with Q-10 in front of the J-8 in dummy.

Missing the Jack-Sixth

If you can spend a perfectly useless afternoon in a perfectly useless manner, you have learned to live.
- Lin Yutang (1895-1976)

Watching the 2008 Canadian National Teams Championships on BBO, I was surprised by the lack of initiative of players holding ♣AKQ10xx when, as is so often the case, they ended up in 3NT making four overtricks. Opposite a singleton spot card, such a suit will provide six tricks more than 50% of the time when the top honors are played from the top. A friend recently provided a rare variation on play in a seven-card fit missing the jack, which nonetheless provides some insight into the calculation of the *a posteriori* odds. Here are the hands which were bid to an inferior contract with an unfamiliar partner.

♠ K Q 10 9 5		♠ A 3
♡ K 7		♡ A J 10 9 6
◇ K Q		◇ 6 5
♣ Q 8 7 4		♣ A K J 5

West	North	East	South
	2◇[1]	2♡	3◇
3♠	pass	4♠	pass
4NT	pass	5◇*	pass
6♠	all pass		

1. Weak, 6-10 HCP.

The initial defense was the ◇A and another diamond to declarer's queen. As there was an excess of vacant places in the South hand, the spade finesse was better than 50%: it was 50% when spades were split 3-3, and 67% when split 2-4. Alas, the finesse lost, and declarer was left to consider whether playing for the drop was the better theoretical play. What are, he wondered, the relative odds of North having a 6331 shape versus a 6322 shape?

It is correct initially to imagine the possible shapes of the North hand, but the *a priori* odds don't apply once a trump is played to the ace and South follows to the second round with another low card. In what follows, to simplify the analysis, we assume North would not open diamonds with a four-card major. Let's consider the six most likely card combinations given the bidding. The relative weights are given at the bottom of the table.

I	II	III	IV	V	VI
♠ 3 - 3	♠ 2 - 4	♠ 2 - 4	♠ 3 - 3	♠ 3 - 3	♠ 1 - 5
♡ 2 - 4	♡ 3 - 3	♡ 2 - 4	♡ 3 - 3	♡ 1 - 5	♡ 3 - 3
◇ 6 - 3	◇ 6 - 3	◇ 6 - 3	◇ 6 - 3	◇ 6 - 3	◇ 6 - 3
♣ 2 - 3	♣ 2 - 3	♣ 3 - 2	♣ 1 - 4	♣ 3 - 2	♣ 3 - 2
60	60	45	40	24	24

Spades are 3-3 on 49% of the combinations, 2-4 on 42%, and 1-5 on 9%, so playing for the drop is indicated. Adding the weights for the cases where the finesse wins (FW) and the drop wins (DW), one finds FW = 132 (52%) and DW = 163 (64%), a clear advantage to playing for the drop due largely to the cases where the ♠J lies doubleton.

A fuller analysis can be obtained which takes into account the imbalance in the vacant places. Mainly there are two divisions of the exclusive vacant places to consider: 4-7 (Conditions I, IV and V) and 5-6 (Conditions II and III). The number of combinations in hearts and clubs, N(3-3) and N(2-4), are in the ratio of 5:7.

Denoting the missing trumps as J, u, w, x, y, and z, the play in spades, after North follows with card u and South with cards x and y, yields the following remaining combinations to be considered.

♡ & ♣ Combinations	N(3-3)	N(3-3)	N(2-4)	N(2-4)
Direction	N S	N S	N S	N S
Generic	uwz - Jxy	Juw - xyz	uw - $Jxyz$	Ju - $wxyz$
Remnants	1	2	2	2
Plausible Plays	6	12	12	12
Probability Weights	2	1	1	1

Probability comes into play in accordance with the strictures of Bayes' Theorem once the spade suit has been broken. The weighted sums of combinations represent the resultant expectations at the point of decision for which the first combination is twice as likely as the others. The weighted sums of combinations for which the drop wins (DW) and the finesse wins (FW) are given by

$$DW = 4 \times N(3\text{-}3) + N(2\text{-}4) \quad \text{and} \quad FW = 2 \times N(3\text{-}3) + 2\, N(2\text{-}4)$$

so that

$$DW - FW = 2 \times N(3\text{-}3) - N(2\text{-}4) > 0 \quad \text{when } N(2\text{-}4)/N(3\text{-}3) < 2$$

The finesse is expected to win 59% of the time, but the drop does better at 66% (under the limitation to these six distributions).

Equality is achieved when the ratio of N(2-4)/N(3-3) = 2, which would occur if the preemptor had held seven diamonds and advancer two, yielding a vacant place discrepancy of 5. This can be seen by noting the following distributions:

♠ 3 - 3	♠ 2 - 4
◇ 7 - 2	◇ 7 - 2
♡ & ♣ 3 - 8	♡ & ♣ 4 - 7

where the 3-8 split contains half the number of combinations as the 4-7 split. The finesse is expected to win in 60% of the occurrences, so the expectation for the drop has decreased from the previously quoted value, whereas that for the finesse has increased slightly.

The Majority Rule Revisited

MARTIN'S MAJORITY RULE: When holding eight cards in a suit including AKQ109, it can be right to finesse even when a 4-1 break would leave the holder of four cards with the majority of cards in the unknown suit(s). The 4-1 break represents an imbalance of three vacant places, so if the split in another suit must result in the same player having the majority, the overall imbalance in the inclusive vacant places must be at least 4 in order to favor the finesse.

In the September 1985 issue of *The Bridge World*, Phillip Martin discusses the situation in which declarer holds eight cards with A-x-x opposite K-Q-10-9-8. The author points out that it would not be right to finesse for the jack simply because LHO is known to hold more cards in the suit than RHO. As most of the time the jack will fall tripleton, declarer has to be sure that the finesse is a better proposition overall. This problem has interest in that it illustrates how to compare the probabilities of success of two lines of play that depend on the splits outside the suit. Here is the deal that raised the question in Martin's mind.

♠ A 6 4 2		♠ Q 10 9 5
♡ K Q 10 9 8		♡ A 7 6
◊ —		◊ 9 6 5 3
♣ A K 8 5		♣ 10 4

West	North	East	South
1♠	pass	2♠	3◊
4◊	pass	4♡	pass
5◊	pass	5♠	pass
6♠	all pass		

North led the ◊2, low from odd, ruffed by declarer. A spade to the ♠9 lost to the ♠K. Declarer was able to ruff the diamond return with the ♠A and draw trumps in three rounds, South following, North pitching his last diamond. Martin entered his hand in clubs, cashing the ♣AK, to which both opponents followed with low cards. Now he faced the problem of how best to play the heart suit. The solution depends on how the clubs are splitting.

The opponents' original shapes can be assumed to be one of the two following sides:

	N	S		N	S		I	II
♠	2	3		2	3			
♡	3	2		4	1		♡ 3-2	♡ 4-1 (0.5)
◊	3	6		3	6		(0.6) ♣ 5-2	♣ 4-3
♣	5	2		4	3		inclusive vacant places are 8 and 4

On the right-hand side are given the two suits of interest, hearts and clubs, whose distributions are not fully disclosed at the point of decision with regard to the heart suit. The numbers in brackets are the number of card combinations relative to the maximum number for the more even splits in the indicated suit.

The greater number of combinations are for the 3-2 heart split (the maximum likelihood distribution in hearts and clubs), so one may be tempted on this basis to play for the drop. However, one can show easily enough that the finesse has a better chance of winning. This is the source of Martin's Majority Rule. To show this, one merely counts up the number of card combinations for each play.

	I	II	Total	Percentage
Finesse wins (FW):	0.6 x 0.6 +	0.40	0.76	69%
Drop wins (DW):	0.6 +	0.10	0.70	64%

This is an interesting result as far as it goes, but there is something missing in the analysis, which is, what happens to the weights if the club suit is played before the hearts are tackled? In Martin's deal, after two rounds of clubs, the remaining possibilities are: Q-J-x-x opposite x-x-x; Q-x-x-x opposite J-x-x; J-x-x-x opposite Q-x-x, and Q-J-x-x-x opposite x-x. All combinations embody six plausible plays, so the original proportions are maintained.

It is not necessary for two suits to have been played out, since the unknown cards could be in two suits. Here is an example of how the analysis can be applied in practice (a deal modified from Martin's example):

♠ K 6 4 2		♠ Q 10 9
♡ K Q 10 9 8		♡ A 7 6
◊ 4		◊ A 6 5 3
♣ A K 8		♣ Q 7 3

West	North	East	South
	pass	pass	2◊[1]
dbl	pass	3NT	all pass

1. Weak, 6-10 HCP.

South leads the ◊Q. North overtakes with the ◊K and returns the ◊2 when declarer ducks, so it appears that South has the ♠A as an entry. It is necessary to take five tricks in hearts immediately. In this situation, which play in hearts has the better chance of success?

Before computing the odds for the various possibilities, maybe getting it right on a good day, declarer does well to play off the top clubs to see if South drops the ♣J. Here are the five most common splits with their ratios of combinations in each suit when the defenders have followed to three rounds of clubs:

I	II	III	IV	V
♠ 4 - 2 (0.75)	♠ 3 - 3	♠ 4 - 2 (0.75)	♠ 5 - 1 (0.3)	♠ 5 - 1 (0.3)
♥ 3 - 2	♥ 4 - 1 (0.5)	♥ 4 - 1 (0.5)	♥ 3 - 2	♥ 2 - 3
♦ 2 - 6	♦ 2 - 6	♦ 2 - 6	♦ 2 - 6	♦ 2 - 6
♣ 4 - 3	♣ 4 - 3	♣ 3 - 4	♣ 3 - 4	♣ 4 - 3

If South plays the ♣J on the third round, a strong indication the clubs were divided 4-3, Conditions I, II, and V apply and the drop of the ♥J becomes the favored play. If North parts with the ♣J, the indication is that clubs were divided 3-4, and Conditions III and IV apply, and the finesse becomes the favored play (even better if the ♣J and ♣10 are played from the same hand). Characteristically, for The Majority Rule to apply, there are only two conditions to be considered. Finally, if South shows out on the third round of clubs, three conditions apply, and playing for the drop is highly favored even though the hand with four hearts holds the majority of black cards.

	I	II	III
	♠ 3 - 3	♠ 4 - 2 (0.75)	♠ 2 - 4 (0.75)
	♥ 3 - 2	♥ 2 - 3	♥ 4 - 1 (0.5)
	♦ 2 - 6	♦ 2 - 6	♦ 2 - 6
	♣ 5 - 2	♣ 5 - 2	♣ 5 - 2
Weights	8	6	3

	I	II	III	Total	Percentage
Finesse wins (FW):	0.6 x 8	+ 0.40 x 6	+ 0.8 x 3	9.6	56%
Drop wins (DW):	8	+ 6	+ 0.1 x 3	14.3	84%

CHAPTER 10

DEMONSTRATOR DEALS

It was not easy… to come around to the idea that a gain in entropy eventually is nothing more or less than loss of information.
- G. N. Lewis (1875-1946)

In this chapter we are hoping to demonstrate probabilistic thinking through the use of some examples. The first one presents a structured approach to the playing of a deal; it might be viewed as an exercise in gathering information in order to reduce uncertainty from an initial state of maximum ignorance to a final state of complete revelation.

ET Plays a Hand

How might an information scientist from outer space describe the game of bridge? Perhaps in this manner.

1) A deck of fifty-two cards is dealt in such a manner that any particular card is equally likely to end up in the hand of any one of four players. This creates an environment of maximum entropy. The purpose of the game is to reveal all the cards according to a peculiar and arduous set of rules, thereby reducing the entropy to zero. Part of the psychological appeal is thought to come from the fact that the process acts in defiance of the Second Law of Thermodynamics.[1]

---

1.   The Second Law states that entropy must increase with the passage of time if no work is being done. (Playing bridge is considered legitimately to be hard work.)

2) The game commences with the players exchanging obscure coded messages ('bids') that describe in general terms the properties of their holdings. Sometimes the fourth player to call has the option of terminating the game at this stage so that the current placement of the cards remains forever undetermined. This deal is said to have reached the condition of Total Indifference.

3) In the next stage, one player is compelled to show all his cards at once to substantiate the bidding after which each remaining player reveals his cards one at a time in a round of play and one player alone is given the responsibility of safeguarding the four cards for future verification, if needed. This is the privilege for which the players compete. As each card is revealed, uncertainty as to its initial placement is removed, thus the entropy is inexorably reduced to zero one card at a time.

4) At the end of play, all the cards have been placed, so uncertainty has been eliminated. The cards may be shuffled to restore a state of maximum entropy for the next deal and the whole process is repeated again and again.

Let's give our extraterrestrial kibitzer a deal to play and see if he manages to navigate to a top matchpoint score.

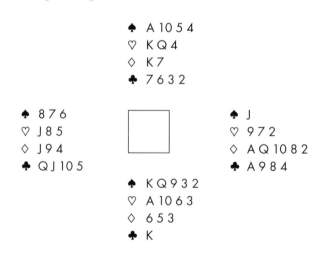

Our ET sitting South opens the bidding with 1♠ and North makes a forcing raise. East-West are silent throughout and West leads a standard ♣Q against 4♠. East plays the ♣A, dropping the ♣K. Noting the advantageous position of his diamond honors, he continues clubs. Declarer sees that 4♠ is a universal contract and ten tricks are easy if the ◇A is onside. Assuming such is the case, he looks for a way to make an overtrick.

An indifferent earthling immediately draws trumps and calculates the vacant places to be twelve against ten, so he believes these are the exact odds in favor of the ♡J being in the East hand. On the third round of hearts, he puts in the ♡10, losing to the ♡J. Down one. Can he blame his failure on the theory of vacant places? No.

The essence of matchpoint success is to take advantage of openings provided by the opponents when they arise, so it is worth a modicum of risk to explore the features of the deal in an attempt to make an overtrick. An intergalactic navigator has learned not to rush. Here the opportunity arises for a preparatory elimination of the club suit. ET goes to dummy's ♠A, dropping East's jack. He ruffs a third club with the ♠9 and goes to dummy in hearts to ruff the last club with the ♠K. The ♠Q is cashed and a second heart to the ♡Q enables declarer to extract West's last trump and produce this ending:

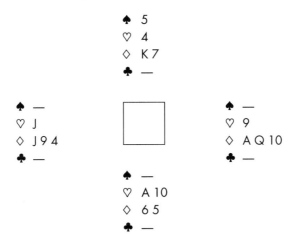

```
                    ♠  5
                    ♡  4
                    ◇  K 7
                    ♣  —

   ♠  —                              ♠  —
   ♡  J                              ♡  9
   ◇  J 9 4        ┌─────────┐       ◇  A Q 10
   ♣  —            │         │       ♣  —
                   └─────────┘
                    ♠  —
                    ♡  A 10
                    ◇  6 5
                    ♣  —
```

With spades proven to have been split 3-1 and the clubs 4-4, the most common splits in the red suits are given below:

	Maximally Likely	Next Most Likely
	W E	W E
♠	3 - 1	3 - 1
♡	3 - 3	2 - 4 (0.75)
◇	3 - 5 (0.8)	4 - 4
♣	4 - 4	4 - 4
Ratio	1	15/16

The vacant places for the red suits are six and eight, an excess of 2 in the East hand. If hearts had not been played, a 3-3 heart split would be more likely than a 2-4 split in the ratio of 16 to 15. However, two rounds have been played and when the ♡4 is led from the dummy in the above configuration, East follows with the last low heart and declarer is at the crossroads with only one significant heart outstanding. This is the situation covered by Kelsey's Rule, which follows as a consequence of the Bayes' Theorem. The odds of the ♡J being in the East hand are given by the relative weights of the diamond splits. Thus, the ♡J is more likely to be in the East hand in the ratio of 5 against 4. Does this mean that ET should take the heart finesse at this late stage? No. This is a case where the adjunct to Bob's Blind Rule applies: if you can find a better play, make it.

The better play in hearts is the one which gives the best chance of yielding eleven tricks. The calculation of the odds for taking eleven tricks must also involve the diamond suit, as there is the possibility of the ♢A being onside, making the ♢K a winner. Thus, considering the heart suit in isolation is not the correct procedure. Here is a table of the probable number of tricks that will be taken if declarer plays the ♡10, finessing for the ♡J, or plays the ♡A, hoping the ♢K takes a trick or the hearts split 3-3, slightly against the odds.

Splits	Weights	Play ♡10	Play ♡A
♡ 2 - 4	5/9	11 tricks certain	11 tricks (1/2 chance)
♢ 4 - 4			10 tricks (1/2 chance)
♡ 3 - 3	4/9	10 tricks (3/8)	11 tricks certain
♢ 3 - 5		9 tricks (5/8)	
Totals for 11 tricks		5/9	13/18

The results in the table show what must be obvious to any good declarer: that in a common contract, it is better to make sure of a plus score while preserving a chance for an overtrick than to risk everything on a slight advantage in one suit, a risk which if taken could lead to a minus score.

As it happens, the correct play of the ♡A is in accordance with Bob's Blind Rule as the 3-3 heart split is representative of the maximum entropy distribution of sides before the heart suit is played. If the opening lead had been a diamond, so that two diamonds and a club were lost at the beginning and the tenth trick could come only from the heart suit, it would be correct to finesse for the ♡J if this were the best remaining chance based on the inferred minor-suit distributions.

The Changing Seascape

> When it is not in our power to determine what is true, we should act
> according to what is most probable.
> - René Descartes (1596-1650)

Often a declarer must adapt to changing probabilities. What is most probable at the start may become irrelevant after further information has been gathered.

Here is a simple example from a deal discussed by Hugh Kelsey in *Test Your Card-Reading.*

♠ 9 5 3 2		♠ 6
♡ 8		♡ A K 10 9 6 3
◊ A K J 6 4 3		◊ Q 10 9
♣ K 4		♣ J 8 3

West	North	East	South
1◊	2♠[1]	3♡	pass
4◊	pass	5◊	all pass

1. Strong jump overcall.

North leads the ♠A and continues with the ♠K, South dropping the queen as declarer ruffs in dummy. The contract might be made by setting up the heart suit, the question being the most likely way of achieving this happy result with only two entries remaining. The hearts must split either 3-3 or 2-4, so one should consider the consequences of each occurrence. Here are the four most likely distributions of sides in order of probability given that spades split 6-2.

	I	II	III	IV
♠	6 - 2	6 - 2	6 - 2	6 - 2
♡	2 - 4	3 - 3	2 - 4	3 - 3
◊	2 - 2	1 - 3	1 - 3	2 - 2
♣	3 - 5	3 - 5	4 - 4	2 - 6
Weights	18	16	15	12

Declarer begins by cashing the top hearts and ruffing a third heart high. If the hearts prove to be split 2-4, then declarer must play for Condition I, returning to dummy with a trump and ruffing a fourth heart high to establish the suit. Now he must hope that the trumps are split 2-2, which remains the most likely condition.

If hearts prove to have been dealt 3-3, declarer should play for Condition II. This is the situation that Kelsey envisions. The hearts have been established, but the trumps most probably are split 1-3, so the correct procedure is to return to dummy with a second trump and play on hearts, forcing a ruff from South. Now a third trump to dummy draws the last trump and hearts provide the required discards.

It is not necessary to calculate the relative probabilities at the table, as one needs only to be aware of which condition is the more likely. A 3-1 split yields two-thirds the number of combinations of a 2-2 split, whereas a 2-6 split yields one half that for a 3-5 combination. Thus, Condition II is more likely than Condition IV, in the ratio of 4:3.

Professor Emeritus Jones Takes a View

In erring reason's spite,
One truth is clear:
Whatever is, is right.
- Alexander Pope (1688-1774)

In this deal we'll see the process of evaluation of a normal opening lead and how it might affect an initial plan of play based on the division of sides.

Professor Emeritus Jones (Mathematics) is a well-beloved figure on the campus; flowing white hair, cape and cane, he has grown into his role of eccentric old codger. His memory is astonishingly clear: he never forgets the name of an old student or a card that has been played in an earlier round. His first recollections of bridge are associated with the smell of sugared raisin cookies, the feel of his mother's stiff dress on his cheek, and the sound of laughter as young wives obliquely talk shop at the weekly home game.

It was the night of the traditional Faculty Club versus Seniors Swiss Teams. Jones was relieved that the gorgeous twins, Minerva and Marguerite (Earth Sciences) had for once let him and his long-suffering partner Ginsberg (Business Administration) get on with it without a frivolous overcall. Their auction was a distillation of all they had learned over decades: Jones 1NT; Ginsberg 3NT; Jones Pass.

After a perfunctory 'any questions?' a pouting Minnie tossed a lowly valentine on the green baize and slouched back in her chair to suck on a strand of her golden hair, after which the Professor was able to turn his full attention to a survey of the dummy. Here were the cards that Jones had available to play after the lead of the ♡3.

Jones		**Ginsberg**
♠ K J 7		♠ A 10 5
♡ K 10 8		♡ A 4 2
◇ A 10 8 7 5		◇ K J 9 6 4
♣ A Q		♣ 10 8

All was well — Ginsberg had provided a balanced hand with honors evenly scattered amongst the suits. Following the habit of many years, the Professor made a quick estimate of the opponents' hidden shapes. Adverse to surprises, he preferred his working assumptions to represent what was the most likely under the circumstances.

The twins held between them seven spades, seven hearts, three diamonds and nine clubs. Yes, he and Ginsberg had an unexplored ten-card fit in a minor, but there was nothing unusual in that. It was rather odd the lead wasn't a club, mused Jones, but the auction had given nothing away in that regard. The maximum number of possible combinations in the suits would occur with the close splits of 4-3, 4-3, 2-1 and 5-4 respectively, so as with the jigsaw puzzles of his long-gone youth, it was just a matter of fitting the pieces together to form a coherent picture.

	I		II		III		IV	
	West	East	West	East	West	East	West	East
♠	3	4	4	3	4	3	3	4
♡	4	3	4	3	3	4	4	3
♢	1	2	1	2	2	1	2	1
♣	5	4	4	5	4	5	4	5

He assumed that even today's female students followed these sensible rules against 3NT: 1) lead from your longest suit, and 2) prefer a major over a minor of equal length.

So Hands I and III were ruled out immediately. Hand II was downgraded because Minerva could equally well have led a spade. It was easy to deduce that the most likely shapes were represented by Hands IV.

If a spade had been Minnie's choice, Hands III would be appropriate. Thus, if a major suit were led, the singleton diamond was most likely to lie with Mogs. If a club had been led, then Jones would assume the singleton diamond lay in the hand with the longest suit (Hands I). Thus the opening lead in one suit leads to an assumption about the distribution of cards in other suits.

Jones' plan was to ride the heart to his king, hoping to kill Mogs' potential entry along the way. He would unblock the ♢J on his ♢A so as to be able to lead the suit four times from his hand, taking careful note of the discards on his left. What a great advantage it is when playing 3NT is to be able to play five rounds of a suit without being forced to make a discard oneself, thought Jones. A spade finesse and elimination would be followed by endplaying Minnie in hearts for a forced return into his club tenace. Making twelve tricks would not be a surprise. As for 6♢ on 29 HCP and no shortage, leave that to the wild-eyed optimists.

Jones always assumes what is most likely on the evidence so far, but bridge is a game of uncertainty, which is why even he sometimes gets it wrong, at which times he recalls for consolation the words of his favorite poet quoted above.

Aim for the Harbor, but Look for the Shoals

Look ere thou leap, see ere thou go.
- Thomas Tusser (1527-1580)

In this deal we shall see how bridge logic must prevail when a choice of plays presents itself. Although Bob's Blind Rule suggests playing with the odds, it does not preclude playing with skill. One book that avoids giving the bad advice of playing against the odds is *Find the Mistakes* by Eric Jannersten. The problems are set in such a way that the reader is not asked to look for eccentric plays in the name of safety; rather the reader is instructed as to how to avoid being defeated when the cards are placed within normal expectation. The emphasis is on foresight and avoidance of awkward situations. Timing is often of the essence, as on the following deal.

North
♠ A Q 9
♡ 9 6 4
♢ A 8 7 2
♣ 9 6 2

South
♠ K 8 3
♡ J
♢ K Q 5
♣ A K J 8 5 3

West	North	East	South
			1♣
pass	1NT	2♡	3♡
pass	4♣	pass	5♣
all pass			

West leads the ♡3, low from an honor, East winning the ♡A. The next heart is ruffed by declarer, who lays down the ♣A to find that West has begun with all four trumps, ♣Q1074. To make his contract, declarer must limit his trump losers to one, which means he must strip West of his outside cards and effect an endplay, forcing a trump lead into an established tenace. How should declarer plan the play? Let's look at the most likely splits for the defenders' hands, given that we know East was dealt six hearts and no clubs.

	I	II	III
♠	3 - 4	4 - 3	2 - 5 (0.6)
◊	3 - 3	2 - 4 (0.75)	4 - 2 (0.75)
Combinations	C	0.75C	0.45C

It is more likely that West holds at least three spades than that he holds exactly two diamonds; however, there is a danger that needs to be anticipated. Declarer ruffs a third heart, stripping West of his last heart, and may play off three rounds of spades with some hope for a successful playdown in that suit, but then he has to turn to diamonds and hope for a further successful playdown in that suit. All goes well if Condition I applies, but the procedure fails for Conditions II and III, as West may ruff in and exit safely.

Jannersten's advice is to play on diamonds first. Declarer needs West to hold at least three diamonds anyway: Condition II represents failure. If he does hold three diamonds and three spades, the strip will work. However, if West holds just two spades, declarer gets an extra chance. Here is the full deal.

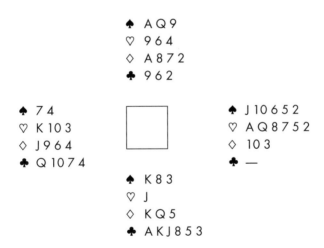

As Jannersten points out, the advantage of playing on diamonds first is that when West has four diamonds, the fourth diamond can be ruffed in the South hand, a necessary move in the elimination process (Condition III). Now spades can be played. West must ruff the third round, and the endplay is effective. If East follows to all three diamonds (Condition I), so three rounds of spades can be played, then a club is finessed into West, who has been stripped of cards outside trumps.

This example shows how declarer must plan the play logically and not rely entirely on probability to see him through; however, if declarer were to assume that the most likely distribution applied (Condition I), he would play as Jannersten suggests because the 4-2 diamond split gives him the extra chance noted. Playing spades first is too committal. Declarer benefits from awareness attached to the most likely (and ultimately successful) scenario.

Odds and Evens

It is a bad plan that admits no modification.
- Publilius Syrus (1st century BC)

A little knowledge can be a dangerous thing, and often experienced bridge players are all too keen to pass on what they think they know. The most common error is a misapplication of the *a priori* odds.

The scene: 4:00 a.m. in a large metropolitan hospital. A grizzled OR surgeon has sutured the last of the knife wounds from the midnight rush of domestic violence and makes his way down the quiet and dim corridors, now devoid of nurses, to the doctors' lounge for a well-deserved break before the dawn ushers in its own set of crises. He is hoping to play a couple of hands of bridge, but when he arrives he finds a game already underway between four of the younger doctors, novices and indifferent players. He has been giving them instruction in the finer points of the game and has found them to be students who can easily absorb the conventional wisdom he expounds. So he sits down to kibitz and advise. The first deal gives him an opportunity to expound on the Nine-Never Rule. This is the situation evoked by Jan Matthew Farber, M.D. in his article 'Doctor Who?' which appeared in the July 2006 issue of *The Bridge World.*

North
♠ 6
♡ A 10 9 8 7 6
♢ 10 8 7
♣ 10 9 4

South
♠ A K 10 2
♡ 5 4 3
♢ A K Q
♣ A K J

2♣	2◊
3NT	4♡
4NT	pass

South declared the contract of 4NT as a result of some confusion in the auction on which the reader is not enlightened. It is amusing to speculate over what branch of standard bidding the protagonists may have stumbled, and a possible auction is shown here.

As we are so often informed after a poor auction, the play's the thing. The opening lead is the ♠3, the ♠Q from East being taken by declarer's ace. On the first-round finesse in hearts, East takes the trick with the ♡K after West has followed with the ♡2. The play of the king halves the probability that East also holds the queen. Declarer takes the spade return and plays a second round of hearts towards dummy on which West plays the ♡J. That halves the probability that West holds the queen. Based on the Rule of Restricted Choice, South decides to go up with the ♡A, with the result that he drops the now singleton ♡Q.

At the point of decision, declarer must choose between two initial lies of the cards:

West	**East**	**West**	**East**
♡ Q J 2	♡ K	♡ J 2	♡ K Q

The guidance author Farber offers is to play for the drop on the basis of the *a priori* odds. A surgeon's strong suit is execution, not diagnosis. He tells declarer that the Rule of Restricted Choice is no more than a 'short-hand way of remembering the *a priori* odds.' This view is most peculiar as it implies that the *a priori* odds are the governing factor, a common enough backward view of little value. Readers of this book know that the worth of the Rule of Restricted Choice lies primarily in its implications for the play of the cards.

Each of the two remaining situations has allowed for two plausible sequences of play. With equality in the number of sequences, the probabilities in the heart suit depend on the distribution of the external minor-suit cards. Yes, another application of Kelsey's Rule where there is just one card remaining to be played, and that a significant card. The question arises, how can one decide on that basis? Of course, declarer can't decide if he hasn't attempted to discover how the minor suits are divided, so he must fall back on the odds that relate to a state of maximum uncertainty. The whole point of the approach to the deal is that further information should be gathered before the critical play in the heart suit is decided. There are circumstances where it is correct to take the finesse.

Declarer realizes that spades are split 4-4. The North-South hands have a distribution of sides 5-9-6-6, so the defenders' sides are 8-4-7-7, an interesting set of sides with a total trick count of seventeen. The most likely divisions of sides for West-East, given that West has followed twice in hearts, are:

I	II	III	IV	V
♠ 4 - 4	♠ 4 - 4	♠ 4 - 4	♠ 4 - 4	♠ 4 - 4
♡ 2 - 2	♡ 2 - 2	♡ 3 - 1 (2/3)	♡ 3 - 1 (2/3)	♡ 3 - 1 (2/3)
◊ 3 - 4	◊ 4 - 3	◊ 3 - 4	◊ 2 - 5 (3/5)	◊ 4 - 3
♣ 4 - 3	♣ 3 - 4	♣ 3 - 4	♣ 4 - 3	♣ 2 - 5 (3/5)
C	C	(2/3)C	(2/5)C	(2/5)C

The numbers in brackets are the fraction of combinations relative to those in the most even splits. The total number of combinations, C, is not important, as it is the ratios that enter the calculations. Playing for the drop is a strong favorite since the combinations for a 2-2 split (Cases I and II) far outnumber the combinations for a 3-1 split (Cases III-V). For enlightenment, declarer should play on the minors before tackling the hearts, beginning with the ♣A, the ◊K, the ◊Q, the first heart finesse, then the ♣K before making the critical second-round play in the heart suit. He can observe the sequence of play by the defenders in the minor suits, having done his best to hide his intentions. Presumably they will signal honestly high-low from an even holding (E), low-high from an odd holding (O). Here are the possibilities for the five distributions given.

I	II	III	IV	V
◊ O - E	◊ E - O	◊ O - E	◊ E - O	◊ E - O
♣ E - O	♣ O - E	♣ O - E	♣ E - O	♣ E - O

If West-East follow one of the first two uncoordinated sequences, then declarer plays for the drop in hearts, but if they coordinate their signals, he should finesse. If their sequences are none of the above, declarer should discount the evidence unless he trusts one of the defenders much more than the other.

Knowledge of the opponents' habits is an important part of the game. In the end, declarer may make the wrong decision, but at least he is going along the right path; you are better off in the long run adopting a regulated way of thinking that is subject to refinement rather than resorting to the *a priori* odds on every occasion, thus reducing your analytic methods to trivialities.

Hey, Mister, What's Your Rush?

Anything worth doing is worth doing slowly.
- Gypsy Rose Lee (1911-1970)

Here is another deal where a decision need not be based on the *a priori* odds if more information can be gathered before taking the plunge. The *Your Queries?* section of the May 2006 issue of *Bridge Magazine* dealt with the probabilities in the play of the following deal by a Mr. Bill Sherman of Alicante:

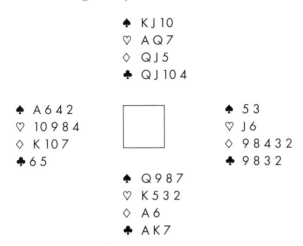

Mr. Sherman had opened the South hand with a bid of 1♡ and got to declare the contract of 6NT on a spade lead. His successful line of play was to knock out the ♠A and cash the ◊A before running the clubs, thus squeezing West in the red suits — a Vienna Coup. Other declarers took a losing finesse in diamonds. David Burn noted that Bill must remain contented solely with his great score, as the *a priori* odds do not favor his line of play — they are roughly 68% in favor of playing off the hearts first then taking the diamond finesse, if necessary, against the 63% in favor of the Vienna Coup.

From our early training, we are discouraged from playing for a 3-3 split when a finesse is the alternative on the basis that the chance of a 3-3 split is a mere 36% whereas the chance of a successful finesse is 50%. However plausible that may seem, experience soon teaches us that playing for the even split often turns out to have been the better approach. Certainly when playing off a suit in which the opponents hold six cards, the odds in favor of the 3-3 split improve as each opponent follows suit. Do the odds for the 3-3 split in one suit improve when one plays off a different suit without incident? Let's see.

Brian Senior gives us a fine example in his book *Step-by-Step Card Play in Suits* where the *a priori* odds of ruffing out a king tripleton or doubleton are seen to be superior to taking a finesse (Hand 57 in the book, discussed in a previous chapter). Now Mr. Sherman provides a related example in notrump play where a squeeze replaces a ruff as the means of manufacturing an extra trick. There are no fewer than three suits that may split 3-3. If they do, the fourth suit is constrained to split 4-4, demonstrating that all four suits cannot be treated as independent.

In 6NT, declarer need not necessarily decide prematurely whether or not to finesse. He may be able to play out the cards in such a way as to determine the splits in both black suits, so as to estimate the probabilities on the basis of what has been learned as a result. Vacant places may have a role to play. The hearts can wait.

Suppose declarer knocks out the ♠A. As long as East does not win and play a diamond through, he can play off the spades and clubs to discover that the clubs are split 2-4 and the spades 4-2. These are the cards remaining with the lead in the dummy once the ♡A is cashed:

North
♠ —
♡ Q 7
♢ Q J
♣ Q

South
♠ —
♡ K 5 3
♢ A 6
♣ —

At this point, declarer can estimate the odds based on what has been discovered. Here are the candidates regarding the division of sides between West and East:

I	II	III	IV	V
W - E	W - E	W - E	W - E	W - E
♠ 4 - 2	♠ 4 - 2	♠ 4 - 2	♠ 4 - 2	♠ 4 - 2
♡ 3 - 3	♡ 2 - 4	♡ 4 - 2	♡ 1 - 5	♡ 5 - 1
♢ 4 - 4	♢ 5 - 3	♢ 3 - 5	♢ 6 - 2	♢ 2 - 6
♣ 2 - 4	♣ 2 - 4	♣ 2 - 4	♣ 2 - 4	♣ 2 - 4
C	0.6C	0.6C	0.12C	0.12C

C is the number of combinations under Case I. The relative numbers of combinations are shown along the bottom. The total number of combinations for all divisions of sides is 2.44C. The question is, what are the (relative) numbers of combinations that favor the diamond finesse over playing for the squeeze/drop? The drop works whenever the hearts are 3-3 and the squeeze takes effect whenever the long heart and the ♢K lie in the same hand.

| Finesse works: | 0.5C + 0.6C + 0.12C | for a total of 1.22C combinations |
| Drop works: | C + 0.45C +0.06C | for a total of 1.51C combinations |

The drop is favored 62% to 50%, so the indicated play is: cash the ♣Q, discarding the remaining low diamond; play to the ◊A and run the hearts if the ◊K has not appeared. An opponent dealt four or more hearts along with the ◊K will have been squeezed. Note that the indicated play is in accordance with the most likely division of sides, Case I.

In the above case, the vacant places available for red cards are balanced between the defenders, so it is to be expected that the ◊K has a 50-50 chance of being with either opponent. Thus the finesse can be expected to be successful in 50% of the combinations.

'That's rather rum,' a sympathetic reader might observe, 'the poor laddie started out at 68% on a finesse and here he has played himself down to 50% without having done anything worthy of conviction.' No need to worry, pal. All the play options are still in place. This roundabout method is the Ringstrasse Variation of the Vienna Coup. The differences in percentages are due to the increase in partial knowledge on which the estimates are based.

Suppose that the play had revealed that the clubs have been dealt four to West and two to East. Under this circumstance, there are five vacant places for red cards in the West hand and nine in the East hand. The finesse must be much better than 50%, but then so must be the play for the squeeze, as length in hearts is also favored to be in the East hand. Here are the possible divisions of sides with their numbers of combinations:

I	II	III	IV	V
W - E	W - E	W - E	W - E	W - E
♠ 4 - 2	♠ 4 - 2	♠ 4 - 2	♠ 4 - 2	♠ 4 - 2
♡ 2 - 4	♡ 3 - 3	♡ 1 - 5	♡ 4 - 2	♡ 5 - 1
◊ 3 - 5	◊ 2 - 6	◊ 4 - 4	◊ 1 - 7	◊ 0 - 8
♣ 4 - 2	♣ 4 - 2	♣ 4 - 2	♣ 4 - 2	♣ 4 - 2
C	0.67C	0.50C	0.14C	0.007C

The finesse for the ◊K succeeds for 65% of the combinations, but the squeeze/drop still offers the better chance (just) at 67%. At the table, the right decision would be reached by conjuring up the most likely division of sides (Case I) and being governed by the observation that 'if the finesse works, there is no need to take it', a favorite phrase often encountered in the beloved works of the late Hugh Kelsey.

Our congratulations to Bill Sherman, who has demonstrated far-sightedness with regard to 3-3 splits. The only grounds for criticism is his timing of the play. Next time, if you gather more evidence in order to distance yourself from reliance on the *a priori* odds before taking the plunge, you may lengthen the game somewhat, but you will shorten the post mortem immensely.

The Abbot's Giant Leap of Faith

> *Faith is believing what you know ain't so.*
> - Mark Twain (1835-1910)

In the definition of a plausible permutation there is a subjective element; declarer must decide how often a defender might have chosen to play his cards in the observed order. It is natural to assume that a defender would play in the same manner that declarer would have chosen if he were put in the same position. Perhaps a better method is to assume a defender would not play an honor card unless he saw that it was necessary to do so. This subjective element was the theme behind a humorous story by David Bird, *The Abbot's Clever Deduction*, which appeared in the June 2006 issue of the ACBL *Bridge Bulletin*. Here is the full deal.

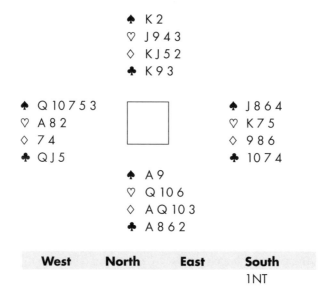

	♠ K 2	
	♡ J 9 4 3	
	◇ K J 5 2	
	♣ K 9 3	

♠ Q 10 7 5 3		♠ J 8 6 4
♡ A 8 2		♡ K 7 5
◇ 7 4		◇ 9 8 6
♣ Q J 5		♣ 10 7 4

	♠ A 9	
	♡ Q 10 6	
	◇ A Q 10 3	
	♣ A 8 6 2	

West	North	East	South
			1NT
pass	2♣	pass	2◇
pass	3NT	all pass	

West led the ♠5. When the dummy came down, the authoritative Abbot, Hugo Yorke-Smith, could see that his only chance to make nine tricks was to get busy in the club suit. He won in hand and played a club to the ♣9, losing to East's

♣10. A spade return cleared the suit, which was seen to have been dealt 5-4. On the play of the ♣K, West dropped the ♣Q, and now declarer had to decide whether or not to play East for the remaining club honor, the ♣J. But not quite yet — the decision need be made only after East has followed to the third round of clubs.

Before the critical play, declarer should gather as much information as possible by playing off three rounds of diamonds ending in dummy. West is found to have been dealt two diamonds, so the situation boils down to two main possibilities:

	I		**II**	
	W	E	W	E
Spades	5	4	5	4
Diamonds	2	3	2	3
Hearts	3	3	4	2
Clubs	3	3	2	4

The probabilities for the club splits are related to the splits in the heart suit, but no information is directly available, as hearts cannot be played with safety. A 3-3 heart split (twenty combinations) is favored over a 4-2 split (fifteen combinations) in the ratio of 4:3. Thus, for the associated clubs, the odds are 4:3 in favor of the 3-3 split. This represents the ratio of the exclusive vacant places. However, these odds do not take into account the play in the club suit, which is governed by Bayes' Theorem.

The Plausible Plays and Vacant Places

Having gathered the information concerning the split in the diamond suit and made a deduction from that, the declarer is in a position to play the third round of clubs, to which East follows with the last remaining low club. Let's look at the play to the critical point. Suppose the defenders had played their clubs in this order: ♣5 - ♣10; ♣4 - ♣Q; ♣7 - ?

The combinations that could give rise to this sequence are as follows:

West	**East**		**Plausible Plays**
♣ Q J 5	♣10 7 4	4 choices	East: 7 or 4 & West: Q or J
♣ Q 5	♣ J 10 7 4	4 choices	East: J or 10 & East: 7 or 4

Assuming that a defender would not play an honor unless required to do so, the observed sequence of plays becomes a random choice between four permutations. There remain just two possibilities, one deriving from a 3-3 split, the other from a 2-4 split. When the third round of clubs is played and East follows with the ♣7, the critical point is reached at which a decision must be made as to whether to place the ♣J in the East hand or in the West hand.

This situation is covered by Kelsey's Rule: when just one card remains to be played and it is a significant card, the probability of the location of that card is reflected in the number of current vacant places. There are six vacant places remaining in each defender's hand to accommodate six hearts and six clubs. Let's trace the evolution of the vacant places as the club suit is played, with the diamonds splitting 2-3 or 3-2.

	Diamonds 2-3		Diamonds 3-2	
	W	E	W	E
Initially	6	6	5	7
After Round 1	5	5	4	6
After Round 2	4	4	3	5
During Round 3	?	3	?	4

With diamonds split 2-3, at the point in the play where East follows with a third club, the odds that West holds the ♣J is the ratio of the vacant places remaining, namely 4:3. This is the ratio of the card combinations in the (untouched) heart suit, the exclusive vacant places. Provided that the Kelsey conditions are met, the current and exclusive vacant places give an exact determination of the odds at the time of decision. If the diamond suit was found to have split three in the West hand and two in the East, there would be an imbalance in the vacant places as shown above so that the ratio of the vacant places gives the odds of 4:3 that the ♣J lies with East, just the reverse of the odds when diamonds split 2-3. Remember that Kelsey's Rule applies only when the number of plausible plays has reached equality for the remaining card combinations.

Subjectivity and Probability

> *Life does not consist mainly — or even largely — of*
> *fact and happenings. It consists mainly of the storm*
> *of thoughts that is forever blowing through one's head.*
> - Mark Twain (1835-1910)

Philosophers argue over the subjective nature of probability. Descartes' opinion was that humans can be thought of as acting mechanically. Mark Twain thought of the human brain as an erratic mechanism over which its possessor has no control. Modern scientists conceive of the brain as a poorly programmed computer, a kludge. If in the above deal the defenders act according to the rule of not playing a club honor unless it is necessary to do so, they are acting blindly in a mechanical fashion, not unlike an early bridge-playing computer. This is the origin of Bob's Blind Rule. This idea coincides with the assumption that the human is acting within the context of maximum uncertainty. Indeed, we see from the hand diagram that the cards are placed according to the maximally likely distribution.

Much of the humor in the aforementioned article derives from declarer's assumption that West would always choose to split his honors from ♣QJ5 when a club was played towards dummy. It is a common tendency to assume that an opponent (or partner) would take the action that you yourself would have chosen in the same circumstances, whereas it is more justifiable in theory to assume the player would take the action that the majority of defenders in the field would take. There are situations where one must judge the action given the known tendency of an opponent, hence the subjective element prevails.

The Abbot's giant leap of faith, which flies in the face of the evidence of many years of play against this particular opponent, is that West knows enough about card combinations to see that the ♣9 in the dummy is a significant card that affects his choices. With balanced vacant places, the Abbot's correct play, if he holds the ♣A10 in hand, is to finesse the ♣9 on the first round, in this way picking up Q-J-x in the West hand for no loser, but without the ♣10, to go up with the ♣K. Thus by not splitting his honors, West is in effect playing his partner for the ♣10. That is the theory. In practice, many players will play low quickly without much thought.

To give high regard to an opponent's judgment is a noble stand, but the Abbot's biggest mistake. He assumed that West would split his honors on the first round if he held ♣QJ5, so he played East for the ♣J and failed to fulfill his contact. Against an expert West, he might have been correct in his assumption. There is a second humorous aspect to the story. As he does not hold the ♣10, the Abbot's best play is to go up with the ♣K initially and attempt to run the ♣9 on the way back, keeping the tenace of A-8 for a final finesse.

This example shows that probability is not entirely a cold science. One must include consideration of the bridge psychology behind the plays. If one assumes that West sometimes will split his honors and sometimes will not, one can assign a probability to his observed play. In practice at the table, one will have to guess his mood and either apply a blind rule or adopt the Abbot's leap of faith.

Better a Bad Map Than No Map

Think of declarer play as equivalent to driving in unknown territory with a sketchy map. The map represents partial knowledge, some of which may be faulty and lead to a wrong conclusion. One decides on a route with an end in view, but one looks for landmarks along the way, being prepared to change direction when appropriate. At a final fork in the road, we make a decision based on what we have learned along the way. Having a faulty map is not as good as a totally reliable map, but it is better to follow the map than to follow one's nose in a state of total ignorance. As far as declarer play is concerned, our general approach is as follows:

1) Determine the most likely division in the suit led;
2) Sketch out the most likely division of sides, taking all suits into consideration;
3) Gather as much information as it is safe to do;
4) Postpone a critical decision to the last possible moment;
5) Favor the division of sides that provides the most card combinations with all suits included unless the defenders' plays indicate otherwise.

Descartes Was Understandably in a Bad Mood

It is necessary to try to surpass oneself always;
this occupation ought to last as long as life.
- Queen Christina of Sweden (1626-1689)

Descartes would be at home in the modern world of artificial intelligence and programmable robots. He would love Disneyland, as his view was that nature is essentially mechanical. One of his famous dictums was, 'When the swallows leave Paris in the spring they act like clocks', to which Queen Christina of Sweden took exception. Imagine the scene one cold, wintry morning in Stockholm in 1650 as Descartes attends Her Majesty in one of his accustomed early morning audiences.

'Monsieur,' Christina says, 'do you see that jewel-encrusted cuckoo clock? Do you agree that it is in fine working order?'

'Your Majesty, I can see clearly it is in perfect working order — 5:07 in the morning exactly, a number which in decimal form is perhaps surprisingly divisible by 3. A most excellent clock — would that my internal workings were as regular.'

'Monsieur, this is my point: I have kept close watch on that clock for three years and it is yet to produce an offspring. Ha ha.'

'All the more regrettable then that Your Majesty was not presented with a pair.'

CHAPTER 11

HOW EXPERTS PLAY THE HAND

Happy the mishap that adds to my renown.
- from *Hannibal* by Philippe Desportes (1546-1606)

If You Want to Play like Zia

Zia Mahmood has a reputation as an imaginative player who makes wondrous plays that are missed by his opponents. We do not think of him as a bean counter obsessed with probabilities. Sometimes simply taking the line of play that is most probable to succeed may appear magical, as the following deal demonstrates.

As reported in the January 2005 issue of *Bridge Magazine*, during the contest for the 2004 Lederer Trophy, Zia Mahmood won the award for the best-played hand for his performance on the following deal. When it appears that a safety play is available involving playing off a top honor before finessing in a suit, one must be careful not to destroy the lines of communication on which the main chance relies. Probability can be used to compare the two lines of play.

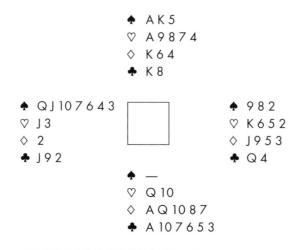

West	North	East	South
		pass	1◊
3♠	dbl	4♠	6♣
pass	7◊	all pass	

Three of five expert pairs bid to the grand slam despite West's devilish preemption, but only one, Zia, made thirteen tricks. Declarers won the spade lead in dummy and considered their chances. Prayers may be offered in other dire circumstances, but experts rely largely on necessary assumptions. If not in a flash then soon, they went after the clubs, assuming a 3-2 spit and may have been surprised to find West holding the third club, necessitating a ruff with the ◊K in the dummy. The question at this point was how to play the trumps.

Considering the diamonds in isolation, the imbalance of vacant places makes the 1-4 split more likely than the 2-3 split by a 5:4 margin. A further hope is that West holds at least one heart so that declarer can make two plays in trumps from the dummy. This is not an independent assumption, as the heart split is reflected in the diamond split. If the bidding is to be believed, these are the relevant distributions of the suits where only the red suits matter:

	I		II
♠	7 - 3	♠	7 - 3
♡	2 - 4	♡	1 - 5 (0.4)
◊	1 - 4 (0.5)	◊	2 - 3
♣	3 - 2	♣	3 - 2

Unsuccessful experts saw the main chance to be a finesse for the ◊J (Distribution II). Their success rate was 60% of the 2-3 combinations, for a relative fraction of 0.24 of the available combinations. They saw an opportunity to make a 'safety play' against a 1-4 trump split with the singleton jack in the West hand (Distribution I). Accordingly, they played a diamond to the ace, which, if the jack appeared, would add 0.1 combinations for a total of 0.34. Unfortunately the lack of entries to the dummy allowed for just one finesse, so these declarers went down, the main chance for success having been destroyed. There are many kinds of failure — theirs was a failure of good intent.

Zia correctly chose to put most of his hope on Distribution I and led a trump to the $\Diamond$8. This would work in 60% of the 1-4 cases, a relative fraction of 0.3 of the combinations available under the two options. It would also work if the diamonds were 2-3 with the $\Diamond$J9x in the East hand, yielding a total combination of 0.42. Zia's play was superior in the ratio of 21:17, as noted in *Bridge Magazine* by Simon Cochemé.

This is nearly the same ratio governed by the split in diamonds (20:16). The difference is small and doesn't affect the decision, the point here being that a simple calculation at the table is possible so that even a modest player (with a bit of practice) can come up with the award-winning decision after a minute of simple arithmetical calculation.

If you don't feel up to that, just follow Bob's Blind Rule and play for the maximum likelihood condition.

If you aspire to play like Zia, there is one quintessential attribute required: you must have the courage of your convictions and not be put off by imagining the embarrassment of losing to the $\Diamond$9 on the first round. It is unlikely that Zia would have won the award in that case, although his play was the best in the best of all possible worlds.

Have the courage of your convictions, but keep this book beside your bed. Probability Theory can come in handy in times of adversity when you were right and everyone else was wrong.

A Shanghai Probability

I play men, not cards.
- Ely Culbertson (1891-1955)

Often when playing against a good player, or even a mediocre one who has your number, psychological factors play a role in driving you off the beaten path. It helps if you turn your thoughts towards probability and away from what you fear most.

Dealer: North
NS Vulnerable

Rosenberg
♠ J 10 7 5 4
♡ 7
♢ Q 10 8
♣ A K J 7

Apteker
♠ A 9 6 2
♡ 10 4 3
♢ K
♣ Q 6 4 3 2

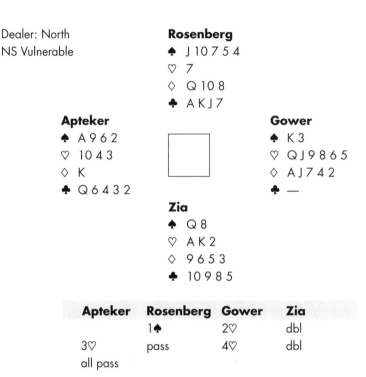

Gower
♠ K 3
♡ Q J 9 8 6 5
♢ A J 7 4 2
♣ —

Zia
♠ Q 8
♡ A K 2
♢ 9 6 5 3
♣ 10 9 8 5

Apteker	Rosenberg	Gower	Zia
	1♠	2♡	dbl
3♡	pass	4♡	dbl
all pass			

This deal arose in the semifinals of the 2007 Bermuda Bowl with USA2 facing upstart South Africa. At the other table, West, Howard Weinstein, was declarer in the same doubled contract. Tim Cope led the ♣A and Weinstein was able to ruff out the diamonds, making an overtrick when the ◊Q dropped on the third round. With East as declarer, Zia made a great start by leading three rounds of hearts, killing the overtrick and putting the contract in jeopardy. Craig Gower had to set up his diamonds without the benefit of a ruff.

The play in diamonds taken in isolation has a very low expected rate of success, around 1 in 4. An expert looks ahead and plans his play based on the assumption that the conditions for success exist. The question was raised on BBO by a British commentator as to whether declarer should play to drop the ◊Q or play to pin the ◊10 by leading the ◊J on the third round. Kit Woolsey replied that one could go back to the *a priori* odds in order to see that dropping the queen was a 3:1 favorite as the relevant four combinations were Q-10-9, Q-10-8, Q-9-8 and 10-9-8, three of which included the queen. This cursory analysis was rather loosely expressed, but it gave the right approach — play off the ◊AK and duck the third round.

Craig Gower started diamonds by leading to the ◊K, and then played a spade to the king and advanced the ◊A. On the diamond leads, Rosenberg played the ◊10 and the ◊8 in that order. So the conditions for success appeared to be in place. Holding Q-10-8, Rosenberg could follow in two ways. Holding 10-9-8, he could follow in six ways. Thus we arrive at the odds of 3:1 that he was dealt ◊Q108 rather than the ◊1098.

Now to the psychological factor. Zia's negative double promised some high card values; might these include the ◊Q? Here is where Zia's bid may have played on the mind of his opponent. In the end, Gower made the correct play.

The analysis can be improved by considering not just the diamond suit in isolation but in the context of the deal as a whole, taking into account the division of sides. This should be the focus of declarer's thinking at the time of decision. First, given the information available, one may form a picture of the most likely candidates in order of their likelihood of occurrence given the known heart split. Here are the most common North-South splits.

	I	II	III	IV	V
♠	5 - 2	5 - 2	5 - 2	6 - 1	6 - 1
♡	1 - 3	1 - 3	1 - 3	1 - 3	1 - 3
◊	3 - 4	4 - 3	2 - 5	3 - 4	2 - 5
♣	4 - 4	3 - 5	5 - 3	3 - 5	4 - 4
Combinations	C	0.8C	0.48C	0.27C	0.2C

The *a priori* odds of a 4-3 split are 62%, double that of a 5-2 split. That advantage has been increased as a result of the bidding, which points to an uneven split in spades. After the double by Zia and subsequent pass by Rosenberg, Condition I appears to be the most likely, so maximum likelihood once again conforms to reality, although generally there is no guarantee.

After the first round of diamonds, playing off the ♠A and the ♠K would have fortuitously dropped the queen doubleton in Zia's hand, giving confirmation that Rosenberg held the ◊Q in order to make up an opening bid on a rather weak spade suit. This represents the gathering of information at no cost. Every bit of information helps, if only to calm the nerves when playing against a master of trickery. Zia's clever drawing of trumps can be turned against him by guaranteeing the safety of this process.

With near certainty, Gower could place the ◊Q with Rosenberg and consider the consequences under Condition I. In fact, if Rosenberg were dealt three diamonds to the queen, the contract is guaranteed on the line recommended by Woolsey. Since North has followed to the ◊K with the ◊10, the remote possibility of a winning variation of Condition II evaporates and one is left with the hope that the maximum likelihood distribution applies.

The analysis using the division of sides is useful in focusing one's thinking at the table on the more probable conditions given the information that is currently available at the time of decision. Yes, some practice is required in the ranking of the probabilities, but as the habit is cultivated, the process becomes easier. It saves time and effort in the long run, and is accurate to a sufficient degree for many situations. Remember, if the odds for two alternatives are nearly 50-50, in a practical sense it doesn't much matter which one is chosen, because the uncertainty is so great. If a mistake occurs, it is more likely to be the fault of the way you have gathered information rather than that you simply guessed wrong in a state of uncertainty.

When Several Honors Are Missing

Usually, when several key cards are missing,
you must manoeuvre first against the lowest.
- J.M. Roudinesco in *The Dictionary of Suit Combinations*

Club players are familiar with the Eight-Ever Rule concerning a finesse for a single missing honor, but are not so clear on the procedure against several missing honors. The tendency is to try impatiently for immediate success when a delayed approach is best. Even world champions might rely too strongly on *a priori* view, as is shown on the following deal from the 2007 Italian Club Championships.

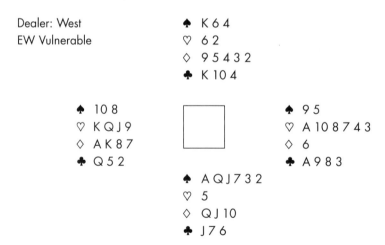

Dealer: West
EW Vulnerable

♠ K 6 4
♡ 6 2
◊ 9 5 4 3 2
♣ K 10 4

♠ 10 8
♡ K Q J 9
◊ A K 8 7
♣ Q 5 2

♠ 9 5
♡ A 10 8 7 4 3
◊ 6
♣ A 9 8 3

♠ A Q J 7 3 2
♡ 5
◊ Q J 10
♣ J 7 6

Both Wests played in 4♡ after opening with a bid of 1NT. The defense began by taking two rounds of spades and switching to the ◊Q. The play was straightforward as trumps were drawn and diamonds eliminated to the point where West was on lead with five cards remaining. North and South could be read for having three clubs each.

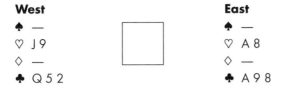

West		East	
♠		♠	—
♥ J 9		♥ A 8	
◇ —		◇ —	
♣ Q 5 2		♣ A 9 8	

The key is to find the ♣K well placed, but one must also take into account the locations of the ♣J and the ♣10. The ♣98 in the dummy can play a role. It would be wrong to think as follows: 'There are 17 HCP missing and I can place 10 of them with South, so the odds favor the ♣K being in the North hand.' That argument is based solely on the *a priori* odds and the play has carried us far beyond that assessment. The only concern is how the club suit may be distributed. Here are the possible combinations where u, v, and w represent low cards:

King in the North

North	KJ10	KJw	K10w	Kvw
South	uvw	10uv	Juv	J10u
Combinations	1	3	3	3

King in the South

North	uvw	10vw	Jvw	J10w
South	KJ10	KJu	K10u	Kuv
Combinations	1	3	3	3

References on the play of suit combinations give conflicting advice on how to play the club suit for two tricks. However, Alfredo Versace had the added advantage that whichever defender won the trick would be obliged to continue the suit or provide a ruff and a sluff. He made the brilliant play of a heart to the ace and the ♣8 from the dummy. The brilliancy lay in recognizing the flexibility this provided, depending on the card with which South followed. In practice, South played the ♣J, so the relevant combinations were as follows:

	Play the ♣Q			Duck
North	uvw	K10w	10vw	Kvw
South	KJ10	Juv	KJu	J10u

Versace covered the ♣J with the ♣Q, losing to the ♣K. On the forced return of the ♣4, the second chance came into play. He finessed successfully by putting in the ♣9 from dummy. The odds were 2:1 that South had not played the ♣J from ♣J10u. This shows why.

	I	II	III
North	♣ K 10 4	♣ K 7 4	♣ K 6 4
South	♣ J 7 6	♣ J 10 6	♣ J 10 7
Plausible Plays	1	4	4
Weights	4	1	1

Assuming South would play the ♣J under Condition I, North must return the ♣4, so there is only one sequence of plausible plays. Under the other conditions, South could have played the ♣10 with equal effect and North could have returned either of his remaining low cards. Hence there are four plausible sequences for each of two combinations.

There is no need to do a full analysis of all the combinations at the table. You simply have to adhere to the advice of Terence Reese based on the Principle of Restricted Choice, namely that, in a critical situation, assume the South player has not played a card (♣J or ♣10) from a choice of equals. When North returns the ♣4, one assumes that he had no choice, as it is his last remaining low card.

Versace earned 12 IMPs as his opposing West (also a world champion) in the five-card ending did not take full advantage of the situation; he went for immediate success or failure by playing the ♣A and then a club to the ♣Q, going down one. No second chance for him. Returning to the distribution of HCP, this can be judged to be a rather shallow play, as the bidding gave a clue that North held the ♣K:

Duboin	Fantoni	Bocchi	Nunes
1NT	pass	2◊	2♠
3♡	3♠	4◊	pass
4♡	all pass		

When he reached his five-card ending, Duboin might have asked himself what was the substance behind Fantoni's raise. Placing the ♣K in the North hand points to Versace's line of play of leading a low club from dummy and attempting to duck a trick to North.

Fear of the Unknown

It is easy to criticize Antonio Sementa's play in going up with the ♣J when it would have been better to keep that honor to cover the ♣9 remaining the dummy. However, if he guessed that Versace intended to duck anyway, the cover would at least give declarer a losing option.

I learned this lesson watching my erstwhile partner, Dr Simon Marinker, superbly playing his favorite contract, 3NT, throughout his late eighties and early nineties. There is a distinct advantage to be had in breaking a suit by leading low from dummy towards the unseen hand, and the more unexpected that is, the better. The confusion this often caused was a wonder to behold. Of course, if no hesitation was observed, that, too, told a story. (Simon's fondest bridge memory was being complimented by Helen Sobel on his declarer play, perhaps after such a move half a century previous.)

It is easy to miss the point that a defender's choice of plays is prompted by the cards that are visible to him. Here is an example from the 2007 Venice Cup.

Dealer: East
Both Vulnerable

Sun
♠ K 6 2
♡ K 9 5 2
♢ 10 7 6
♣ Q 10 3

Sanborn
♠ A J 10 5
♡ 8 7 4
♢ A Q J 4
♣ 6 4

Bjerkan
♠ Q 3
♡ Q J 3
♢ K 8 2
♣ K J 9 7 5

Wang
♠ 9 8 7 4
♡ A 10 6
♢ 9 5 3
♣ A 8 2

Sanborn	Sun	Bjerkan	Wang
		1♣	pass
1♠	pass	1NT	pass
3NT	all pass		

Commentators can see all four hands. They may publicly reject computer programs that possess the same facility, but often the temptation is too great for a human to resist and their analysis becomes flawed. This deal is a case in point, as success depends on a play in a key suit that is obvious with all hands on view. The question becomes: is the right play justifiable on the evidence available to declarer?

First, what should South lead against 3NT? The bidding has warned against a black-suit lead, so it is a choice between a passive diamond and an active heart. Hongli Wang, like most, chose a passive ◇9. Cheri Bjerkan won the ◇Q in dummy and led the ♣4. If Ming Sun had played a low club, it is easy to see that putting in the ♣9 would have given declarer three club tricks to go along with a spade, a heart, and four diamonds. Would declarer have played to the ♣J, as did Bob Hamman after the same lead in his match against Italy? That leads to down one as South can switch to a heart, giving the defense three hearts, a spade and a club. On the other hand, when Bruce Neill for Australia put in the ♣J, the Indonesian defender ducked — giving up the contract as declarer could now safely play on spades.

It is clear that most declarers assumed three tricks in spades, and decided they needed just one trick in clubs. One commentator, true to the principles of his avocation, suggested the play of the ♣K on the first round. Roudinesco would not approve.

Superficially, you might think that playing to the ♣9 gives you three ways to lose, to the ♣A, the ♣Q or the ♣10. Surely playing to the ♣J reduces that to two chances, so should be better. That thinking is along the lines of the advice to play to the ♣K, which loses only to the ace. It all assumes there is just the one opportunity to succeed, but declarer has two chances to lead a club from dummy, and two chances are better than one. If the king loses to the ace, there is no recovery position on the second round.

One further point: in isolation, the best play for one trick is the same play as for three tricks, namely put in the nine, guarding against strength in the North hand. Declarer also has to think about what happens if the hearts are cleared before the spade finesse is taken. Now a losing spade finesse dooms the contract.

How circumstances change the odds is well illustrated by Ming Sun's unexpected play of the ♣Q on the first round of the suit. This was covered by the king and won with South's ace, after which the defense played three rounds of hearts. The greater the surprise, the more information the play contains, so it pays to give extra thought to what may be happening. What had she in mind — that declarer would take a deep finesse in clubs? The play of the queen from a holding including the ten is one of the most common deceptive plays, so on that basis alone, the circumstances of Sun's play might have given rise to some deeper analysis concerning the most likely splits given the passive lead of a diamond from South. Here are the main candidates of the North-South splits.

	I	II	III	IV	V
♠	4 - 3	3 - 4	4 - 3	4 - 3	3 - 4
♡	3 - 4	4 - 3	4 - 3	4 - 3	4 - 3
◇	3 - 3	3 - 3	3 - 3	2 - 4	2 - 4
♣	3 - 3	3 - 3	2 - 4	3 - 3	4 - 2
Combinations	C	C	(3/4)C	(3/4)C	(9/16)C

Condition I may be ruled out, as South would have led a heart. Condition II may be included because on the auction, South would have been reluctant to lead a spade. (Rodwell against Italy did lead the ♠8, but on a different auction.) Note that Condition II was indeed the actual division of sides, so maximum likelihood once again conformed to reality. Condition III is more likely than Condition IV, as the ◇9 lead would be somewhat unusual from a four-card holding. One concludes from a cursory analysis that clubs 3-3 is much more likely than clubs 4-2, perhaps with odds as high as 2:1, enough to get on with.

Now let's examine Sun's plays when clubs are 3-3. There are two cases.

	Sun	Wang	Permutations
Case I	♣ Q 10 x	♣ A x x	1
Case II	♣ Q x x	♣ A 10 x	2

The first case is twice as likely as the second; as in Case II, Sun could have played either of her two low cards on the second round, whereas in Case I she had to play her one remaining low card — a prime example of the rule of restricted choice.

Logically, declarer should have put in the ♣9 on the second round of clubs, especially since the play to that point had pretty much marked North as the danger hand with the long heart. Losing to the ♣10 might have been a matchpoint disaster, but here would still have left declarer with chances. In effect, she was playing for North to have begun with ♣Qx and South with ♣A10xx (Condition III).

Perhaps the most interesting question, from declarer's point of view, is why did Sun play the ♣Q on the first round? Surely she would be more likely to do this looking at the ♣10 in her own hand, as she would know that Bjerkan might be taking a successful deep finesse. This is similar to the situation faced by Versace on the previous deal, but here Bjerkan had an alternative play in spades that dissuaded her from pursuing the club suit. She cashed out her diamonds, played a club to the jack and banked everything on the spade finesse, finishing two down.

Jason Hackett's Direct Approach

The best plan is to profit by the folly of others.
- Pliny the Elder (23-79)

The play in 3NT is often a race between defenders and declarer to determine which side can establish the requisite number of tricks. If the opening lead is passive, the race is not so much a sprint as a marathon in which the two sides can give up the lead a couple of times in hopes of eventually gaining an advantage at the end. Some declarers are especially adept at looking ahead and applying gradual pressure. Other experts like to make their moves early, applying pressure before the defenders have been able to exchange information.

Here are two game swings manufactured by Jason Hackett in the finals of the 2007 English Open Team Trials. He is a declarer who often takes a direct approach to good effect. In this first deal, he demonstrates a knowledge of the best odds for developing tricks in a suit in which three honors are missing.

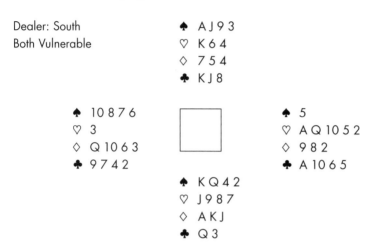

Dealer: South
Both Vulnerable

♠ A J 9 3
♡ K 6 4
◇ 7 5 4
♣ K J 8

♠ 10 8 7 6
♡ 3
◇ Q 10 6 3
♣ 9 7 4 2

♠ 5
♡ A Q 10 5 2
◇ 9 8 2
♣ A 10 6 5

♠ K Q 4 2
♡ J 9 8 7
◇ A K J
♣ Q 3

At both tables, South opened a strong 1NT and North raised to 3NT without investigating the possibility of a 4-4 spade fit. At the other table, the opening lead was an attack on the diamond suit, giving away a trick to the ◇J. With four spades and three diamonds in the bag, it appears that the best play for nine tricks is to force two tricks in clubs, but for reasons best known to himself, declarer led a heart to the ♡K in dummy. It may be a clever play at matchpoints where a stolen overtrick counts for much, but at Teams, bad timing can lead to a disaster, as it did here. A wide-awake East won the ♡A and returned the ♡2. Declarer put up the ♡J only to discover he had set up four tricks for the defense to go along with the ♣A.

At his table, Jason Hackett got a passive spade lead, which had the merit of giving nothing away except a tempo. Declarer looked to hearts for tricks. According to Jeroen Warmerdam's program, 'SuitPlay', there is a 73% chance of making two or more tricks in hearts if the ♡9 is run from the South hand. As the cards lie, this would be unsafe, as East can establish heart winners while still in possession of an entry with the ♣A.

In keeping with his usual style, Hackett made an immediate pressure play by leading a low heart away from the dummy and towards the closed hand. This assured the contract. East rose with the ♡Q and returned a diamond to declarer's ◊A. A spade to dummy and a low club towards the ♣Q3 provided the essential club trick. A heart to the ♡K revealed the bad break, but it established the ♡J9 as a tenace against East's ♡105. In the end, a satisfying overtrick was recorded.

In his handling of the heart suit, Jason Hackett gave a demonstration of technical skill that one would expect to be praised by the BBO commentators; however, they seemed more impressed by his treatment of the next deal, even though success on this occasion depended on an error by the East defender. Once again, the 9876 spotcards played a part.

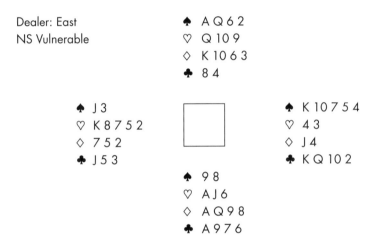

Dealer: East
NS Vulnerable

```
                    ♠ A Q 6 2
                    ♡ Q 10 9
                    ◊ K 10 6 3
                    ♣ 8 4

♠ J 3                              ♠ K 10 7 5 4
♡ K 8 7 5 2                        ♡ 4 3
◊ 7 5 2                            ◊ J 4
♣ J 5 3                            ♣ K Q 10 2

                    ♠ 9 8
                    ♡ A J 6
                    ◊ A Q 9 8
                    ♣ A 9 7 6
```

South opened 1NT and, after a Puppet Stayman sequence, played in the contract of 3NT. The lead was the ♡5, won by the ♡Q in the dummy. This was not an effective start for the defense, as West had no outside entry to enjoy heart winners.

The spade finesse could wait, and there seemed to be time to try a diversion in the club suit, so Hackett played the ♣8 from dummy at Trick 2, once again putting pressure early on the defender. The contract could have been defeated if East had put up a club honor, but sleepily he played low. Jason overtook with the ♣9, losing to West's ♣J. Now declarer was home: he could eliminate the red suits from the East hand and endplay East in clubs, forcing him to lead a spade away from the king.

This demonstrates that a declarer needn't always gather information before making a critical play. Playing off a couple of rounds of diamonds is safe enough, but it does give the defenders a better idea of where their tricks are going to have to come from. Ducking a trick early turned out to be a safety play of sorts and a preparation for the eventual end position.

Common-sense Probability

Truth will sooner come out of error than from confusion.
- Sir Francis Bacon (1561-1626)

The October 2007 issue of *Bridge Magazine* contained an article entitled 'The Principle of Vacant Places' in which Michael Akeroyd discussed a deal played successfully by British expert David Gold. A major point of discussion was how discards in a side suit affect the estimation of probabilities based on vacant places. Our treatment is rather different, as it is based on the direct application of a study of the most probable distribution of sides. Here is that deal.

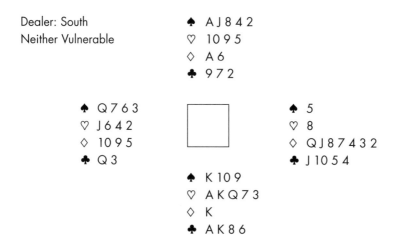

Dealer: South
Neither Vulnerable

♠ A J 8 4 2
♡ 10 9 5
◇ A 6
♣ 9 7 2

♠ Q 7 6 3
♡ J 6 4 2
◇ 10 9 5
♣ Q 3

♠ 5
♡ 8
◇ Q J 8 7 4 3 2
♣ J 10 5 4

♠ K 10 9
♡ A K Q 7 3
◇ K
♣ A K 8 6

South opened the bidding with 1♡ and jump-shifted to 3♣ on the next round. After North showed a diamond control, RKCB followed and the North-South pair reached the heart slam. West led the ◇9, which was won with the ◇K. When the hearts were found to be 4-1, David Gold played off four rounds to surrender a trump trick to West. A diamond was continued to the ace in dummy. The decision now faced by declarer was which way to finesse for the ♠Q.

   Akeroyd points out that based on the known split in hearts, there is a vacant place imbalance of 3, which points to playing East for the ♠Q. However, this doesn't take into account East's discard of three diamonds on three previous heart tricks. Surely this points to East's holding more diamonds than West, and so the discards act to even the vacant place count. The process becomes confused since the whole argument depends on adjusting the vacant places appropriately. This gets away from the fundamental properties of the play and obscures the reasoning to no great purpose. It is better if one abandons the vacant place argument altogether, as the mathematics behind the vacant place calculation of probabilities depends on a random choice of plays by East whereas in fact the discards are based on bridge logic and do not mirror the action of dealing the cards.

The Discards in Diamonds

As noted previously in the discussion of Bayes' Theorem, a discard changes the current number of vacant places, but might not change the odds of finding a particular card in a particular location. Those odds depend on the known (or assumed) distribution of the sides. The above deal is another application of the general principle. The first point to be addressed is whether East's discards can be judged to have been made at random from the cards held. Clearly not. A look at the dummy tells East that a spade cannot be spared if for no other reason than that it might expose West to a marked finesse. A club cannot be spared, as the ♣J10 need to be protected. The conclusion is that East's discards may be at random, but they are confined to the diamond suit in which he holds many insignificant cards. East's action cannot be thought of as a reproduction of the dealing process in which all three suits could be chosen at random.

From the evidence of the defense, declarer may assume that East holds many diamonds and should make use of this indication, not by adjusting vacant places, *per se*, but by making a tentative hypothesis about the number of diamonds dealt to each defender and, on this basis, calculating the odds of the ♠Q being on the right. The consequences to a possible finesse can be evaluated numerically. The result remains tentative, but provides a realistic assessment consistent with the confidence assigned to the original assumption.

To begin, we can assume conservatively that the diamonds were dealt four to West and six to East. Here are the most probable distributions of sides at Trick 6 with the lead in dummy, hearts known to split 4-1.

	I	II	III	IV
♠	2 - 3	3 - 2	1 - 4	4 - 1
♡	4 - 1	4 - 1	4 - 1	4 - 1
◇	4 - 6	4 - 6	4 - 6	4 - 6
♣	3 - 3	2 - 4	4 - 2	1 - 5
Combinations	C	(3/4)C	(3/8)C	(3/20)C
Weights	40	30	15	6

Weights for ♠Q on the left	16 + 18 + 3 + 5	Total 42
Weights for ♠Q on the right	24 + 12 + 12 + 1	Total 49

For these four distributions, the ♠Q is more likely to be in the East hand, which points to a finesse through that defender. But this is not the end of the story. The plays in the spade suit are fundamentally different, since finessing through East, declarer needs to run the ♠J immediately, whereas the other way declarer can first test spades by playing the ♠K. Let's look at the effect of this by considering the success of each process given the six distributions shown above.

	2 - 3	3 - 2	1 - 4	4 - 1	Total
Running the ♠J wins	24	12	0	1	37
Playing ♠K and finessing wins	16	18	3	6	43

The superiority of the ♠K play derives not from the vacant places directly, but from the advantage gained when the spades split 4-1 or 1-4. With spades 4-1, this play always succeeds, as a singleton ♠Q in the East hand will be dropped. In order to make the correct decision at the table, declarer should recognize the consequences of the 1-4 splits, for most of which four spade tricks cannot be taken as declarer can't afford to overtake a spade honor to get back to dummy. The specifics are important and any argument concerning the definition of vacant places serves only as a distraction.

Having solved a simple problem in this manner, a declarer may now consider the consequences of assuming the diamonds had been dealt 3-7. No detailed calculation is required, as one can see that this split will be even more favorable to playing the spades first from the South hand. Thus, one concludes that Sir Francis Bacon was correct and that it is better to apply a method and be wrong than to argue obscurely in a confused manner without advancement of awareness. In this case, David Gold got it right both in theory and in practice.

A Dubious Signal

> *What is madness? To have erroneous perceptions and to*
> *reason correctly from them.*
> *- Voltaire (1694-1778)*

By tradition and by temperament, many veteran experts are opposed to the concept that every card played by the defenders conveys a message. In his (1991) book *More Tips for Tops*, George Rosenkrantz, always thoughtful, suggests that a defender shouldn't signal if the information transmitted is of more use to declarer than to his partner. Marshall Miles, in his recent book *Inferences at Bridge* (Master Point Press, 2002), confesses that he preferred throughout his long and successful bridge career not to signal profusely when declarer initiated a suit, rather playing his defensive cards at random, and thus, as we know, giving away the least information. Martin Hoffman puts it this way in his 1985 foreword to *Defence in Depth*:

Constant signalling, whether to show length or strength, is the mark of second-rate players. Trust your partner to know what is going on; don't add to declarer's information.

Bridge is not a game of certainties and the more information partner has the more likely he is to make the right decision, so there is a compromise to be reached. Today, among long-standing partnerships competing in tournaments at the highest levels, there is an opportunity to develop the art of signaling to a previously unrealized high level of excellence. Potentially, every card sends a message. So how are they doing? The following deal demonstrates that there is still some area for improvement.

In the final of the 2008 Spingold, the eventual champions sitting East-West disadvantaged themselves greatly by a dubious signal.

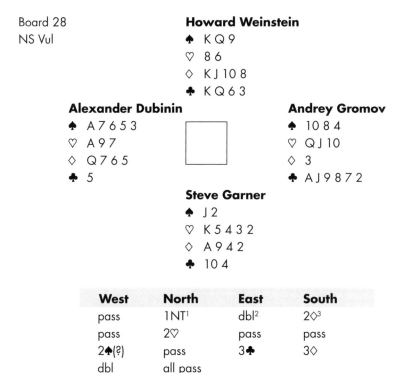

Board 28
NS Vul

Howard Weinstein
♠ K Q 9
♡ 8 6
◇ K J 10 8
♣ K Q 6 3

Alexander Dubinin
♠ A 7 6 5 3
♡ A 9 7
◇ Q 7 6 5
♣ 5

Andrey Gromov
♠ 10 8 4
♡ Q J 10
◇ 3
♣ A J 9 8 7 2

Steve Garner
♠ J 2
♡ K 5 4 3 2
◇ A 9 4 2
♣ 10 4

West	North	East	South
pass	1NT[1]	dbl[2]	2♡[3]
pass	2♡	pass	pass
2♠(?)	pass	3♣	3◇
dbl	all pass		

1. 14-16 HCP.
2. One-suited.
3. Transfer.

With five boards to play, the Russian-Polish team had an 18-IMP lead. The final session had been quiet and there was no apparent need to look for swings. On the other hand, there was no need to alter their aggressive stance, so Gromov took a light action over a 14-16 1NT opening bid to show a one-suited hand. In the passout position, Dubinin balanced with modest values and a five-card spade suit. Gromov may have thought Dubinin's bid was encouraging in a pass-or-correct mode. Nonetheless, Garner was not one to give up easily when his side held the majority of the HCP, and he rescued the East-West pair from their misfit.

The defenders had enough tricks in hand to set the contract and avoid disaster (♠A, ♣A, a club ruff, and two hearts), but there was more madness to come. The lead of the ♣5 was taken with the ♣A. With all hands on view, it is obvious to play the ♡Q at Trick 2, but Gromov may have thought that declarer held the ♡A. He returned a club for Dubinin to ruff, and this is where one must conclude that signaling was not at the forefront of his thought processes, for he returned the ♣2, which should clearly indicate suit preference for hearts. This would be a safe return if Dubinin held the ♡K.

Dubinin scored his ruff and thought a long time over whether to believe his partner's signal or his opponent's bidding. If he believed Garner's bidding, he could play safely by cashing his ♠A and awaiting developments in the heart suit. If he believed his partner's signal, he could get another club ruff. In the end, he gave away the contract, and with it 11 precious IMPs, by returning the ♡7, allowing the ♡K to score a trick. As a result of this, the match wasn't decided until the last hand was played, a 1♡ contract by Garner that was brilliantly defeated by Gromov and Dubinin, who regained their form just in time.

The main point to be made is that even experts have difficulties in providing clear signals to their partners. The second point has to do with the nature of the information conveyed by suit-preference signals. The information they contain should relate to the signaler's holding (hard information), not to what he thinks others may hold (soft information).

With regard to count signals, there are two states to be conveyed: odd number held or even number held. There are few times when the exact number is ambiguous. With regard to attitude signals, there are three states: Yes, No, and Maybe. With suit-preference signals, there are three states: higher suit, lower suit, neither. The 'neither' category is ambiguous, as on rare occasions a trump return is desired. A suit-preference signal was appropriate from Gromov, as he had shown a six-card suit in the bidding, so had ample scope for expressing his preferences. Here is a list of the five possible preference messages on his second play of the suit:

♣ J	spades, definitely	♣ 7	hearts more than spades
♣ 9	spades more than hearts	♣ 2	hearts, definitely
♣ 8	neither spades nor hearts		

One can see that the ♣7 would have expressed his major-suit holdings rather better than the ♣2.

CHAPTER 12

HIGH CARD POINTS AND ALL THAT JAZZ

The best in this kind are but shadows,
and the worst are no worse, if imagination amend them.
- from A Midsummer Night's Dream
by William Shakespeare (1564-1616)

Everyone is familiar with the assignment of high card points on the scale of 4-3-2-1. Bids in popular systems are defined in terms of the range of the HCP content; for example, an opening bid of 1NT may have a range of 12-14 HCP in one system and 15-17 HCP in another. So when a player picks up a hand, he sorts it into suits to discover the pattern of suit lengths and then proceeds to count up the HCP. This yields the two major pieces of information that he will use to describe his holding. How that information is used to evaluate the playing strength of the hand is a matter that will be considered later in the chapter. First we wish to treat HCP content purely as a descriptor which feeds into the complex matter of flexible hand evaluation.

Shannon's link tells us that information is inversely related to probability; the total information contained in a hand is related to both the shape probability and the HCP probability. But one must be careful in the definition of HCP probability, as one does not mean the total number of points held in all suits. That would be too easy. The average number of HCP held is independent of the shape. The relevant HCP probabilities are those linked to the length of each suit taken individually.

There is a relationship between the number of cards held in a suit and the average number of HCP held. If N is the number of cards in a suit, then the *a priori* expectation is that the number of HCP held in that suit is N times 10/13. Often we first show our shape, not our strength, in the hopes of finding a fit. So if partner opens the bidding with a five-card major, the expectation is that on average he holds at least 4 HCP in the suit. Of course, we have all upon occasion opened with a topless five-card major, because our bidding system required that bid, but we don't envision that initially and one's partner doesn't expect it. One's partner is entitled to assume that our five-card suit will contain close to the average number of HCP, as that is the most likely situation. Sometimes this working hypothesis is greatly flawed and leads to difficulty later in the auction unless the initial impression is corrected.

Expectations of HCP Distributions

Given the number of cards in a suit, what is the probability those cards include a given number of HCP? This is the expectation of HCP in a suit without regard to the composition of the deal as a whole. The following table shows how those *a priori* single-suit probabilities vary.

Percentage with Given HCPs

Suit length	0	1	2	3	4	5	6	7	8	9	10	Mean	Deviation
1	69.3	7.7	7.7	7.7	7.7	0.0	0.0	0.0	0.0	0.0	0.0	0.769	0.973
2	46.2	11.5	11.5	12.8	12.8	2.6	1.3	1.3	0.0	0.0	0.0	1.539	1.774
3	29.4	12.6	12.6	15.7	15.7	6.3	3.5	3.5	0.4	0.4	0.0	2.308	2.071
4	17.6	11.8	11.8	16.8	16.8	10.1	6.3	6.3	1.3	1.3	0.1	3.078	2.269
5	9.8	9.8	9.8	16.3	16.3	13.1	9.3	9.3	2.8	2.8	0.7	3.846	2.392
6	4.9	7.3	7.3	14.7	14.7	14.7	12.2	12.2	4.9	4.9	2.1	4.615	2.451

The percentages for longer suit lengths can be obtained easily by reversing the line for 13 minus the suit length. So for suit length 8, look at the line for suit length 5 and go backwards. 0.7. 2.8, and so on for values of 0, 1, 2, ... HCP. The average values are easily obtained from the formula 10 x N/13, where N represents the known suit length.

The table shows that the spread of values about the mean is 'normal' for lengths of 5 and 6, but is skewed to the right for lengths below 5. Statistically, it is better to deal with the 'middle' values rather than the mean. The variability as measured by the standard deviation rises rapidly as the suit length increases from 1 to 3, but flattens out thereafter.

The skew, graphically displayed with the appearance of a breaking wave flattening out when moving from left to right, is due to the fact that the range of HCP is limited for suit lengths under three cards. When dealing with a singleton, there are just two states: either no court card is held (9/13 probability) or a court card is held (4/13). The full range of 0 to 10 HCP isn't possible until four cards are held. This skew feature, which results from restricted choices, is encountered also in the statistics of Total Tricks, discussed in the next chapter.

The *a priori* distribution of HCP in hands consisting of four suits can be obtained from this table, since the distribution of HCP in a particular suit is independent of the other suits. The average value is always 10 HCP. The variances are additive and vary with the composition, but one can see from the following table that the effect of the shorter suits is not that great.

Shape	Standard Deviation	Shape	Standard Deviation
4333	4.24	4441	4.05
4432	4.21	5431	4.01
5332	4.18	5521	3.94
5422	4.14	5530	3.97

For most common shapes, the mean total of HCP is 10, with a standard deviation close to 4. The *a priori* probability without regard to shape of holding 10 HCP is 9.41%, whereas the probability given a 5440 shape is 9.42%, an insignificant difference. The figures for 16 HCP are also close, 3.31% and 3.28% respectively, even though in the latter situation, 10 HCP have been removed from consideration because of the void.

It is not just the total of HCP that is important, but how those points are distributed amongst the suits. For example, consider a hand with 13 HCP and a 6-3-3-1 shape. The expected values for points in each suit follows the distribution exactly: 6, 3, 3, and 1. This would be an example:

♠ A Q 9 7 6 4   ♡ K 7 3   ◇ Q J 8   ♣ J

If the ♣J were reduced to x status and the long suit became ♠AQJ976, a bridge player would say that the hand had improved considerably. Moving 1 HCP to the six-card suit has not changed the overall probability (of a 6331 13-count) from the original 12.2%. However, the hand with 6 points in the long suit and 0 in the singleton is much more likely to be dealt than the one shown above. Probabilities are affected to a much greater extent by the conditions in the short suits than by those in the long suits.

The median values of HCP for a given suit length are a rough guide. This is hardly necessary for the experienced player, but the process does give focus to the main idea that hands vary in quality due to the placement of points within a given hand pattern.

Suit	Median HCP	Pattern (9 HCP)	Pattern (12 HCP)	Pattern (16 HCP)
6	5	6	6-7	8-9
5	4	4	5	7
4	3	3	4	5
3	2	2	3	4
2	1	1	1	2
1	0	0	0	1

One may use the Median Patterns to calculate departures from what can be expected in the way of HCP for a given distribution of cards containing a total given number of HCP, as was done above. Large departures represent large discrepancies from what partner expects from the bidding of the hand. Positive discrepancies in the long suits are considered to be 'good', in the short suits, 'bad'. These departures are the cause of many errors, as the information content of the bids is low. Your 1♠ opening bid will be the same whether your suit is headed by a ten or a powerful combination of honors.

Even after the bidding has disclosed the shape of a hand, the partners are often still guessing about how the HCP are distributed among the suits. It is expected that the distribution of HCP mirrors the length of the suits. If such is the case, there will be no surprises in the dummy and little more need be added to the description of the hand through subsequent bids. If the distribution of HCP differs greatly from expectation, then partner may be very surprised by what comes down in the dummy unless otherwise informed. Surprise and information are linked: the greater the surprise on disclosure, the greater the information disclosed. To illustrate the general principles, let's examine a once popular limited opening bid that is fairly well defined with regard to distribution.

Information and Flannery 2◇ Bids

Information resides in departures from the norm.

The Flannery 2◇ opening bid is defined as showing 11-15 HCP with four spades and five hearts. A responder envisions 4-5-2-2 shape and may assume with some hope of consistency that the bidder has 13 HCP that are distributed four in spades, five in hearts and four in the minors. Let's look at two hands with 13 HCP that both qualify under the definition of an opening Flannery bid.

Hand I	HCP	Departures	%	Hand II	HCP	Departures	%
♠ AJxx	5	+1	10.1	♠ Jxxx	1	-3	11.8
♡ AQxxx	6	+1	9.3	♡ Qxxxx	2	-3	9.8
◇ xx	0	-2	46.2	◇ AJ	5	+3	2.6
♣ Qx	2	0	11.5	♣ KQ	5	+3	2.6
Sum of Departures		4				12	

The percentages shown are taken from the table of *a priori* percentages of HCP in a suit taken in isolation. The product of the percentages gives a rough guide as to the relative probabilities of the two conditions. On this basis, Hand I is about six times more likely than Hand II, the critical factors being the unexpectedly high number of HCP in the short suits of the latter.

The sum of the departures from the expected number of HCP in each suit is a good indication of the amount of information that still remains to be disclosed even though the two distributions fall within the narrow definition of the bid. The sum represents the number of points displaced from their expected location.

The Flannery 2◇ bid is limited to five possible shapes with the following probabilities of occurrence:

4-5-2-2	43%		
4-5-3-1	26%	4-5-1-3	26%
4-5-4-0	3%	4-5-0-4	3%

Although the single most likely shape is 4-5-2-2, overall the probability of shortage in a minor is 57%. An inquiry bid of 2NT is available for determining which shape applies, but that still does not specify the departures of the HCP from their expected values. To alleviate possible problems, you might restrict the 2◇ opening to hands where both majors represent playable trump suits. In particular, you could require that the spade suit be headed by the queen or a higher honor, since the quality of the trump suit is much more important in a 4-4 fit. This eliminates about 20% of the qualifying hands, the obvious alternative for the exclusions being a 1♡ opening bid. An alternative approach is to retain the full range of departures from normality, but design the responses to the 2NT inquiry bid to include information about the quality of the spade suit, along the lines of the Ogust inquiry after a weak-two opening bid. Departures from the norm in the heart suit are less critical.

The Obligation to Inform

I never saw any good that came of telling truth.
- John Dryden (1631-1700)

The holder of a limited hand has the obligation of informing his partner of any disparity between the expected normal holding and reality. The Principle of Fast Arrival has a different basis, which is a jump to game with a minimum in the context of the bidding so far. The jumper makes his best estimate based on what he can see before him and on what partner has told him. The weaker hand represents the weaker component and shouldn't attempt to manage the auction, but rather should be informative.

As noted by Amalya Kearse in her wonderful compilation *Bridge Conventions Complete*, in earlier days, a jump to 4NT (the Culbertson 4-5NT convention) *showed* a minimum holding of three aces or two aces and a king in a suit bid naturally by the partnership. This allowed either partner to make decisions based on the information provided by the jump. Since its introduction, the simpler Blackwood 4NT has dominated and the Culbertson 4NT has lost favor, one reason being that the user needn't be restricted by such requirements. Some players love to make decisions above all else, often leaving their partners and the defenders in the dark. Their argument has always been that it is wrong to give away information that reduces the chances of making the contract. Let's see how that worked in an example from top-level play. I think you might guess the answer already.

In the 2007 European Mixed Teams, the Russian pair of Alexander Dubinin and Tatiana Ponomoreva showed how full knowledge of the suit strength allows for an accurate evaluation in the slam zone.

Dubinin
♠ A K J
♡ A K 9 4
◇ Q 10 5 4
♣ A 8

Ponomoreva
♠ 10 7 4 3
♡ —
◇ A K J
♣ K Q J 7 5 4

Ponomoreva	Dubinin
2♣	2◊*
2♠	2NT*
3NT*	4♣*
5♣*	7NT

The 2♣ opening was Precision, showing 11-15 HCP and usually six clubs, and 2◊ was an enquiry with game-going values. Ponomoreva continued to show her distribution with 2♠, a four-card suit. This is rather a misdescription in that she held no HCP in her major suit. No problem this time, as Dubinin didn't expect much there and he could enquire further with a forcing 2NT. The 3NT response showed diamond values; 4♣ asked about clubs and 5♣ showed length and strength in the suit. This asking bid has been around a long time, being described by Ron Andersen and C. C. Wei in their 1983 book, *Match Point Precision*. Knowing where the values lay, Dubinin could blast to 7NT without fear of correction. The bidding was routine rather than brilliant. Accuracy, not brilliance, should be the aim in slam bidding.

To state that asking bids can at times provide the information necessary to get to the appropriate level in the appropriate strain is stating the obvious in the manner of moms lecturing on mittens, hankies and scarves. If one thinks of bids as providing information rather than deciding a contract, one is on the right track.

Conflicting Methods at the USBC 2007

Failure is a foundation for success.
- Japanese Proverb

Historically, even during the glory days of the Italian Blue Team, British experts have been very much opposed to asking bids. The British view has been that natural auctions are shorter, which is usually true, and more accurate, which clearly on the evidence isn't. When two strong-willed individuals involve themselves early in decision-making, there is twice the chance of getting it wrong in the end.

One of the most amusing deals of the century so far occurred on a slam combination where the lengths and strengths were in conflict, so the deal will serve as a good illustration of the phenomena. Meckwell were involved, this deal contributing to the eventual victory of their team in the trials for US representation at the 2007 Shanghai World Championships. First let's consider how a pair using standard methods might bid a pair of hands with 13 HCP each that conform to expectations of strength within length.

```
♠ A 8 7                              ♠ K J 9 3
♡ A 7 5 3          ┌─────┐          ♡ K Q J 10 9 8
◇ 3                │     │          ◇ K 6 2
♣ K Q 5 4 3        └─────┘          ♣ —
```

1♣	1♡
2♡	2♠
4◇	4♡
pass	

Both players have 13 HCP distributed nearly according to the length of their suits. The bids are natural and conform to shape. This should be a situation where natural bidding methods based on normal expectations do well. Responder may be tempted to proceed farther on the strength of the ♠KJ combination, but it appears there is wastage in the minors and slam may be no better than a finesse and not worth bidding. Without aces, he has no convenient bid, unless 3NT over 3♠ can be taken as a mild slam try, an agreement suggested by Kit Woolsey. Let's look at an actual layout from the 2007 USBC trials (hands rotated) where the shapes are the same but the distribution of the HCP do not conform to expectations. Natural methods may, as expected, not work well.

```
♠ A K J                              ♠ Q 9 6 3
♡ A 7 5 3          ┌─────┐          ♡ K Q J 10 9 8
◇ 3                │     │          ◇ K Q 2
♣ J 8 5 4 3        └─────┘          ♣ —
```

Martel	North	Stansby	South
1♣	pass	1♡	pass
2♡	pass	2♠	pass
2NT[1]	pass	3♡	pass
3♣	pass	4♣	pass
4♡	all pass		

1. Artificial, showing maximum for a single raise.

The expert cooperative auction didn't come to grips with the conflict between length and strength in the club suit.[1] Neither player was able to take charge and each had reservations about the minor-suit situation. That is to be expected

---

1. Note: a different auction is presented on page 17 of the Jan 2008 issue of *The Bridge World*.

even with an expert pair. Can they guess better than the rest of us? Maybe, but they still require basic information. The artificial Meckwell Precision auction provides the required asking bid methods and the amusement.

Meckstroth	Rodwell	
2◇[1]	2NT[2]	
3♠[3]	4♣[4]	(dbl)
pass[5]	4◇[6]	
4♡[7]	4♠[8]	
5◇[9]	6♡[10]	

1. Precision 2◇, short in diamonds, 11-15 HCP.
2. Asking bid.
3. 3-4-1-5 and a maximum.
4. Nebulous slam try.
5. No club control.
6. Agrees hearts, 'tell me more'.
7. Top heart.
8. Keycard enquiry in hearts.
9. Two keycards without ♡Q.
10. With the ♠K opposite, slam must be a laydown.

The action was broadcast via Bridge Base Online with expert commentary provided by Kit Woolsey, who plays Precision 2◇ with his regular partner, Fred Stewart. Early on he stated, 'There is absolutely no way to investigate on this hand.' He may have been correct with regard to bids with a natural base, but what if Meckwell could employ asking bids to discover there were no wasted values in clubs?

The auction did not develop that well, as Rodwell reached the four-level before he could show slam interest, whereas in the other room Stansby had used the bid of 2♠ to start the slam inquiry. But now Rodwell got some help from the opposition. Baseball fans may be reminded of outfielder Jose Canseco's effort, when, going back on the warning track for a routine catch, he lost sight of the ball at the last instant, with the result that said ball took a lively bounce off his skull up into the stands for a home run. Here, the victim of his own efforts was Brad Moss, who felt an uncontrollable urge to inform his partner that he had a good holding in clubs. Like Jose, Brad temporarily lost sight of the ball. Meckwell were informed as well. This allowed them the space for the extra asking bids that eventually led to the slam that was obvious to the viewers. If Moss and Gitelman can join in the laughter, I predict a world championship for them in the not-too-distant future.

Let's belabor the point. If a partnership bids naturally, they are bidding in accordance with normal expectations with regard to the distribution of HCP among the suits. Partners are allowed to assume what is most probable. However, if the distribution of HCP features large departures from normalcy, even experts will have difficulty conveying this to a partner without the use of asking bids. Clearly it is not a good strategy on the part of an opponent to volunteer the information that he has a good holding in a long suit they have been bidding naturally, unless it is too late in the auction for them to take corrective action.

Let's look at the departures in the two 13-HCP hands.

Suit	Meckstroth			Rodwell		
	Length	HCP	Departure	Length	HCP	Departure
♠	3	8	+5	4	2	-2
♡	4	4	0	6	6	0
♢	1	0	-1	3	5	+2
♣	5	1	-4	0	0	0
Total Departures			10			4

Rodwell's hand conforms well to the expectation in the distribution of HCP, so one expects his bidding to be informative even in a natural setting. Meckstroth's hand has a large departure from normality of which Rodwell is unaware. The problem in a slam auction is how to inform Rodwell of this abnormality — strength in spades, nothing wasted in clubs. This is where the essential information resides.

Long Suits versus Short Suits

The HCP content of a hand is correlated to the length of the suits. If one considers the division of sides as indicating two long suits and two short suits, the division of the HCP can be expected to be related to the difference in the number of cards in the long suits and the number in the short suits. Thus if the division is 8765, there are 15 cards in the long suits and 11 in the short suits, so the HCP should be divided roughly in the same proportion. With 21 HCP held, expect 12 in the long suits and 9 in the short suits. If there are proportionally more in the long suits, the conditions are favorable for bidding higher, whereas if there are proportionally less in the long suits, one should subside. The normal case is where one needs to exercise judgment based on statistical analysis and personal experience. Here are the three situations exemplified:

	I Above Normal		II Normal		III Sub-Normal	
♠	A Q x x x	♠ K x	A x x x x	♠ K x	Q x x x x	♠ K x
♡	K Q x x	♡ A x x x	K x x x	♡ Q x x x	A x x x	♡ J x x x
♢	J x	♢ x x x x	K x	♢ x x x x	K x	♢ A J x x
♣	x x	♣ Q x x	Q x	♣ A x x	K x	♣ x x x

Case I Long Suits 18 Short Suits 3. This is a situation where bidding to the three-level should be correct. Making ten tricks is not in the cards as it might be if the opener had shortness in diamonds. Note the attractiveness of a holding of K-Q-x-x in a 4-4 fit.

Case II Long Suits 12, Short Suits 9. The hearts are on the weak side, but nine tricks may be made if the ◊K lies behind the ◊A, or the defenders help out in some way.

Case III Long Suits 10, Short Suits 11. The minor-suit honors may produce defensive tricks that defeat 3♣ by two tricks and could also help in a heart contract, but the weakness of the heart suit itself is problematic.

A critical factor to consider when contemplating playing in a 4-4 fit is the quality of the intermediate cards. Tens and nines are of prime value when present in conjunction with higher honors. A 4-1 split of the defenders' holding in the suit is fairly frequent, in which case one needs to be able to withstand adverse conditions.

The Single Raise in Competition

The need for accuracy is not as great in competitive bidding as in constructive bidding because one is not certain which side will become the declaring side. Pushing the opponents over their limit is one of the aims, so one can profit from misjudgment fed by misinformation. That seems to be the theory behind many bad bids. On the other hand, good defense is based on reliable information. If you overcall on a bad suit, you must be prepared for a costly opening lead from a trusting partner.

A common occurrence is a single raise of partner's bid suit meant to remove bidding space from the opposition as well as stake out an area for further competition, if appropriate. What does a single raise promise? Usually three trumps, but what about honors? Is the support Q-x-x or better?

The Support Double is a popular way to show the number of cards held in support of a responder's suit after an opponent interferes in one's auction:

West	North	East	South
1◇	pass	1♡	1♠
dbl			

Opener's double shows three hearts.

In effect, the Support Double gives opener two ways to make a single raise of responder's suit. Is attitude possible? Must opener double even if his hearts are three small? This risks getting overboard at the three-level if spades are raised. In his book *Double! New Meanings for an Old Bid*, Mike Lawrence suggests opener may judge to pass with three small hearts, but should double even with a minimum opener if all the HCP are 'working', his example holding being ♡Q106. This advice is in keeping with normal expectations in which the HCP lie in the suit bid. If one bids otherwise, the information conveyed is less and the uncertainty is greater.

Four-Card Raises

May you live in exciting times.
- ancient Chinese curse

There is widespread approval of 'weak' jump raises to the three-level when holding four-card support for partner's five-card suit. With a nine-card fit, the three-level is not only safe, but also appropriate, it is thought. The argument applies in competition as well as in constructive auctions without interference. The situation is simplified by the fact that the responder and defenders hold four cards in the suit, which makes the analysis easy.

Suppose that the initiator holds a suit headed by A-J. Here are the normal expectations within the suit for responder's hand with regard to honor cards (without regard to the full deal). Probability estimates are very rough, as no account is taken of the tens and nines.

Initiator	Responder	Probability	Rough Estimate of Probable Losers 0	1	2	3
AJxxx	KQxx	21%	1.0	—	—	—
	Kxxx	29%	0.6	0.4	—	—
	Qxxx	29%	0.27	0.6	0.1	—
	xxxx	21%	—	0.53	0.37	0.1
	Overall		0.46	0.41	0.1	0.02

Responder is expected to hold the king half of the time. Roughly four times in nine, the initiator expects to lose no tricks. Losing two tricks in the suit happens roughly one time in ten. As shown next, with touching honors in the long hand, the situation is better. Responder is expected to hold the ace half of the time, which greatly increases the chance of no losers in the suit.

			Rough Estimate of Probable Losers			
Initiator	Responder	Probability	0	1	2	3
KQxxx	AJxx	21%	1.0	—	—	—
	Axxx	29%	0.95	0.05	—	—
	Jxxx	29%	—	0.95	0.05	—
	xxxx	21%	—	0.76	0.19	0.05
	Overall		0.49	0.45	0.05	0.01

The key holding in constructive bidding is a first- or second-round control, an ace or king. Aces and kings are known as 'controls' and are given full value in the following method of evaluation.

LTC — The Losing Trick Count

The very simplicity of the LTC makes some people suspicious.
- M. Harrison-Gray (1900 -1968)

The Losing Trick Count (LTC) is a method of hand evaluation related to Jaynes' Principle, in that the user bases his evaluation on what is most probable given the current state of partial knowledge. This is not the place for a full description (such as is given in Ron Klinger's *The Modern Loser Count*), but the method is a major advance in hand evaluation in the context of trump suit contracts. It has a basis in probability theory, but we are concerned here with why it works rather than how it works, so only a cursory treatment of techniques is presented.

Most readers will be familiar with the LTC concept, a method devised in 1935 for estimating the number of winning tricks available in trump contracts when small trumps are promoted to the status of winners through the process of ruffing losers from the hand opposite. As with The Law of Total Tricks, there are no absolute guarantees. The method is valid when playing in a trump suit that cannot be depleted to a critical level by the opponents leading trumps. The secret of success is to project the play in terms of what is most probable, and thus there is a connection with Bob's Blind Rule.

A major promoter of the method was Maurice Harrison-Gray, a leading player and authority of his time. In his August 31, 1961 column in *Country Life* he wrote, 'A good player does not make the same call in the same context on two hands with a marked difference in quality.' By this, he meant that two hands with the same number of HCP can differ greatly in their capacity for taking tricks, so bidding methods must be capable of conveying this difference. This is the antithesis of the approach of the late Al Roth who often expressed the wish, 'if I can only get through this round', indicating that his hand was not well described in the structure employed. Here is an example given by Harrison-Gray to support his argument.

West		East
West		**East**
♠ A K J 8		♠ 10 9 5 3 2
♡ 9 8 2		♡ 10 5
◇ 4 3		◇ A K 10 7
♣ A K 9 3		♣ 6 2
6 losers[1]		8 losers

West	North	East	South
1♣	pass	1♠	pass
2♠	all pass		

Two British teams of international standard stopped in a contract of 2♠ when eleven tricks were available. Both agreed the game was unbiddable with just 15 HCP opposite 7. Harrison-Gray thought otherwise. West should have bid an encouraging and descriptive 3♠ to show a six-loser hand, he maintained, so East could have bid game automatically, five trumps in an eight-loser hand. The number of tricks expected according to the LTC method is twenty-four minus the total of losers (fourteen), namely ten. Is that too simple? How does one count losers and why subtract from twenty-four? We shall get to that shortly.

Opening Light in a Natural Setting

It is often observed that the side that opens the bidding has a distinct advantage during the auction. This advantage is heightened if the expectations created reflect reality, that is, if the HCP go along with the long suits. Natural bidding should work well under these circumstances, systems allowing, so it is surprising to see that in many cases even expert players are inhibited by HCP restrictions. It is better to use the losing trick count in trump contracts when strength matches length. In the following deal, a grand slam is possible on a mere 24 HCP. The deal, from *The First IPBM Book of Bidding Hands* (1983), featured the famous actor Omar Sharif in partnership with Patrick Sussel.

---

1. The rationale for this evaluation will be explained shortly.

	♠ J 4 3 2		♠ A 7
	♡ —		♡ J 4
	◇ A Q 8 7		◇ K 10 9 6 5
	♣ K 10 9 7 3		♣ A Q 8 6
	6 losers		6 losers

Sussel	North	Sharif	South
pass	pass	1◇	pass
2♣	pass	3♣	pass
3◇	pass	3♠	pass
4♡	pass	5♣	pass
5♡	pass	5♠	pass
6◇	all pass		

The opponents added a certain degree of uncertainty by not entering the bidding with eleven hearts between them! If West doesn't open the bidding on this rich hand, how does he subsequently show the full potential? A jump to 4◇ over 3♣ bypasses the usually desirable 3NT, but with East known to have at most four cards in the majors, that's not such a bad thing here. The critical point in the auction came after Sussel bid a non-forcing 3◇, hoping to get into one more round of bidding, and Sharif stretched to show a spade control, hoping perhaps for 3NT if some secondary help in spades was forthcoming. It may have appeared to Sharif that clubs was the agreed suit, but Sussel showed otherwise.

The bidding might have been more relaxed if West had opened the bidding in a minor suit. The point to be made is that the HCP in the two long minor suits are up to expectations, and the fact that there is a point or two fewer in the majors than might be expected is not a major concern. The loser count of twelve indicates that twelve tricks may be available. Once the double fit is discovered, the partnership may well realize that there is potential for even more. This method works well when the HCP strength and suit length are well matched in the suits being shown, which is the essential advantage gained by the LTC method.

Counting Losers

How do you count losers? You consider only the top three cards in each suit: aces and kings and accompanying queens are defined as winners. Any others count as losers up to a maximum of three. Let's look at Harrison-Gray's 'unbiddable game' example:

West		Losers	East		Losers
♠ A K J	- ♠8	(1)	♠ 10 9 5	- ♠32	(3)
♡ 9 8 2		(3)	♡ 10 5		(2)
◇ 4 3		(2)	◇ A K 10	- ◇7	(1)
♣ A K 9	- ♣3	(1)	♣ 6 2		(2)
	Total	7		Total	8

Harrison-Gray subtracted a loser in the West hand on the grounds that he held half of the controls in the deck. The correct rebid in that context was therefore 3♠. East with eight losers would then know to raise to game. It works often. Why? We shall discuss this in terms of the suggestion that one should consider playing for what is most likely (Bob's Blind Rule).

Of course, potentially there are really 3.25 losers in each suit, since there are thirteen potential tricks to lose on each deal, but these numbers are awkard to handle — besides, we are striving for simplicity (the 4-3-2-1 HCP count is itself a simplification). It is simplest to round to three, giving us a maximum total of twelve losers per hand, or twenty-four in all. A non-loser is a winner, so we can approximate the number of winners available by adding the losers from the two hands and then subtracting the total from 24. In Harrison-Gray's example, we have (after adjustment) 6 + 8 = 14 losers, and therefore ten potential winners: enough for game in spades.

Ron Klinger's discussion in *The Modern Losing Trick Count* gets more involved, and he advises players to add and subtract 1/2 losers under some circumstances. My view is that the LTC should be treated as empirical and kept simple: it's a rule of thumb, not a micrometer.

Inside the 12-Box and Outside the 12-Box

When one limits the cards included in the loser count to twelve, one puts twelve cards 'inside the box', no more than three in any suit, so there remains initially one or more cards 'outside the box'. Let's illustrate the process with simple examples where seemingly insignificant cards are denoted by an 'x'. Spades are trumps.

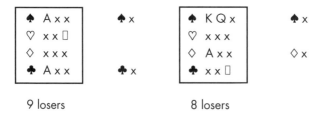

9 losers   8 losers

The truncation of the suits to at most three cards inside the box in this situation leaves two cards outside the box. An empty space inside the box, denoted by ▯, must be filled from outside the box. As one envisions the play, with trumps moved inside the box, a heart and a club can be ruffed, bringing the total number of winners to seven, provided there are no overruffs as a consequence of bad splits. The absence of bad splits is the most probable situation, as discussed earlier with regard to Jaynes' Principle. The loser count (24 - 17 = 7) therefore gives the correct number of winners under these favorable, but normal, conditions. Let's consider a change that affects the relationship: let's give the East hand a 4333 shape.

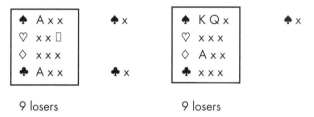

9 losers   9 losers

The LTC indicates just six tricks are available (24-18), but one can count, on straightforward play, three spades, a heart ruff, two aces, and a remaining trump from outside the box of the East hand that serves as a winner on the thirteenth trick, provided the opponents' trumps are split 3-2. Another approach to combining the losers from the two hands is to look at the 'cover cards' in the East hand — of which there are three. Subtracting those from West's nine losers gets us to six losers, or seven tricks.

The Number of Total Tricks

The above hands form a side of 8765. It is interesting to see if the LTC gives the same prediction for the opponents' hands, which are also 8765. The Law of Total Tricks[1] indicates that the sum of total tricks should be sixteen, so if there are seven tricks available in spades, the opponents should be able to take nine tricks with hearts as trumps. Let's assume the distribution of the sides is 'normal'.

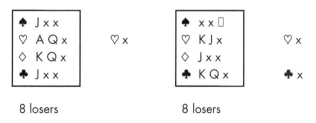

8 losers   8 losers

---

1.   The LAW is discussed in more detail in the next chapter.

The expectation is that these hands will produce nine winners (25 - 16) as the trump outside the West box counts as an extra winner. Or you could say that the East hand produces four cover cards — three high cards and the missing spade — leaving West with four losers and therefore nine tricks.

How to Outperform the LTC

One may do better than the LTC indicates by making full use of the trumps by establishing a long side suit or by crossruffing. Another way to play is not to draw trumps early and to convert a trump companion card into a winner. Here is an example of an 8855 deal where spades are trumps.

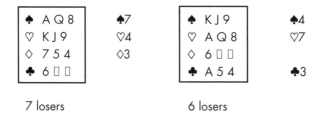

♠ A Q 8	♠7	♠ K J 9	♠4
♡ K J 9	♡4	♡ A Q 8	♡7
◊ 7 5 4	◊3	◊ 6 ☐ ☐	
♣ 6 ☐ ☐		♣ A 5 4	♣3

7 losers   6 losers

There are two losing clubs, but only one trump available 'outside the box' that can be used for ruffing. Similarly for diamonds. Eleven tricks appear to be the limit. However, the quality of the major suits may allow for an extra ruff before trumps are drawn. Suppose a top diamond wins the first trick and the defender switches to a trump. West (declarer) wins with the ♠Q, plays the ♣A and takes a ruff. A heart can be played to dummy and another club ruffed, then the process repeated, taking a third ruff with the ♠A. A diamond ruff gets declarer back to dummy to draw the remaining trumps with the ♠KJ while pitching a losing diamond, which has become a companion card. In this way, twelve tricks can be taken.

An LTC Horror Show

The advantage of being declarer is that there are three ways to win:
either you get it right or the defenders get it wrong
... and there are two of them.

Dealer: North
Neither Vulnerable

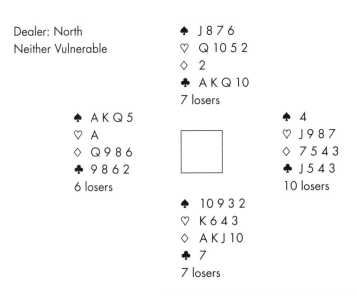

```
                    ♠ J 8 7 6
                    ♡ Q 10 5 2
                    ◇ 2
                    ♣ A K Q 10
                    7 losers
   ♠ A K Q 5                         ♠ 4
   ♡ A                               ♡ J 9 8 7
   ◇ Q 9 8 6                         ◇ 7 5 4 3
   ♣ 9 8 6 2                         ♣ J 5 4 3
   6 losers                         10 losers
                    ♠ 10 9 3 2
                    ♡ K 6 4 3
                    ◇ A K J 10
                    ♣ 7
                    7 losers
```

West	North	East	South
	1♣	pass	1♡
dbl	2♡	pass	4♡
all pass			

North-South bid according to their loser counts. South thought that seven losers plus seven losers amounted to ten tricks. He checked his 'points' and counted fourteen opposite an opening bid. So he bid game and was disappointed when West defeated the contract immediately by leading spades, giving East a ruff on the fourth round. There was still the ace of trumps to lose, so South made just eight tricks, two fewer than expected.

This horror story illustrates what can happen when controls are lacking. The sides are 8855, usually a good sign for those who would bid aggressively, but, against the odds, the side suits are divided 4-1, not 3-2. Furthermore, the side suits contain the vast majority of HCP, this too being unusual. A deal like the one shown is very rare compared to the majority of deals in which most of the HCP lie favorably in the long suits.

Expert players use multiple hand evaluation methods, not just one exclusively. They look at HCP and shape, consider loser count and the texture of the hand, and upgrade and downgrade their holdings based on the auction and, above all, on their own judgment based on experience. Empirical methods exist which attempt to make parts of this process simpler for lesser players; these include the LTC and the Law of Total Tricks — of which we'll see more in the next chapter.

CHAPTER 13

PROBABILITY, STATISTICS AND THE LAW

Science is built up of facts, as a house is built of stones,
but an accumulation of facts is no more a science than
a heap of stones is a house.
- Henri Poincairé (1854-1912)

The world divides itself into two main groups: those who judge according to what should have happened, and those who judge according to results. Probability exists in the cloudy realm of the idealist. It provides the blueprint of what should be but often isn't. Statistics provide the concrete foundations for the realists; it represents the hard facts of what has happened and is likely to happen again. The main objective of data analysis is to derive practical conclusions to guide our future actions.

Bridge scores are the rough stones of experience, and if we are to make full use of them, they must form part of a coherent structure. Looking at the results from a single session may not be enlightening, as the overall pattern is obscured by human fallibility. Over the long run, experience is what guides us. What works today gets repeated tomorrow and what doesn't work is discarded. Slowly our methods evolve, in a random fashion, unless we seek guidance from experienced players who can present a reasonable explanation that somehow makes sense of our observations. It is the Darwinians against the Intelligent Designers.

On the basis of experience over a few sessions, you may conclude that if you are dealt a singleton, it will most likely be a club. Now, while this may be true of the data on which the conclusion is based, it is a statistical fluke. The next hundred deals may not bear this out. Although one may note the occurrence as a curious fact, it does not provide a basis for action in the future. Easley Blackwood used statistical tests on various prejudices concerning hand-shuffled deals, like the superstition that the ♣K is more likely to be a singleton than the other kings. He knew better, but the fact that he felt the need to disprove it was a sad reflection on the players of his time.

It is worthwhile to examine the process of statistical analysis, because even today in more enlightened times there is a profound misunderstanding of the process, especially with regard to the Law of Total Tricks, the subject of this chapter. Let's first look at the simple question of what conventions one may wish to incorporate into one's bidding system. Surely a statistical survey can help in deciding which ones are worthwhile, if only one could interpret the statistics properly.

Let's suppose one wishes to address the question of whether or not to adopt the Flannery 2◊ opening, which was discussed in the previous chapter. A natural first step would be to extract from a storehouse of past tournaments those hands that were opened with the Flannery 2◊ and compare the scores obtained with those obtained on the same boards by players who didn't use the convention. Surely that would be a prerequisite for the adoption. Suppose that the Flannery users outscored the field on those hands. That is to be expected because the bid is very informative, but that in itself would not tell us that the Flannery bid was a worthwhile addition to a bidding system, because it comes up infrequently. To complete the analysis, one has to look at the much greater number of hands where the Flannery pairs couldn't open 2◊ to show something else. Did the supposedly good results from Flannery get swamped by bad results when not being able to open 2◊ otherwise?

A further difficulty is that the players who used Flannery may be a different class of player from those who didn't. There may be a generation gap, for example. So the validity of any conclusion drawn from statistical analysis must be considered in terms of the uniformity of the database. Thus, the question becomes very complex and not easily resolved by a simple test of results.

Statistical analysis is best directed towards looking for answers to very specific questions. For example, one might ask whether there was degradation in the results when Flannery was used with large HCP departures from expectation, as we surmised in the previous chapter. There is a reason to believe that this might be the case, the reason being that the information content in this situation becomes degraded as the uncertainty is increased. If this hypothesis is tested with data, attention is focused solely on the group of players who employ Flannery, so the results should be meaningful. The study might show that Flannery was equally effective despite the loss of information, thus putting one theory to rest while suggesting others.

Statistics and the LAW

Statistics are like lampposts: they are good to lean on,
but don't shed much light.
- Robert Storm-Petersen (1882-1946)

Theories arise as a means to arrange facts into a structure. The Law of Total Tricks says the total number of tricks taken by both sides, each playing in their longest trump fit, equals the total number of trumps in the two suits declared. Of course, this is a mis-statement of the results obtained by Jules René Vernes, the Frenchman who first observed in a statistical survey of deals from world championship play that the correlation between the number of tricks taken and the number of trumps held was much greater than that between the number of tricks and the division of HCP.

Vernes' observation was based on very few deals. With computer simulations, the database can be greatly expanded — albeit within the restriction that the results are dependent on the degree to which computers can reproduce 'realistic' situations. One such statistical study, involving over 400,000 simulations, was reported by Matt Ginsberg in the November 1996 issue of *The Bridge World*. He concluded that 'provided that the trump lengths combine to twenty cards or fewer, the Law of Total Tricks will lead you to correct decisions approximately 70% of the time.' What the characteristics were of the 30% of the deals for which the LAW did not provide the correct decision was left unexplored. Perhaps the failures were random and unpredictable, but one would be reluctant to make such a conclusion, rather hoping that more directed statistical studies might lead to further enlightenment.

The results of a statistical study do not produce laws; they produce trends within limits of uncertainty. Attacking the LAW as being subject to variation is silly and addresses solely the gullible few who believe in it absolutely. Statistics are a compilation of data subject to variation due to hidden factors such as the skill level of the players (or computer programs) involved. The trick for obtaining insights of general validity lies in the collection process and how the categories are defined.

No matter that the LAW is not Platonic in its perfection, the consequences of Vernes' revelation (and Larry Cohen's brilliant exposition of it in *To Bid Or Not To Bid*) is that many have taken it to heart and invented bidding schemes based on its relevance to competitive action. There is no doubt that the emergence of vigorous competitive bidding is a major change to duplicate bridge at all levels that has been influenced by the LAW and is still developing, with some way to go. It's what they believe rather than what is true that moves the masses. The real question is this: knowing that there is a correlation between the total number of tricks and the total number of trumps, how does one apply that knowledge in a competitive auction? Specifically, when do the odds favor bidding on and when not?

This is where hypothesis testing comes to the fore. Good players know what factors favor bidding on, so it is a matter of testing hypotheses under the various favorable conditions to see which are most influential with regard to the LAW.

The Classification of Results

Statistics are a potentially dangerous distillation of results. The constituents must be clearly labeled.

When drawing conclusions from results, you have to make clear what process is used to judge a result. Often an analyst looking at all four hands can see what is the ideal result, but is this a fair assessment? The results may not lead to a conclusion of what is right or wrong even where experts are involved. Here is an example from real life, Board 17 of the 2007 Spingold Semifinals, where there are twenty total trumps, double fits. At the two tables, both sides got into the bidding and had to judge at a high level. As there were ten tricks theoretically available to East-West in 4♠, the North-South pairs should do well to sacrifice in 5♡.

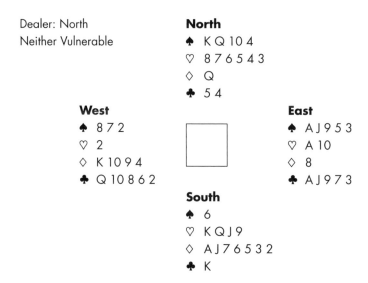

Dealer: North
Neither Vulnerable

North
♠ K Q 10 4
♡ 8 7 6 5 4 3
◇ Q
♣ 5 4

West
♠ 8 7 2
♡ 2
◇ K 10 9 4
♣ Q 10 8 6 2

East
♠ A J 9 5 3
♡ A 10
◇ 8
♣ A J 9 7 3

South
♠ 6
♡ K Q J 9
◇ A J 7 6 5 3 2
♣ K

In the first match, North-South took nine tricks in a contract of 5♡, while at the other table East-West took nine tricks in 4♠, so the Total Tricks came to eighteen, two fewer than predicted. In the other semifinal match, both East-

West pairs played in 4♠, and one declarer guessed the club position to bring home his contract. Can all this be classified as evidence of a failure of the LAW?

The point to be made with regard to this deal is that there is no clear right or wrong with regard to the North-South decision at the table to defend or sacrifice. From South's point of view, the heart lead looks solid, and there are certainly ways for East to go wrong. The ♣K may provide a trick for the defense, and did so on two out of three occasions. So within the bounds of uncertainty, a decision to defend appeared correct to three semifinalists. With regard to a statistical classification, can one say The LAW was upheld, or not? Three results point to a total of eighteen tricks, two fewer than predicted by the LAW; however, the fourth piece of evidence is that ten tricks can be made in spades on astute play.

It should be noted that in *To Bid Or Not to Bid*, Larry Cohen advocates bidding one more than the LAW suggests on 'freak' hands with double fits. The LAW does not fit well with the results obtained from extremely distributional hands. Board 17 might be so described. It is safer for South to bid on with a double fit than to rely on The LAW, which applies more happily to the more frequent flat hands.

Presumably on the evidence of played hands, there will be some doubt as to whether the deal was played to full advantage by defenders and/or declarers. If experts can make mistakes, how about the results with average players? Reality is messy. On the other hand, if computers bid and play the hands, the results will reflect the methods employed in the software. These can be controlled so that each deal is played in a uniform manner. This situation is controllable from the outside, so is preferable for testing hypotheses. Trends can be more easily identified, methods more easily tested. In reporting test results, the researcher must state fully the methods employed. Once methods are refined, the real test is to apply them to real data in great quantity so as to gauge the degree of uncertainty.

Refining the LAW

In their book *I Fought The Law of Total Tricks*, Mike Lawrence and Anders Wirgren discuss ways to improve the prediction of the number of tricks available in a deal. They note that it is not so much the number of trumps one side holds but the number of trumps that can be used successfully for ruffing that is important. Their title is misleading, as they don't fight the LAW so much as attempt to stay on the right side of it. Anders Wirgren has undertaken extensive surveys using a computer program to do the work of playing out the hands (presumably when the numbers of HCP were approximately balanced). The results confirmed the relation of tricks to trumps in this respect: the most likely number of total tricks was always the total number of trumps. Here are two examples of how the statistics play out.

When the total trumps equals 14					
Total Tricks	12	13	14	15	16
Percentage (%)	—	5	56	34	4

When the total trumps equals 16					
Total Tricks	14	15	16	17	18
Percentage (%)	5	17	44	27	6

When there are fourteen total trumps, there is only one relevant division of sides, 7766, which comprises about 10% of all deals. Normally these hands should be played in notrump contracts, as there are few if any ruffs available. Under the conditions of the computer simulation, the range of variation is not large, so the statistics stack up under just two categories. When there are sixteen total trumps, various conditions apply and a wider range of results is possible. In this situation, the statistical distribution flattens while maintaining a peak in the middle. It looks like a normal (Gaussian) shape with a median value between 16 and 17. This has more to do with the statistics of random variables and so-called 'degrees of freedom' than it does with bridge, *per se*.

If Wirgren's computer results are accepted, they clearly indicate that the best estimate of total tricks is the number of total trumps. This represents the 'normal' condition and therefore you should 'normally' accept the LAW. The results for sixteen total trumps show that there are as many results for sixteen tricks as there are for fifteen tricks and seventeen tricks combined, so why would you estimate otherwise? However, if you do decide to deviate, it pays to be aggressive, as seventeen tricks are half again more likely than fifteen tricks.

Let's look at how the cards would most likely be divided when 7-6-6-7. The relative numbers of combinations for each set is given beneath the distribution shown.

I	II	III	IV	V	VI
♠ 4 - 3	♠ 4 - 3	♠ 4 - 3	♠ 5 - 2	♠ 4 - 3	♠ 5 - 2
♡ 3 - 3	♡ 3 - 3	♡ 2 - 4	♡ 3 - 3	♡ 4 - 2	♡ 2 - 4
◇ 3 - 3	◇ 2 - 4	◇ 4 - 2	◇ 3 - 3	◇ 1 - 5	◇ 4 - 2
♣ 3 - 4	♣ 4 - 3	♣ 3 - 4	♣ 2 - 5	♣ 4 - 3	♣ 2 - 5
1	0.75	0.56	0.36	0.23	0.20

The vast majority of distributions could be described as 'notrump' types. The proportion that would end up in a suit contract is small, and depends on the bidding system being used. So if one were to do a computer simulation, the final contract should be determined by the result of an auction. If one includes some bidding options, one obtains a different picture of possible distributions. Which distributions would give rise to the sequence 1◇-1♡; 1♠ if one were employing a five-card major system?

III	VII	VIII
♠ 4 - 3	♠ 4 - 3	♠ 4 - 3
♡ 2 - 4	♡ 2 - 4	♡ 1 - 5
◇ 4 - 2	◇ 5 - 1	◇ 5 - 1
♣ 3 - 4	♣ 2 - 5	♣ 3 - 4
0.75	0.13	0.09

Shortages become more relevant, and shortages are what favor playing in a suit rather than in notrump. Let's imagine a 7766 deal where both sides might declare in their best seven-card fit, one side with shortage and the other side without. Which side do you think will take more tricks?

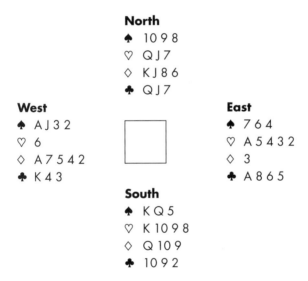

North
♠ 10 9 8
♡ Q J 7
◇ K J 8 6
♣ Q J 7

West
♠ A J 3 2
♡ 6
◇ A 7 5 4 2
♣ K 4 3

East
♠ 7 6 4
♡ A 5 4 3 2
◇ 3
♣ A 8 6 5

South
♠ K Q 5
♡ K 10 9 8
◇ Q 10 9
♣ 10 9 2

If East-West get to play in their 4-3 spade fit, the result will be beyond normal expectations, as West can take ten tricks on any lead. For North-South, six tricks is the limit in diamonds.

The LAW is out by 2, since the total trumps are fourteen and the total tricks sixteen. The East-West hands play extremely well, one major advantage to declarer being the possession of all four aces.

Although both sides held 20 HCP, North-South lacked the normal quota of controls, only three versus East-West's nine. North-South possessed no shortages, whereas East-West had complementary singletons. North-South held the most likely distribution of sides, 4333 opposite 4333, whereas East-West held a distribution with fewer than one-tenth the number of combinations. This deal illustrates specifically these five points with regard to trick-taking potential:

1) Most hands are flat in a 7766 side;
2) Shortages are important, as they allow for ruffs;
3) One side having shortage doesn't promote shortage in the other side;
4) Controls are important as they enable ruffs;
5) Honors in the trump suit are important, as they reduce the effectiveness of the opponents' trump leads.

The Losing Trick Count and Total Tricks

Martin, if dirt were trumps, what hands you would hold.
- Charles Lamb (1775-1824)

The previous deal can also be used to illustrate evaluation according to the losing trick count, details of which are given in *The Modern Losing Trick Count* by Ron Klinger. An important feature of the method is the emphasis placed on shape and controls: two sides with 20 HCP and 7766 distribution may have greatly different potential depending on the shapes of the individual hands.

North	South	West	East
♠ 10 9 8	♠ K Q 5	♠ A J 3 2	♠ 7 6 4
♡ Q J 7	♡ K 10 9 8	♡ 6	♡ A 5 4 3 2
◇ K J 8 6	◇ Q 10 9	◇ A 7 5 4 2	◇ 3
♣ Q J 7	♣ 10 9 2	♣ K 4 3	♣ A 8 6 5
9 losers	9 losers	7 losers	8 losers

Because of their flat shapes, North-South have a total of eighteen losers, which indicates they can take six tricks, in exact agreement with the actual total. East-West have a total of fifteen losers, which indicates they can take nine tricks. However, one loser can be deducted because East-West hold nine controls, an exceptionally high total, so one arrives at a total of ten tricks expected to be taken. This, too, is in exact agreement with the actual total. Therefore, the number of total tricks agrees with the totals predicted by the respective losing trick counts as described by Klinger. The simple conclusion is that bidding systems can justifiably be based on *a priori* probabilities and the LAW as a general guideline, but in practice players should evaluate their hands according to their current losing trick count, that being a better estimate of the potential of the hand before them.

An Appropriate Statistical Approach

Nothing is beautiful from every point of view.
- Horace (65-8 BC)

The LAW is not perfection. It is an observation based on a statistical study of selected deals, so the validity of the result on any particular deal should be viewed in the context of variability within the bounds of uncertainty. Such bounds depend on the method of classification: the narrower the constraints placed on the classification, the more accurate will be the predictions. In practice, one may apply constraints on the number of HCP held, but HCP alone may not be the most suitable measure to use. Using only HCP classifications is inherently unsound, so variability must be expected in the resulting predictions. The efficiency of one's methods of hand evaluation will be paramount, and many experts have sought to improve that aspect with specific rules including controls and distributional features. The Losing Trick Count is one such method.

Mike Lawrence and Anders Wirgren presented five hands that illustrated that the number of total tricks in a deal may vary greatly depending on the distribution of a side. The North-South hands were fixed and the East-West distribution was allowed to vary within the constraints of the fixed distribution of sides. Here are the North-South hands:

North
♠ K 7 6
♡ A K 7 3
◇ 7 4 2
♣ A 8 4

South
♠ A Q J 10 9 3
♡ 8 5 2
◇ 9
♣ K Q 6

The side is 9-7-4-6 with 26 HCP. The Losing Trick Count is 20. There are eleven easy tricks in a contract of 5♠, but we are told that the opponents have competed to the five-level in diamonds. The question posed by the authors is this: should South double or take the push if vulnerable against not? Is the Law of Total Tricks a reasonable guide for these five deals?

Here are the five East-West hands they provide for comparison. We provide the Losing Trick Count at the bottom of each deal.

Deal I

♠ 4 2	♠ 8 5
♡ Q J 10 9	♡ 6 4
◇ A Q 8 6	◇ K J 10 5 3
♣ 5 3 2	♣ J 10 9 7
8 losers	8 losers

Deal II

♠ 4 2	♠ 8 5
♡ Q J 10 9	♡ 6 4
◇ A Q 8 6 5	◇ K J 10 3
♣ 3 2	♣ J 10 9 7 5
7 losers	8 losers

Deal III

♠ 4 2	♠ 8 5
♡ Q J 10 9	♡ 6 4
◇ A Q 8 6 5 3	◇ K J 10
♣ 2	♣ J 10 9 7 5 3
6 losers	8 losers

Deal IV

♠ 4 2	♠ 8 5
♡ Q J 10 9 4	♡ 6
◇ A Q 8 6 5	◇ K J 10 3
♣ 2	♣ J 10 9 7 5 2
6 losers	7 losers

Deal V

♠ 4	♠ 8 5 2
♡ Q J 10 9 4	♡ 6
◇ A Q 8 6 5 3	◇ K J 10
♣ 2	♣ J 10 9 7 5 3
5 losers	8 losers

The playability of the contract in diamonds depends largely on the quality of the West hand. The raw loser count has been lowered because of the prime fit in trumps. The number of losers in the East-West hands varies from sixteen to thirteen, so one expects a wide range in the results of the play. The relative probability of occurrence depends on the shapes.

	I	II	III	IV	V
♠	2 - 2	2 - 2	2 - 2	2 - 2	1 - 3
♡	4 - 2	4 - 2	4 - 2	5 - 1	5 - 1
◇	4 - 5	5 - 4	6 - 3	5 - 4	6 - 3
♣	3 - 4	2 - 5	1 - 6	1 - 6	1 - 6
Frequency	54%	33%	7%	4%	2%
Total Tricks	17	18	19	20	22

From the relative frequency of these various shapes, it can be seen that Deals I and II constitute a frequency of occurrence of 87%. For the great majority of cases with these five configurations, the Law of Total Tricks offers a good estimate, and South should double for penalty. This corresponds to the advice often given, that 'the five-level belongs to the opponents.' Deal III is borderline, and South should bid on to 5♠ if vulnerable against not. Deals IV and V are the exceptions to the general rule and South should bid on since the penalty will not be adequate to compensate for the lost game bonus.

In only a small minority of the hands (1 in 16) will The LAW provide bad advice. The average number of total tricks for this set is 17.7, so on average the LAW is correct to predict eighteen total tricks. Sometimes, not often, a disaster occurs. Think of it this way: if a line of play can provide a 15/16 chance of success, you would be wrong not to take it on the argument that sometimes it will fail. No matter how refined one's guess, there will always be some degree of danger due to the inherent uncertainty.

Beware of Quacks

It would be useful if one could judge consistently when to take a pessimistic view and bid cautiously within the guidelines of the LAW. Detailed statistical analysis would be a great help in uncovering the main indicators. Experts have given us some advice, the easiest to follow being, 'Beware of quacks in the short suits.' Vernes observed that there were more tricks to be expected if both trump suits contained the top four honors. What of normal trump suits that contain the majority of HCP in the suit? As we have seen previously, this is the normal condition, so one would expect a normal result, that is, the LAW holds. Based on this reasoning, one would expect fewer tricks when the trump suits are deficient in HCP. Is it so? Statistics would guide us further.

Goren's guidelines for hand evaluation based on HCP don't distinguish where the HCP lie. The advice is this: count the HCP, then add distribution points as follows: 1 for a doubleton and 2 for a singleton. Thus, for Goren, both these hands have 14 points.

Hand I	HCP	Departures	Hand II	HCP	Departures
♠ A x x x x	4	- 1	♠ A K x x x	7	+2
♡ Q J	3	+1	♡ x x	0	- 2
◇ K x x x	3	- 1	◇ K Q x x	5	+1
♣ Q x	2	0	♣ x x	0	-2
8 losers			6 losers		

The departures from normal expectations are modest at best. Obviously from the losing trick count, the hand on the left, where the departures in the long suits are negative, is much less powerful than the hand on the right, where the departures in the longer suits are positive. With regard to the LAW, the presence of the ♡Q and the ♣Q in Hand I preclude the opposition achieving purity in their presumed long suits. This is a hand for applying the LAW conservatively.

Hand I has close to a normal correlation between HCP and suit length, whereas Hand II is overloaded in favor of the longer suits, 12 HCP to none. In addition, it retains the possibility of trump purity for both sides. This is a hand to bid strongly in expectation of a greater number of tricks than indicated by the LAW.

The same logic applies when bidding a weak hand in competition. Raises that are based on a normal holding in the trump suit can be made with the LAW as a basis for reasonable expectation, but raises on hands that are weak in the trump suit are dangerous, as the total number of tricks available may be fewer than expected normally. There is a double whammy effect. Whatever HCP are held in the short suits are defensive in nature and tend to reduce the number of tricks available to the opponents playing in their best fit.

A fine discussion of Vernes' results and the relationship between the LAW and the Losing Trick Count is presented in *Bridge: TNT and Competitive Bidding* (1981) by Dick Payne and Joe Amsbury, an early discussion that has been neglected by analysts. There is need for much more numerical evidence to be added to this topic.

Probability in Competition

The noblest answer unto such,
Is kindly silence when they brawl
in *After-Thought* by Alfred, Lord Tennyson (1809-1892)

As with declarer play, one should use Jaynes' Principle as a guide during competitive bidding. The technique is to assume a rough estimate of how the cards lie based on what is most likely given the partial knowledge available. As the bidding proceeds, one adjusts according to what has been disclosed. Estimates are expected to change, sometimes radically, but it is easier to adjust from a central position where necessary rather than start without assumptions and make a blind guess at the end. Furthermore, a partnership has an understanding as to what each partner expects and so can adjust during the auction in accordance with that understanding.

We begin an auction with the assumption that we have an eight-card fit or better, an 83% chance before anyone looks at the cards. The Law of Total Tricks indicates that if both sides have an eight-card fit, they should be prepared to bid to the two-level when the HCP are more or less evenly divided. If the opponents have an 8+-card fit, the odds are 8:1 that your side also has an eight-card fit. If the opponents deny an eight-card fit during the auction, then the odds are 2:1 that your side has at best a seven-card fit, so balancing against a 1NT bid in competition is somewhat dangerous.

The most common division of sides is 8765, occurring on 23.5% of the deals. Each side has this pattern, so no advantage can be assumed in that regard; however, the distributions of the sides can be different, with the advantage going to the side that has more ruffing power. This translates into the number of cards held in the short suits, an observation developed fully by Lawrence and Wirgren in *I Fought The Law of Total Tricks*.

To estimate one's chances at the beginning, one may place partner with the most likely shape, 4432, and place his cards so that the side is 8765. No guarantees, of course, but it is a sensible start based on a likely occurrence. Here are three examples for which the opening bid is 1♠.

	I	II	III
♠	5 - 3	5 - 2	5 - 2
♡	3 - 4	4 - 4	4 - 4
◇	3 - 2	2 - 4	3 - 3
♣	2 - 4	2 - 3	1 - 4
Combinations	C	C	(2/3)C

For Case I, there are no fears of missing an eight-card fit in spades, so let's consider Cases II and III where the eight-card fit occurs in a second suit.

West	North	East	South
1♠	2♣	dbl	3♣

The double relates to holding four hearts, so in Cases II and III, the opening bidder is assured of an eight-card fit in hearts, the only question being whether to take the push to the three-level. The Law of Total Tricks taken by itself suggests not competing to the three-level when the Total Trumps equal 16. This is the type of decision that is treated in detail by Lawrence and Wirgren. Their advice is to look at the number of cards in each partner's shortest suits before deciding. In Case III, opener expects a total of three cards in the two shortest suits, so it is worthwhile considering a bid of 3♡. In Case II, there are too many losers to contemplate bidding on, so a pass is appropriate.

In Defiance of The LAW?

> Mrs. Bertram: *That sounds like nonsense, my dear.*
> Mr. Bertram: *Maybe so, my dear; but it may be very good law for all that.*
> - from *Guy Mannering* by Sir Walter Scott (1771-1832)

A present difficulty in competitive auctions is that there seems to be no way to punish transgressors who overbid in the hope that both sides can take enough tricks that overbidding becomes worthwhile. One bridge writer has recently suggested playing more frequently for penalties by having responder pass at the two-level with hands that contain invitational values even when holding three-card support for partner's five-card major suit. This is contrary to the LAW, which suggests that a side should compete to the level that represents the number of trumps held; where eight trumps are assured, one is advised to bid at the two-level. In his article 'The Cooperative Pass', appearing in *The Bridge World* (Sept 2007), Philip Martin suggests otherwise. After

West	North	East	South
1♡	2◇	?	

He suggests a pass with

♠ A 3   ♡ J 8 7   ◇ K J 10 3   ♣ K 9 7 5

The idea is that the opening bidder will not balance if he holds at least a doubleton in diamonds. The opponents may not have found their best fit, in spades. If the opener doesn't balance, the deal may be played in 2◇, in which case the defending side has a better chance of scoring well, as 2◇ is surely going down. It is unLAWful to balance with a double with length in diamonds, as the opponents are likely to be able to escape to an eight-card fit in spades.

To compete further on moderate trumps risks a minus score, says Martin, in agreement with our previous observation that adequate support for hearts is Q-x-x. Is this a sign that the pendulum has begun to swing back towards trapping, seeking to take advantage of an adverse lie of the trump suit, or is merely a sign of frustration at being outbid by aggressive opponents with the LAW behind them?

This suggestion can be tested using computer simulations with real deals. For all sequences that begin as suggested above, one may require responder to pass with a poor three-card raise and four cards to two honors in the overcaller's suit. Then one can track what happens subsequently. The data would, of course, be flawed insofar as the computer's actions do not match human reactions in the same situation. Although imperfect, such a simulation could provide some grounds for accepting Martin's suggestion, which is most suited to a system of limited opening bids.

Finally, one notes that Martin is not in defiance of the LAW, but is following it when he caters for a situation where the overcaller's suit is not well supported by his partner's hand. The opposition may have an eight-card fit, but not in diamonds, so if left alone, they are not going to play in their best fit.

A Consultative Double

Progress may have been all right once, but it has gone on too long.
- Ogden Nash (1902-1971)

Marshall Miles in his 1992 book *Stronger Competitive Bidding* comments that it pays to assign meanings to doubles that occur frequently rather than adopt *beautiful descriptive bids* that seldom arise. There is a paradox in expecting partner to make a good decision on the basis of a nebulous double when good decisions are based on exact information. The 'do-something-sensible' double is a trap. However, a consultative double is a sensible approach if partner has a clear-cut alternative given the information available from the action to that point. To be considered 'consultative', the primary attribute of the double must be that it provides useful information. (The same is true of defensive signals.) A partner cannot make a sensible decision unless he has been given information on which to base it. The conclusion is that the meaning of doubles, being based on alternatives, will be well defined, but that the definition will vary with the auction. The common ground will be that of expectations based on probability considerations.

The concept of doubling to provide one's partner with an alternative has many applications, one of which came to light in the 'Marks and Comments' feature conducted by Sally Brock in the August 2007 issue of *Bridge Magazine*. Experts were asked to choose a call for the West hand given below, North-South vulnerable, IMPs scoring:

♠ K 10 3
♡ 7
◊ A 9 8 7 3
♣ A 10 9 2

West	North	East	South
1◊	1♡	1♠	4♡
?			

Experts' Advice:	pass (14)	4♠ (5)	dbl (1)

Only one expert, John Armstrong, voted for Double, the reason being that he knew the correct answer from experience. He and Graham Kirby, playing Precision, were for years a strong partnership on British international teams. It was Kirby who doubled on this hand many years ago; Armstrong was able to correct to 4♠, which made on this layout:

Kirby	Armstrong	Totals	Hypothetical
♠ K 10 3	♠ A Q x x x	8	♠ A x x x x
♡ 7	♡ x x x	4	♡ x x x
◊ A 9 8 7 3	◊ K x x	8	◊ K x
♣ A 10 9 2	♣ x x	6	♣ Q x x

The meaning of the double was 'I want to bid 4♠, but I am happy if you prefer to defend.' As Sally Brock commented, this was a way to have your cake and eat it, too.

Without such an agreement, many of those experts who passed held the view that they weren't strong enough to bid 4♠ on minimal values, but expressed the hope that their partner might take further action with a double, in which case a bid of 4♠ would be justified. Thus there was no way to take a vulnerable penalty even if East's double was penalty-oriented and showed defensive values behind the long suit. The hand on the far right is a possible penalty double with 8-4-7-7. There the penalty could be substantial, but there would be no way to achieve it. At any rate, East would have passed on the actual hand, and a game would have been missed at minimal cost to the preemptor.

The idea that one may pass a consultative double for penalty is against the LAW when the opponents have bid and raised a suit in a partscore situation. Thus, the double will often be pulled unless the opposition have made the gross error of bluffing on very little, certainly a possibility. The defensive value of such doubles is that they suggest a penalty double on the next round if the opponents try to steal the hand.

Ms. Lee Regrets...

A well-ordered mind is a tranquil mind.
- Marcus Aurelius (121-180)

In her blog at www.bridgeblogging.com, Linda Lee wistfully voiced some regret concerning one of her decisions when Canada faced Germany in the quarterfinals of the 2007 Venice Cup. How could she have guessed the winning action on

Board 26 after highly charged competition from the famous pair of Auken and von Arnim? In fact, only one player in the field, it seems, found the right answer, so it is worthwhile to investigate this interesting deal further from the point of view of available information.

First, here is what happened on the same deal in the Bermuda Bowl when Italy faced South Africa. If you expected fireworks, you would have been surprised.

Dealer: East
Both Vulnerable

Fantoni
♠ Q 5
♡ A K Q 8 7 5 3
◇ Q 8
♣ A 7

Holman
♠ K J 10 9 7 4 2
♡ 4 2
◇ 9
♣ 10 4 2

Cope
♠ 8 6 3
♡ 9 6
◇ A K 4 3 2
♣ Q 8 3

Nunes
♠ A
♡ J 10
◇ J 10 7 6 5
♣ K J 9 6 5

West	North	East	South
Holman	Fantoni	Cope	Nunes
		pass	2◇¹
pass	2♡	pass	3♣
pass	3♠	pass	4♠
pass	4NT	pass	5◇
pass	5NT	pass	6◇
pass	7♡	all pass	

1. 10-13, unbalanced, diamonds.

South Africa was the surprise team of the tournament, frequent employers of semi-preemptive pressure bidding, but here Holman went the other way with a passive-aggressive pass over 2◇. It worked wonders, as the Italians propelled themselves into a hopeless grand slam. Cope was deceived into not doubling.

The Venice Cup match of Great Britain versus China produced the highly competitive auctions that one has come to expect when both sides hold long major suits.

West	North	East	South
Liu	Dhondy	Wang	Smith
		pass	pass
2◇*	3♡	3♠	4♡
4♠	5♡	all pass	

Liu began with a Multi 2◇ (weak two in a major), then gave herself a raise, a dangerous practice, but Dhondy was not to be denied her right to declare the hand. The result was a normal 650. Apparently there was no way to suggest the possibility of defending 4♠, a reasonable possibility with the two queen-doubletons representing defensive values in short suits. Some partnerships have a useful agreement in this situation: a pass forces a double, after which North may pull to 5♡ to show slam interest, whereas a direct double is cooperative.

The winning action was found by the South player for China on the following auction: her penalty double picked up a score of +1100.

West	North	East	South
Teshome	Zhang	Jagger	Gu
		pass	pass
3♠	4♡	4♠	dbl
all pass			

The defense was ridiculously easy: ♡A, ♡K, ♣A, ♣J, ♣K and a fourth club to promote the ♠Q in the North hand.

South players in a similar situation, like Linda Lee, may look back and wonder if they, too, might have found that lucrative double. The singleton ♠A is both an offensive and defensive asset, but the jacks and tens are purely defensive in nature. Surely 4♠ will be defeated, but will it be enough?

The problem is that there is insufficient information available to be certain, but even at this late stage, there may be ways to exchange information with partner and come to a decision based on the joint holdings. Obviously, a double cannot show a trump stack, but it can show a hand with defensive potential, leaving a bid of 4NT for takeout. The ♠A is a huge asset on defense, as it enables one to adjust the defensive strategy if the opening lead is a disappointment.

If a double in this position could be construed as cooperative, North with two black queens in the short suits and a 7222 shape would be happy enough to leave it in. From North's point of view, the ♠Q is not expected to take a trick, but there is an indication that it may supplement South's holding. The anticipated opening heart lead may hold the trick, so the follow-up can be adjusted according to what appears in the dummy. With five losers, the hand pretty well conforms to what is expected from the bidding, so the defense should progress smoothly. Such decisions are too much of a guess to be left to one partner alone.

CHAPTER 14

BIDDING SYSTEMS:
INFORMATION AND COSTS

Most contracts can be made. However,
most contracts can also be defeated....
from *Play Better Bridge* by Rixi Markus (1910 - 1992)

In this final chapter, we come at last to a topic that so far has been neglected in this book, which is the consideration of probable cost versus probable gain. This critical factor in decision-making depends on the method of scoring. The Bob's Blind Rule approach is most suitable to matchpoint scoring where the frequency of success is an overriding consideration. Traditional advice in bridge texts is slanted more towards IMP play where the safety of the contract is foremost in the mind of a declarer. There is no need here to repeat the lessons they provide with regard to card play. Therefore, we shall consider more fully cost versus gain in the context of bidding.

The early bridge masters were schooled in rubber bridge. As many veteran players have noted, playing for stakes you cannot afford is the quickest way to learn, because a minus score represents money flowing the other way. It is natural then that early bridge writers had safety at the forefront of their thinking. This attitude prevails at IMP scoring where it is not uncommon to see an expert in a partscore play with extreme caution to score eight tricks and a +110 result when at the other table declarer in game goes all out to take ten tricks and score +420.

At rubber bridge, there is a continuity from one deal to the next. A partscore is worth more than its face value. Playing in a minor-suit partial is useful, especially when that represents the safest partscore. Even 2NT is a respectable vulnerable contract, as 120 below the line with 30 above puts pressure on the opponents to prevent the completion of the rubber, often with disastrous consequences to them. Nowadays duplicate bridge dominates the scene and this has had a profound effect on how probability is applied. At duplicate scoring, the result on each board stands on its own without carry-overs, so taking twelve easy tricks in a game contract is more than merely a missed opportunity for even greater profit — it can represent a real loss. Scoring nine tricks in a contract of 2NT must usually be considered something of a disaster. Minor-suit contracts serve as a last resort. This affects one's approach to bidding.

In the middle of the twentieth century, Rixi Markus was a familiar figure at the rubber bridge tables of famous clubs in London, yet her approach was suitable for today's duplicate game. As is evident from her quote cited above, she saw the game as fiercely competitive, each side being pushed to the limit of safety. This is in line with today's reliance on the Law of Total Tricks to justify taking chances in order to push opponents to a losing position. She did not imagine that the purpose of bidding was to rest in a safe haven. 'Bid boldly, play safe' was her adopted motto. She bid her games and slams, leaving it up to the defenders to find a way to set the contracts. If they did, Rixi could shrug off the result, because she did not expect to be successful every time.

Nonetheless, perfectionists often treat failing games or slams as errors. They consider deals separately rather than in the overall context of the totality of deals played. Taken alone, a failed game may be considered a consequence of a bidding error, but in the context of probable gain versus probable loss, in the long run there should be frequent occasions when a voluntarily bid game will fail. Obviously if you never fail in game you are not bidding enough close games. The question then becomes: what is the optimum failure rate? To consider this point, let's look at some results from a recent tournament involving the best American players.

In June 2008, the Nickell Team won the USBF trials for representation in the Beijing world championships. The anchor pair of Eric Rodwell and Jeff Meckstroth played 345 deals, so their results may serve as a guide to a successful strategy. They declared a game contract 101 times, a 29% rate. They failed 33 times, a 1 in 3 failure rate. From this evidence, we conclude that bidding a failing game contract at a rate of 1 in 10 boards is very good bridge.

Their opponents bid game on 87 boards, 14 fewer than Meckwell and a 25% rate, but it was not swings produced by the different contracts that proved decisive. On those boards, the IMPs flowed equally in both directions, sometimes a big swing for Meckwell being offset by many small swings to their opponents. The difference in favor of aggression was probably a psychological one, as the defenders were conscious of the fact that they would frequently be put to the test of defeating a close game contract that might not be bid in the other room.

Meckwell's greatest gain was declaring a contract of 3NT: 31 times with success, gaining 110 IMPs, and 9 times with failure, losing 28 IMPs. The swing per board was roughly 3 IMPs in either case, but the high success rate in 3NT when played in both rooms provided the margin of victory in two of their three matches.

We may conclude that a paradoxical situation exists: you want to bid accurately in order to maintain a fairly high rate of success in game, but you do not wish to give away information that would help the defense defeat the close contracts. The conflict is between maximizing the potential gain and maximizing the amount of information transmitted during the auction. Designers of bidding systems are caught up in this conflict. Rixi Markus did not advocate a complex bidding system, although she recognized its value in the hands of experts. The secret perhaps lies in having a complex set of agreements available, as do Meckwell, then choosing not to use them when the situation demands simplicity. Those who bid crudely without the benefit of an informative system do not have this option.

Those who play a two-over-one system without the benefit of limited opening bids must treat each game-going hand as having slam potential, which requires informative exchanges at the early stages of bidding before appropriate limits are established. Long auctions to a game contract provide defenders with useful information. Those who open light within a Big Club system that immediately establishes limited resources can bid crudely to game with some hope that a slam has not been missed in the process. They have the advantage of the lesser risk when no slam is viable.

When Scores Are Relative

You should always bid to the level equal to the combined number of trumps held by your side.

Try not to let the opponents play at a level equal to their number of trumps.
- excerpts from *To Bid Or Not to Bid* by Larry Cohen

Whereas in early days the emphasis in bidding was on what you thought your side could make, in modern times the rationale has changed to include what you think the opposition can make. In order to win, one must occasionally beat par and one way of achieving this is to push the opponents beyond their level of safety. This should be attempted even when one's side does not possess the majority of the HCP. Larry Cohen's two maxims, quoted above, grossly exaggerate the importance of the total number of trumps relative to the deal as a whole, but they set the tone in what is now understood to be a finite interdependent world.

If one thinks along the lines above, the emphasis shifts from HCP to LTC (losing trick count). Although with a 4432 shape the probability of finding a 4-4 fit in one of the long suits is 60%, there is no shortage to enhance the loser count. This common shape is classified as a notrump hand. With a 5431 hand, the probability of having an 8+-card fit in one of the longer suits is 74%; one expects the singleton will enhance one's chances as declarer, and consequently the LTC becomes the primary method of hand evaluation. This leads to opening hands 'light' in HCP content, a common practice that still baffles some conservatives, even though light opening bids have a long history.

Observing a roomful of bridge players at play in my club, the conclusion that here we have a gathering of fervent admirers of the poet, Ovid, is not obvious, yet it is so. They have engraved on their hearts his saying, '*Media tutissimus ibis*' (*One goes most safely in the middle*). They adhere to the current bidding fashion, which is UGF, Undisciplined 2/1 Game Forcing. This may not be the best approach taken in isolation, but they know that if the auction lands them in a bad contract at least they can expect an average result. The aim is to minimize cost rather than maximize gain.

Kludge Rhymes with Fudge

> *I bet the human brain is a kludge.*
> - Marvin Minsky

kludge: 1) An ill-assorted collection of poorly matched parts forming a distressing whole.

2) A quick fix to a computer system that is inefficient, inelegant, or even unfathomable, but which nevertheless works, more or less.

We have already introduced Dr Minsky's views on the patchwork evolution of the human brain. In that regard, I observe that the North American male is currently being kludged from tough cowboy to tender nanny. Will social pressures be enough to effect a more or less successful conversion over ten short generations or will random acts of violence continue to mar the landscape?

As a computer scientist specializing in artificial intelligence, Minsky is familiar with the patches to which the second definition refers. All PC users are familiar with the ever-evolving Windows operating system. Outwardly, from version to version, the basic functions seem to operate in a similar fashion, since each new version must remain more or less compatible with earlier ones, but upgrades are required to accommodate unanticipated new functions, such as internet communications. At the core, Windows remains its old inefficient self, susceptible to penetration by killer viruses.

Bidding systems present us with classic examples of kludges. The evolution of the species is not through fundamental restructuring, but rather through the addition of multitudinous conventional patches to cover up weaknesses. The Support Double is one such patch that advances a pair's ability to compete against interference. On the other hand, Jacoby Transfers represented the onset of a fundamental change towards relay bids, evolution away from the natural to the artificial, from the inefficient to the efficient. A system based on relays is a fundamental step upward in the development of better bidding systems. The general playing public wedded to natural bidding is getting left behind and, it appears, is in the process of becoming extinct.

Do Bidding Systems Make a Difference?

Only he who finds empiricism irksome is driven to method.
- Johann Wolfgang von Goethe (1749-1832)

David Bird has commented (gloomily?) that bidding systems are like religions: one sticks to what one is born into. Of course, he refers to the masses. Recent public opinion surveys show that most Brits are non-religious but do believe in Heaven; it's just that they can't agree on how to get there. They are not happy unless they are miserable. Otherwise, why rebuild a modern theater by the Thames with no seats in the pit and no roof to cover it?

A bidding system is not, however, a religion; it is the language by which partners communicate. The meanings of the bids are sometimes in doubt, but the frequency of the bids determines the amount of information they contain. Some authors have the opinion that a good bid is one that may lead to several different conclusions; that is, a bid that is flexible. Nebulous doubles in competition are a breed of this type. Such vague bids, by not being specific, are less informative than closely defined bids. The exchange of information has parallels in bidding and cardplay — the more possible sequences in defenders' play, the less likely is a particular division of the cards. A highly unusual bid, like a highly unusual play, is informative. Commonplace activity is not greatly informative, because it is much to be expected.

Although some argue that languages don't make a difference, they do. How one defines the cost of communication determines how the system operates. We'll demonstrate this below, but first, here is a comment by a British expert, Eric Crowhurst, appearing in his *Precision Bidding in Acol* (1974):

> Fourteen world's championships in the last seventeen years is a record that is unlikely to be ever equalled, and since the Italians have employed a series of big club systems throughout this period, the doubtful conclusion has been drawn that therein lies the key to their success... there is no evidence to suggest that they would not have won all their fourteen world's championships if they had adopted a natural bidding system like Acol and developed and analyzed it with their customary thoroughness.

It is true there is no evidence of the type alluded to, nor will there ever be, but that is not a good reason for ignoring the evidence we do have before us. Why not adopt a winning approach? Howard Schenken, the greatest American player of his era, after losing to the Italians, came to an entirely different conclusion from Crowhurst — that the Italians won because of their bidding systems. The Italians themselves thought as much.

So what is it that makes the difference? We shall show that it is something that is often overlooked in a discussion of bidding systems — it is the *pass rate*, a measure of how often your side opens the bidding. The lower your pass rate, the more aggressive you are as a player.

Determine Your Pass Rate Comfort Zone

Is it nothing to you, all ye that pass…?
Lamentations 1:12

Here is a test you can perform on a rainy afternoon to determine the pass rate with which you are personally comfortable. From the printouts of three 32-board sessions of computer dealt hands, take the ninety-six hands that were dealt to South. Divide these equally into two categories of forty-eight hands each, good and bad. Now divide each of the forty-eight hands into good and bad, yielding four categories of twenty-four hands each. Lastly, divide those equally to yield eight categories of twelve hands each. This gives you a profile as follows:

Category	Classification	Category	Classification
1	best	5	not-so-bad
2	good	6	poor
3	decent	7	bad
4	so-so	8	worst

If your pass rate is 50%, you would pass on hands in Categories 5-8 and open the bidding with Categories 1-4. This is considered somewhat aggressive. If you would bid on half of the Category 4 hands, your pass rate is a mainstream conservative 56%. If you would bid on half of the Category 5 hands, your pass rate is 44%, which is considered fairly aggressive. The theoretically optimum pass rate, strictly from an information standpoint, is approximately that which is achieved by bidding on all hands in Categories 1 through 5. This is considered overly aggressive, but has been achieved at times in matches of over 100 hands.

Having performed the test and gauged your preferred style, don't fight it: adopt a system that fits your natural tendency. Keep partner informed. I have done this test and have found my own tendency to be on the side of aggression. Most systems have you opening with good hands and passing the obviously bad hands, so the pass rate is determined by what you do with the middle categories. My own guideline is to open all hands with 12 or more HCP. With less than 12 HCP, open all hands with fewer than eight losers, and most of those hands that have eight losers and three or more controls. Some hands with nine losers and four controls might be opened.

My test over ninety-six hands produced the following hands as the critical cases. See how many you would like to open, non-vulnerable, if there were a suitably descriptive bid available.

1	**2**	**3**	**4**
♠ A Q 9 8 2	♠ K 10 9 8 4 3	♠ A 10 9 4 3	♠ Q J 8 6 4 3
♡ A 9 7 6 5	♡ 6 4	♡ A J 8 7 4 3	♡ 7
◇ 2	◇ 7 3	◇ 6 5	◇ 6 5
♣ 7	♣ A Q 6	♣ —	♣ K Q 8 6

5	**6**	**7**	**8**
♠ A 9 6 2	♠ A J 10 9	♠ 10	♠ K 9 6
♡ —	♡ Q 8 6 4 3 2	♡ A 5 4	♡ A 8 5 4 3 2
◇ A 8 2	◇ K J 7	◇ K 10 7 5	◇ A 9 4
♣ Q 10 9 8 6 5	♣ —	♣ A 7 5 3 2	♣ 3

9	**10**	**11**	**12**
♠ J 8 7 5 4 2	♠ K Q 5 4 2	♠ —	♠ A 6 5 3 2
♡ K J 9	♡ —	♡ Q 9 8 6 4	♡ A 6 3
◇ 7 6	◇ Q 10 8 5 4	◇ 10 3	◇ 7 3
♣ A 10	♣ 8 5 2	♣ A J 9 7 6 3	♣ K 4 3

13	**14**	**15**	**16**
♠ 9 7 3	♠ A 8	♠ 10 8 7	♠ K 9 8
♡ Q	♡ 10 9 6 3	♡ K Q J 2	♡ 7 6 4 3
◇ A J 10 7 5	◇ Q 8 2	◇ A 9 5 4	◇ K 8
♣ K 10 7 4	♣ K Q 9 8	♣ J 8	♣ K J 9 8

17	**18**	**19**	**20**
♠ 7 5	♠ A 10 9 3	♠ A K 7 3	♠ K J 9 7 6
♡ 10 7	♡ A 10 8 3 2	♡ 8 6	♡ 10 6
◇ A K 8 7 5	◇ 4	◇ J 10 7 6 3	◇ A 10 7 6
♣ Q 10 4 3	♣ 8 5 2	♣ 4 3	♣ 5 4

21	**22**	**23**	**24**
♠ A 8 5	♠ A Q 9 6	♠ K Q 7 6	♠ A K J 8 3
♡ J 9 7 4 3	♡ J 6 2	♡ A 9 8	♡ 8 7
◇ A 7 6	◇ K 10 4	◇ Q 8 2	◇ J 9 5
♣ 10 7	♣ J 7 6	♣ 7 6 2	♣ 7 5 3

There are another thirty-six hands in my sample that will be opened since they contain 12+ HCP. Add to that number the number of hands from these twenty-four on which you would open the bidding. The bid rate is that number divided by 96. The pass rate is 1 minus the bid rate. On my test, I would have liked to open on twenty of these twenty-four hands, non-vulnerable, so my pass rate is 41%. If I had chosen to open on all twenty-four hands, my pass rate of 37.5% would have been near the information-theoretic optimum that maximizes the contribution of a single call to the overall entropy of the system.

You should also ask yourself whether there are hands you would open in third seat, but not in first or second seat. If there are a significant number of these, your bidding system cannot be considered seamless, so adjustments in the response structure are required. The Drury convention is one obvious choice for a third-hand opening bid structure.

Average Information Related to the Pass Rate

Determine the pass rate and you know whether a system can be classified as conservative or aggressive. Conservative pairs will pass on more than 56% of the hands dealt, whereas aggressive pairs will pass on fewer than 50% of the hands dealt them. The two types have a different estimate of how costly it is to pass. One of obvious modern change has been to reduce the pass rate by altering the meaning of two-level openings, removing them from the strong category to the weak twos advocated by Howard Schenken.

To see how a lower pass rate yields a more informative bidding system, let's look at a simplified strong notrump model for which the constructive bids are limited to 1♣ through 1♠. Opener passes, bids a strong 1NT, or bids his best suit. Bids at the two-level are ignored, but as these are rare in most systems, their omission is not mathematically significant for demonstration purposes. We look at three pass rates and their effect on the average amount of information (the entropy) transmitted in an opening call.

Type	pass	1♣	1♦	1♥	1♠	1NT	Average Info
			Probability of Choice				
Conservative	0.56	0.10	0.10	0.10	0.10	0.04	1.00
Aggressive	0.48	0.12	0.12	0.12	0.12	0.04	1.09
Very Aggressive	0.40	0.14	0.14	0.14	0.14	0.04	1.16

A conservative system is informative when the hand is opened with a bid, but uninformative when a pass is made. That makes sense as regards cost effectiveness. Why give away information if you don't rate to declare the hand, some ask. In a very aggressive system, the suit bids are less informative, but the information contained in a pass call more than compensates. Overall, the very aggressive approach yields more information by 16%. The hope is that one may compete more efficiently if the opponents enter the auction. If partner has passed, he must have a very bad hand, leaving one more freedom for preemptive action.

Bidding Space: The Basic Cost of Information

An opening call transmits information about the cards held by the player, so can be thought of as the message, selected from a small number of possible messages, that most closely describes the hand he or she holds. Each call has associated with it a probability of being selected as the most appropriate descriptor, and, as some call must be selected, the sum of these probabilities is unity. The designer of a bidding system normally begins by defining which hands fall within the category of a given bid, the consequence being that this definition automatically determines (in theory) the probability that this call will be chosen at the table.

The information in a bid has an inverse relationship to the probability that the given bid will be selected from all possible bids. The rarer the bid, the more the information transmitted; the more frequent the bid, the less it conveys. We do not need to know what a given bid means in order to calculate the amount of information it contains. Also, in the initial stages, we do not need to estimate how useful this information is.

The average information for a system of bids, termed the entropy, equals the sum of the information in each call multiplied by its probability of occurrence. To communicate efficiently, a system must possess the property of high entropy, meaning that the calls must be designed so that on average they transmit information to a high degree. The principle of maximum entropy is well established and methods are available for determining how to maximize average information under various constraints — in other words, how to assign probabilities to the various calls for maximum effectiveness in this regard.

Strong Jumps Must Be Informative

When she had passed, it seemed like the ceasing of exquisite music.
from *The Day is Done* by
Henry Wadsworth Longfellow (1807-1882)

Strong jumps to game are expensive because they use up bidding space and put pressure on one's partner. System designers do well to avoid them unless they are narrowly defined. Goren strong two-bids are things of the past. The two-level is now used for opening with weak hands, so the cost in bidding space is turned into an asset when the hand belongs to the opponents. In such circumstances, one wishes to open at the two-level as often as possible, removing from the pass category suitable distributional candidates. A recent expert trend is towards two-suited two-level openings, as the hands for them occur more frequently than traditional weak twos. Of course, the more a bid is employed, the less information it conveys, so a weak, wide-ranging jump bid can backfire when the hand belongs to the side that has preempted. Again we see there is a compromise involved.

When one part of a system is changed, the effects are felt through a range of bids. One effect that crops up with regularity is that a simple opening bid made on a four-loser hand leads to problems. Here is an example from the English Ladies Trials in February 2008.

Duckworth		Cook
♠ A K 4		♠ 10
♡ K		♡ A 8 7 5 3
◇ A K Q 10 4 3		◇ 8 5
♣ K 9 4		♣ A J 6 5 2

Duckworth	Cook	
1◇	1♡	
3NT	pass	Making 520

In defense of Duckworth's action, a rebid of 3NT certainly describes the trick-taking potential of her hand, but it is very difficult for her partner to find a bid over 3NT. Jumping past twelve units of bidding space is not cost effective in a constructive auction. She could instead have lied and jump-shifted into 2♠. My major objection to this approach is that I know when I am lying, but how do I know when it's my partner who is exercising her option? Striving always to tell the truth is less complicated. On this hand, opening an under-strength 2♣ proved to be the lesser risk, as slam was easily bid at the other table after that beginning. One can imagine the questioning as Ms. Cook is brought before the Bridge Inquisition to explain her action.

'Of course, I knew Ducky had a four-loser hand, and I did recognize the fact I held two aces, but four minus two equals two, so there were two losers still, weren't there?'

'No, my dear, you are mistaken: four minus two does not equal two.'

This problem is not unique to Acol. In the February 2008 issue of the ACBL *Bridge Bulletin*, the same auction was presented in a quiz. Kerri Sanborn thought the following four-loser hand was a possibility:

♠ A 6 3   ♡ 3   ♢ A K Q 9 8 3 2   ♣ K 2

This would be her suggested auction in that case:

ACBL		Sanborn
♠ A 6 3		♠ J
♡ 3		♡ A K 10 9 6 5
♢ A K Q 9 8 3 2		♢ 7 4
♣ K 2		♣ A Q J 6

ACBL	Sanborn
1♢	1♡
3NT	5♣[1]
5♠	7NT

1. Ace-asking.

The fact that Sanborn feels the need to ask for aces implies uncertainty as to the requirements for the jump. I am not sure how one establishes hearts as trumps in the situation where opener has ♡Qx and responder is void in diamonds. The situation cries out for a redefinition within the system in which a less costly rebid by opener is forcing and opens the possibility of a useful exchange of information below the game level.

Information and Cost in Modern Systems

The Immutable Law: The more hands that can be described by a given bid, the less information the bid contains. A bid rarely used is ipso facto highly informative.

One cannot make decisions based solely on the probability of success, the reason being that cost also enters as a consideration. A bidding system is a compromise between maximizing the information content of bids (reliability and definition) while minimizing the cost — which touches upon many factors, some of them of a psychological nature.

The following table shows estimates of the frequency of various opening calls in five-card major systems employed by five famous partnerships participating in the Cap Gemini IMP Pairs Contest during the late 1990s. These represent five different ways of coping with cost.

	Opening Call						
	Pass	1♣	1♦	1♡	1♠	1NT	Other
Levy-Mari	.55	.12	.12	.07	.07	.05	.03
Zia-Forrester	.51	.13	.10	.07	.04	.04	.10
Chagas-Branco	.51	.10	.10	.08	.08	.07	.06
Berkowitz-Cohen	.46	.08	.16	.06	.06	.10	.09
Meckwell	.42	.09	.19	.07	.04	.09	.11

In bridge terms, the ultra-conservative French champions Alain Levy and Christian Mari were miles apart from the super-aggressive Jeff Meckstroth and Eric Rodwell. Levy-Mari were classically conservative preemptors who required full values for their constructive opening bids in first or second seat, whereas Meckwell stretched to open the bidding — they employed the Kamikaze No Trump, 9-12 HCP, non-vulnerable versus vulnerable. Berkowitz-Cohen used an aggressive system conservatively. Zia-Forrester played a conservative system aggressively, while the superb Brazilian pair of Gabriel Chagas and Marcelo Branco can be thought of as the epitome of the happy median. The three pairs with the lower pass rates employed the weak notrump, as is evident in the higher frequencies of that opening bid.

In his *Bridge World* article 'What Shall We Play?' (June, 1999), Larry Cohen argued against detailed bidding agreements, yet admits he and David Berkowitz had seventy pages of Precision system notes which had to be committed to memory. What he did emphasize is partnership predictability: be aggressive or be passive, but be consistent. Predictability bears upon the information content of a call: bidding consistently according to prior guidelines is a means of passing reliable information to one's partner. In other words, the looser the bidding, the less information it conveys. Intuitively, it would appear that the more informative a bidding sequence, the better the result should be on average, and Cohen's seventy pages appear to support this notion. On the other hand, if the claim is correct that modern bidding systems are more or less equally effective (or ineffective), the specific information a bid contains is of secondary importance.

Books on bidding systems emphasize the details of the opening bids and the ways to respond to them, while missing the most important characteristic of system, which is the pass rate. As far as winning a tournament is concerned, one has to do well on the deals on which one's side has begun with a pass in first or second seat if for no other reason that these deals far outnumber the deals for which the esoteric details of responding to other bids will make a difference. This point was made in my article 'The Winning Edge' that appeared in the 2000 December issue of *Bridge Magazine*, and the evidence from the Cap Gemini tournaments bears this out in dramatic fashion.

Consider the opening bid of 1♡ in the hands of the five expert pairs. The probability of opening 1♡ is very much uniform across the field, which means the amount of information in that bid is much the same for all pairs. Can a few details in the schedule of responses bear much fruit? Hardly likely, is it? There aren't that many hands that are opened with a bid of one of a major. On the other hand, a pass occurs about half of the time. Let's concentrate on that.

What Did They Gain by Passing?

A bid is a bid and a pass is a call, but both actions are messages that transmit information. The pass rate affects the information content of the system taken as a whole. Here is the information content of a pass for four famous pairs playing in the Cap Gemini. It is reasonable to ask how successful these pairs were when they began with a pass.

Pair	Pass Rate	Information	Relative Info
Levy-Mari	0.56	0.580	0.86
Chagas-Branco	0.51	0.673	1.0
Berkowitz-Cohen	0.46	0.777	1.16
Meckwell	0.42	0.892	1.33

The amount of information in an initial pass is -log (pass rate). Relative to the happy median, the Meckwell pass contains 33% more information and the Levy-Mari pass contains 14% less. How does this relate to the number of IMPs won or lost across the field of sixteen experts?

IMPs Won or Lost 1997-1998		
	Pass	Preempts
Levy-Mari	-43	-7
Chagas-Branco	60	16
Meckwell	46	9

The conservative French style was not conducive to gathering IMPs. This analyst prefers that Meckwell had achieved results superior to the Brazilians, but notes that Meckwell perhaps were too swingy in their approach. Certainly Chagas-Branco competed well using a moderate pass rate. Normally one does not expect to do well when both partners pass. On sixty-six deals of this type, Levy-Mari lost 40 IMPs. The Brazilians won 14 IMPs on forty-seven deals, a good margin above average. Meckwell gained 44 IMPs on forty-four deals, an amazing achievement.

Here is how three top competitors in the Cap Gemini scored using various opening calls for the two years, 1998-99, in which Zia-Forrester participated.

Registering a positive score against an expert field is a major accomplishment and a pair scoring 100 IMPs in the event was in contention for first place.

IMPs Won or Lost 1998-1999

	Pass	1♣	1◊	1♡	1♠	1NT	Total
Chagas-Branco	60	17	6	0	-5	24	113
Zia-Forrester	92	-41	-8	25	18	6	134
Berkowitz-Cohen	101	-38	12	13	-4	48	155

The consistent measure of success is how well the partnership did after an initial pass. The proportion of IMPs won after a pass by partner is high for Zia-Forrester, fully 69% of the IMPs won by them belong to this category. The partnership with the lowest pass rate did the best after they made their relatively infrequent call. Surprisingly, the Precision pair suffered a significant loss with their strong club bid, the part of their system that must have taken up many of their seventy pages of notes. Both weak-notrumpers significantly outscored Zia-Forrester's strong notrump opening.

The Cost of Passing

To conquer fear is the beginning of wisdom.
- Bertrand Russell (1872-1970)

It is often said by those of a cautious mind that the winners of matches are those who make fewer mistakes. What, however, is a mistake? Is it a reasonable play that happens to result in a bad score? No. Bridge is a game of probabilities, so playing with the odds doesn't always win. Often those who win in a long match are those who employ cost-effective bidding methods. It can be costly to pass. There is a tendency among commentators to overemphasize the risk that comes from the possibility that those who open light will be penalized. Here is an illustration from the finals of the 2007 Spingold with Russia-Poland versus the USA. The opening bid was light by most standards and one British commentator on BBO was moved to ask if anyone could explain the rationale behind it. The results on the board provided an answer. A question that might have been better asked is this: what is the cost of passing with a hand that could be opened?

One cost is self-inflicted: after passing in first or second seat, the passing player finds that in a constructive auction without interference he has been unable to express the full value of his 11 HCP. The temptation is to bid too high even if the value of the hand has not substantially increased. S. J. Simon, a writer with a high degree of insight into a bridge player's psychology, noted this tendency and formulated the Principle of the Lesser Risk: there is less risk in opening the bidding light than in passing and overbidding later. This is true of any system. So it proved.

$$\spadesuit A 5 \quad \heartsuit K 6 3 2 \quad \diamondsuit K J 5 \quad \clubsuit 10 6 4 2$$

Vulnerable, Rodwell opened this thin hand with the nebulous Precision 1◊. Meckstroth with a decent 12 HCP hand containing ♠Q98742 made a game try, which Rodwell declined to pursue. By the time they had reached the three-level they had exchanged enough information to realize they should have stopped two levels sooner. 'Aha!' thought some, 'now Meckwell will receive just punishment for their flagrant over-bidding.' Undoubled, Meckstroth went down two for a loss of 200.

With the same cards, Andrew Gromov began with a prudent pass and was due, so it seemed, to gain IMPs on the merit of the safety of his action. However, after Dubinin had shown six spades, Gromov considered he owed his partner a tentative raise. Dubinin took him seriously and suggested a contract of 3NT in the hope that his partner could supply stuffing in spades. Nickell, holding ♠KJ103 behind the long spades, doubled.

As it turned out, Gromov was able to escape for down one instead of the down two that was possible on the layout, so in the end the board was pushed at -200. No cost to either side, an inconclusive result, but a close call for the Russians, who had taken the greater risk. Of course, Gromov could have passed 2♠ for a small gain, but matches are not won by a series of small gains, especially against the aggressive Meckwell. Jeff Meckstroth has noted in his book *Win the Bermuda Bowl with Me* that it is better to start with an slight overbid rather than to pass. Whether or not Rodwell's control-rich 1◊ was 'slight' in the overbid category, one leaves to Meckwell to decide.

The Majors-First Movement

Let me stand to the main chance.
- John Lyly (1554-1606)

The principle of Majors-First is incorporated directly into the modern bidding structure. It is recognized in practice that overall the partnership that holds the most spades has an advantage that should be employed as quickly as possible. Minor suits are given less value in the scheme of things, an attitude related to the scoring system, not directly to the probabilities alone. The modern principle is described this way in *On Bidding* (the 1964 classic by Albert Morehead revised in 1990 by Alan Truscott and Phillip Alder):

The primary objective is to find an eight-card or better major-suit fit; but within that framework, it is more important to show the general strength of the hand than to show the location of the strength or the distribution of the hand.

We can interpret this advice as: having found a major fit, don't give away detailed information. Bids have come to reflect hopes and aspirations rather than reality. Slams are bid on general strength, with the aid of Roman Keycard Blackwood to uncover the quality of the trump suit. While investigating for a game in a major suit, a partnership may stumble into a slam on a 4-4 fit, whereas while investigating for 3NT, it is difficult to stumble into a minor-suit slam on a 4-4 fit. Most don't even try. In what follows, we shall investigate, with regard to probability, the consequences of the modern spin approach to a series of fundamental issues.

Biddable Suits

In early days, opening with four-card majors was the dominant style in the USA. Great players found merit in that style, and a very few adherents to the methods of the Neapolitan Club, Bob Hamman in particular, still do. The main assumptions were that a partnership bid to play in their best trump suit and to avoid large penalties. Thus, one opened in one's best suit, even if it were a minor suit. In order to be classified as 'biddable', a suit needed to qualify with regard to length and strength. A four-card opening bid in a suit required that the suit be at least as good as Q-J-x-x, that is, that the suit met the expected median strength for that length. A five-card suit could be opened when headed by the jack. To rebid a five-card suit, one needed to hold at least K-J-x-x-x; again, the expected median strength of 4 HCP. Any six-card suit was deemed rebiddable.

Spades or Clubs?

Experts have argued over whether to open in spades or clubs when both suits are five cards in length. Nowadays bidding spades is a top priority, but this may be a situation where the relative strengths are a deciding factor. True to his British bridge roots, in the 2007 Bermuda Bowl Final, Zia opened 1♣ on the following hand:

♠ A K 9 6 2   ♡ A 3   ◇ 5   ♣ Q 9 6 5 3

so perhaps this is not a dead issue. Opening with the lower suit provides the partnership with more bidding space, thus facilitating an informative auction. Also, if opener has a very big hand, a 1♣ opening provides less risk of being passed out than starting with 1♠.

Because it is easier for the opponents to overcall 1♣ than to overcall 1♠, most agree that opening 1♠ has the tactical advantage. It appears to me that the side that holds length in spades need not worry greatly about interference, as they can expect to outbid the opponents, who, through ineffective bidding, may have given away vital information that will help in the play of the deal.

Opening Bids

What do commentators mean when they state that the modern style is to open light? How has bidding changed in that regard? Certainly old-timers were not shy on opening distributional hands with only 10 HCP. Charles Goren in *Contract Bridge for Beginners* (1953) suggested opening 1♠ on this collection:

♠ A Q x x x   ♡ A 10 x x x   ◇ x x   ♣ x

The modern Rule of 20 advises opening the bidding on hands that contain ten cards and 10 HCP in the two longest suits. It helps if one of the long suits is spades. This does not fit well into conservative systems whose structure is defined in terms of HCP alone, but perhaps the light opening bids often derided are flat hands that contain few controls. The weak notrump (11-14 HCP) opening bid can be used to avoid passing with featureless, flat hands, thus reducing the gap between a pass and an opening bid. This is the type of bid that is justifiably categorized as a light opening bid on the basis of its high LTC.

Finale: Kit's *Cri de Coeur*

> *So much easier if you describe your hand... and 10 more IMPs go away.*
> - Kit Woolsey commenting on the bidding from a deal from the
> 2007 USA Senior Teams Finals

For our final example, we turn once again to Bridge Base Online, that incomparable source of data. Of course, if you watch expert bridge on the Internet long enough, you will find evidence to back any prejudice, so you have to view the proceedings with as open a mind as possible. What works one time, fails another: all the more reason to adopt a probabilistic point of view. Kit Woolsey has long been a renowned director of the 'Master Solvers' Club' feature in *The Bridge World*. He strongly advocates bidding descriptively, so when the following deal came up during the 2007 match to determine the USA representatives to the world's championships in Shanghai, he couldn't help but express his exacerbation.

Berkowitz
♠ K Q 3
♡ 5
◇ J 9 8
♣ Q J 7 6 4 3

Bates
♠ 10 9 8 6 5
♡ K Q 9
◇ K Q 4 3
♣ 2

Sontag
♠ 7 2
♡ A 6 3
◇ A 10 7 6 5
♣ A K 8

Lair
♠ A J 4
♡ J 10 8 7 4 2
◇ 2
♣ 10 9 5

Bates	Berkowitz	Sontag	Lair
pass	pass	1NT	pass
2♡*	pass	2♠	pass
3◇	pass	4◇	pass
5◇	all pass		

Other Room

West	North	East	South
pass	pass	1◇	pass
1♠	2♣	pass	3♣
3◇	all pass		

The actions of Alan Sontag and Roger Bates, Precisionists, appear to be so blindingly obvious as not to require comment. The watcher's mind drifts back to thoughts of food, drink, and sex, not necessarily in that order. In the other room, however, a vulnerable game is missed.

Anarchists might approve of what they see as an attempt by East in the other room to swing some IMPs his way under the extraordinary circumstances of being down 36 IMPs with hopes fading. Others would maintain that trying to analyze East's actions is futile — maybe it was a senior's moment. It is not surprising, then, that some purists reject statistics as being tainted by state-of-the-match mentality and are forever wedded to the idea that the results are randomly attributable to luck. These are the Platonists whose ideal world remains untouched by experience.

Our preference is to consider the evidence as the primary source. Down 36 IMPs with twenty-eight boards yet to be played is not a hopeless situation unless you think it so. What has been lost over several boards cannot be regained on one. East's actions demonstrate that unilateral actions are not optimal, and that playing against the odds most often leads to a further decline. Mistakes are made, and disasters occur, when emotions outweigh common sense and probability. These are not predictable. This deal is evidence that, as Woolsey notes, decisions will usually turn out better if they are based on an accurate description of the partnership's resources. It is surprising how many rational commentators don't draw the obvious conclusion and adopt this view as gospel.

Not telling more than is necessary is another matter altogether. Philosophers may have trouble defining the difference, but politicians make an easy distinction every day.

A Final Thought

As I finished reading through the final version of this book in page proofs, I realized that much of my thinking on these subjects has advanced since I began writing the book. It is perhaps not even the same book I would write if I were to begin today. However, we have to cut it off at some stage, then get on with creating new stuff. Readers interested in the further development of these ideas can follow my blog on www.bridgeblogging.com, and can also download free supplemental articles from www.ebooksbridge.com.

Master Point Press on the Internet

www.masterpointpress.com

Our main site, with information about our books and software, reviews and more.

www.masteringbridge.com

Our site for bridge teachers and students — free downloadable support material for our books, helpful articles, forums and more.

www.bridgeblogging.com

Read and comment on regular articles from MPP authors and other bridge notables.

www.ebooksbridge.com

Purchase downloadable electronic versions of MPP books and software.